RESCUE ME

RESCUE ME

Your Step-by-Step Guide
to Starting an Animal Rescue

SANDRA PFAU ENGLUND, ESQ.

First printing 2017
ISBN: 978-0-9970878-2-6 (printed version)
ISBN: 978-0-9970878-3-3 (mobi and epub versions)

Photos: AStylePhotography.com (Amanda Myers)
Cover and interior design by Adina Cucicov, Flamingo Designs.

Disclaimer
This book provides information and resources to help you start-up a nonprofit animal rescue. This book does not provide legal advice. Please contact a licensed legal professional if you need help.

Use of information provided in this book is voluntary and should be used based on your own analysis of its accuracy and appropriateness for your intended use.

While effort was made to ensure the accuracy of the book's content at the time of publication, the information, rules and laws may have changed, or errors or omissions may occur.

Reference to specific commercial businesses, products, or services by trade name, trademark, manufacturer or otherwise in this book are for informational purposes only and does not imply the endorsement, recommendation, or favoring by the author.

Dedication

*To my daughter, Maggie and son, Jack who
insisted we get a dog; and to Tottenham,
our not-so-miniature Miniature Schnauzer,
and Stella, our Shih-poo,
who have enriched our lives ever since.*

APPRECIATION

I t takes a pack to pull a book together. My sincere appreciation goes to my assistant, Kathy Weideman, who keeps my calendar up-to-date and spent hours upon hours putting together and formatting the state-by-state laws found in Appendix A. Thanks too, to Kathy's mom, Norma Green, who read through the text not once but twice looking for spelling, grammar and punctuation mistakes. My son and law clerk, Drew Englund, also deserves a pat-on-the-back for conducting research and otherwise supporting numerous tasks in the writing of this book. And to the entire team at myRENOSI™ who also helped edit this book and work hard every day to help animal rescues and other nonprofits handle the mountains of government paperwork required to operate a public charity.

ABOUT THE AUTHORS

Sandra Pfau Englund, Esq. ("Sandy") has represented non-profit organizations for over twenty years. She is a sought-after speaker and subject matter expert and has been quoted by *Forbes*, the *Wall Street Journal* and the *Today Show*. Her first book, *School Fundraising: So Much More than Cookie Dough* was published in 2016. In December 2016, her documentary, *The Embezzler Next Door* was released, shining a light on the problem of embezzlement from volunteer-led school fundraising groups. As CEO of myRENOSI™ Inc. she helps nonprofits keep their tax-exempt status and not get revoked by providing an innovative at-a-glance internet platform that educates volunteers about federal and state registration and annual filing requirements.

Sandy's second book, *Rescue Me: Your Step-by-Step Guide to Starting an Animal Rescue*, focuses on the increasing need for specialized animal welfare organizations and provides the guidance you need to stop chasing your tail and get your rescue group off the ground before any more dog-years go by.

For information, or to book Sandy and Tott
call 844-346-8412, or email: kathy@myrenosi.com

CONTENTS

Find more great tools and tips on the
book website at www.sandrapfauenglund.com.
Use registration code: ResQme2017!

Ψ Ψ

PART I

RESCUES NEEDED

1

ONE HUNDRED SIXTY MILLION AND GROWING....

Pet ownership in the United States has exploded. It's estimated that sixty-five percent (65%) of all American households have one or more of the 164 million domesticated dogs and cats in our country. My house is one of them serving as home to two dogs, Tott our not-so-miniature Miniature Schnauzer, and Stella, our queen-of-the-neighborhood-thank-you-very-much Shih-poo. The growing popularity of family pets also has led to the growing need for help with abandoned animals.

Nearly 7.6 million animals are taken to public and private shelters each year with half (an estimated 3-4 million) never making it to a forever home. Some animals have more difficulty being adopted than others. Kittens and puppies, for example, are much more likely to be adopted than full grown animals. If you are a black cat you are twice as likely to remain unadopted and face euthanasia than other cats. Some animals, largely due to mistreatment by former owners, have behavior problems and cannot be adopted unless their behavior can be modified.

There is hope. The Animal Humane Society posted encouraging news for the 2014–2015 year: a startling 90% adoption rate. The largest portion of the animals that were euthanized (66%) were unhealthy and untreatable. The animal welfare movement began with the formation of the American Society for the Prevention of Cruelty to Animals (ASPCA) in 1866. The movement hit full-stride in the 1970s as more and more veterinarians began the push away from euthanization of animals in shelters. Yet the need for involvement and action remains great, and is getting greater as the popularity of companion animals increases.

10-SECOND TAKEAWAY

1. Pet ownership is growing exponentially throughout the world.
2. Over 7 million pets enter shelters every year.
3. Roughly half of all rescued animals are given new homes.
4. Approximately half of all rescued animals are euthanized.
5. There is a growing need for rescue organizations.

2

MANY DOG-YEARS AGO...

There are a wide variety of animal rescue organizations including public tax-funded shelters, large nonprofit organizations such as the local societies for the prevention of cruelty to animals (SPCA), and small, private, nonprofit rescues set up by individuals on their own. This book focuses primarily on privately funded nonprofit rescues.

Historically, animal shelters arose in colonial times. Lost live-stock were gathered up and held in what became known as "pounds" until the owners came to reclaim them. A reclaiming fee was typically charged. Animal shelters later evolved to house stray dogs and cats. These shelters were publicly funded because dogs and cats often would go unclaimed, especially if fees were charged to reclaim them. As a result, many of the unwanted animals were euthanized. [1]

Today, shelters may be broadly classified as either public animal shelters, funded primarily by local and state tax dollars, and private, nonprofit shelters funded primarily by individual donations. Public shelters typically must accept any animal brought in and commonly have little information about the animal's history or habits. Publicly funded shelters may rely on euthanasia due to funding and facility limitations. Private shelters include those defined as "no-kill" shelters that do not engage in euthanization, and a variety of other types. Note, however, that some "no-kill" shelters have been accused of wordplay by labeling some animals as "unrehabitable" and excluding these unrehabitable animals that are euthanized from the "no-kill" statistics.

Shelters also are distinguished by the type of animals accepted, the community served, and/or the work conducted. For example, a shelter may accept only cats, and even a particular breed of cat, or a particular breed of dog, or other animals such as birds, rabbits and so forth. I have a client, for example, that focuses on abandoned and abused Catahoula dogs; another client rescues dogs from high-kill shelters in a specific state, and trains the dogs to work with military personnel suffering from post-traumatic stress syndrome. Another one of my clients set-up an organization to take care of the companion animals of people going through medical treatment. Other rescues find new homes for companion animals of people who have recently died.

In addition to shelters, animal welfare organizations include groups that provide transportation services to move animals to new homes and fostering groups. There are organizations that train and provide service animals for the blind, the police and the military. Some groups provide veterinarian services and others educate the public about how to properly take care of companion animals.

Animal sanctuaries generally focus on providing long-term care and homes for animals that are not "adoptable"—including older animals, exotic pets that may be illegal, and other animals such as wolves, wild cats, horses, primates and rare birds.

Common to all of these groups are people passionate about ensuring animals are treated humanely. This book focuses on providing the tools, tips and resources needed to successfully set-up, maintain, and operate an animal rescue, sanctuary or other similar organization.

10-SECOND TAKEAWAY

1. Animal "pounds" began in colonial times to collect stray animals and return them to their owners for a fee.

2. Public tax-funded "pounds", later called "shelters" relied on euthanasia due to limited funds and facilities.

3. Privately funded shelters began in 1866 with the ASPCA.

4. Animal shelters, rescues and sanctuaries come in a wide variety of types, distinguished by the animals accepted, community served, and work conducted.

5. Most shelters and rescues are started and managed by people passionate about animals who are in need of tools, tips and resources to help them successfully set-up, maintain and operate their animal welfare organizations.

PART II

YOUR RESCUE
START-UP GUIDE

3

FIVE QUICK STEPS TO GET YOUR RESCUE OFF AND RUNNING

The truth is, few of us are good at everything and many of us shudder at the very whisper of the acronym IRS. The reality is that obtaining and maintaining 501(c)(3) tax-exempt status is a key hurdle to getting your rescue started, and keeping it going. In this chapter we provide you a map to keep you on the road to rescue success. Subsequent chapters provide you with the details you need.

Step 1: Choose your niche. Just as the pet population has exploded, the number of rescues popping up also is growing rapidly. That's a good thing, but your chances of success (including raising donations) is better the more "niched" you are. Chapter 4 provides help on how to pick a niche.

Step 2: Gather your pack. The IRS requires that you have an independent board of directors to govern your nonprofit tax-exempt organization. So gather your friends, experts in your niche, and others to build a pack of support for your organization. Chapter 5 discusses the IRS requirements for your nonprofit board of directors.

Step 3: Structure for success to keep your organization purring. The IRS and your state government have rules for how you set-up an animal rescue, and get and keep it tax-exempt. Making sure that you, and your board of directors understand the legal requirements will help keep your organization purring year-after-year. Chapter 6 provides a step-by-step guide to completing the IRS tax-exemption application, Form 1023EZ or Form 1023.

Step 4: Raise support. You can't go far without support. Chapter 7 provides a guide to the dos and don'ts for keeping a continuous fundraising program in place.

Step 5: Risk management & insurance. Chapter 8 provides information on how to control the risks involved with operating an animal welfare organization and the types of insurance you should consider obtaining.

4

CHOOSE YOUR NICHE

There are over 13,000 animal shelters and rescues in the U.S. However, with the pet population soaring, there is a need for more shelters, rescues, sanctuaries and other animal welfare groups. To make your work stand-out and gain the attention of donors and funders, it's important to find the right niche.

WHAT IS NICHE MARKETING?

A niche is a specialized product or service that you provide to a focused portion of your target market. Generally you look for a product or service that is not currently being provided by mainstream organizations or other providers, a community of people in need of help. For example, temporary boarding of cats for women going through breast cancer treatment.

WHY NICHE YOUR RESCUE?

There are a number of reasons to niche your work rather than opening a general rescue or shelter. Let's look at four:

1. **You can't save all the animals.**

   You cannot serve everyone and save every animal. By focusing on a specific need of a targeted group of people you are able to better understand their needs. You will learn what they read, where they shop, what's important to them. It also helps protect you from the dangers of spreading yourself too thin.

2. **You need partners, funders and clients.**

   Focusing on a smaller pool of people and their particular needs helps you focus your marketing and fundraising efforts. For example, doctors, hospitals and clinics may be a great source of referrals for women needing temporary care of their cats. It also helps with fundraising. Funders and other donors like new ideas and supporting something different from the ordinary. In addition, your pool of funders expands. For example, now breast cancer survivors and their families, in addition to people passionate about cats, may support your work.

3. **It's easier to become an expert.**

   The better niched you are, the better known you will become for what you do and for whom. For example, you are no longer the founder of another animal rescue. You are now an expert in providing temporary fostering of companion animals for active military while on deployment. Your visibility and profile will naturally increase while your competition will decrease.

4. **You will get better referrals.**
   Because you are very clear about what you do and who you do it for, you will get more and better targeted referrals. By telling people exactly who you serve—for example breast cancer patients or active military—people are more likely to stop and think about who they know that fits that profile and may be in need of your services.

You may wonder whether you can pick too small of a niche? Could over-niching limit the future growth of your work? Not at all. Once you become known for a niche you can start adding new products and services. In addition, often related business comes your way due to your new expert status. And while working in your niche, and listening to your target clients, you may learn about new opportunities and new ways to serve the community better. You also can add partners in related areas of work.

SELECT YOUR NICHE

When selecting a niche for your animal welfare organization the possibilities are nearly endless. As a result, pursuing what you are most passionate or knowledgeable about is usually a good place to start. Also consider where the need is greatest, and don't forget to consider the likelihood of obtaining donations and other funding for your project.

To help you get started thinking about a niche, take a look at the "Pick Three" chart below and select one item from each column. Choose a category or type of animal you are passionate about, a community which you would like to serve, and the type of work you are most qualified to do.

Pick Three

ANIMALS	COMMUNITY	WORK
Dogs—all	General public	No kill shelter
Dogs—specific breed(s)	Military (e.g. all active, active deployed, veterans, disabled veterans)	Rehabilitation
Dogs—types (e.g. retired police dogs)	Sick—all	Sanctuary
Cats—all	Sick (e.g. all cancer, breast cancer, pancreatic cancer)	Foster, rehoming
Cats—specific breed(s)	Sick (e.g., terminally ill, hospice patients)	Temporary fostering
Cats—types (e.g. feral)	Elderly	Veterinarian services
Horses—all	Disabled—all	Spay, neuter
Horses—types (e.g. retired race horses)	Disabled—specific (e.g., blind, quadriplegic, deaf, mental illness)	Education—public, all
Exotic animals (e.g. snakes, wolves, rare birds)	Disabled—children	Education—children

Your Niche

The result is your niche or focus area—the intersection of your main interests, such as temporary fostering of cats for breast cancer patients.

Next steps will include determining the people and organizations that might provide funding or otherwise support your work, and how you reach out to this community. But before you go there, you must first gather your team (Chapter 5) and set-up your organization (Chapter 6).

5

GATHER YOUR PACK

To qualify for federal 501(c)(3) tax-exempt public charity status your rescue must have an independent board of directors. Essentially this means you need to pick a team of people that will be responsible for key decisions of your organization, including approving your annual budget, your salary, and your annual action plan. I find that a board of about five (5) is a manageable size, particularly when first starting out. While you may be tempted to keep your board close—tapping family to serve—to meet Internal Revenue Service (IRS) rules you will need an independent board (meaning people unrelated to you). This is necessary so that you have non-family members to approve your salary and show that your rescue is not engaging in "private benefit" activities (activities that financially benefit you, your family, other founders and decision makers and their families).

The IRS defines "family" as an individual's spouse, ancestors, children, grandchildren, great-grandchildren, and the spouses of children, grandchildren, and great-grandchildren. A legally adopted child of an individual is treated for these purposes as a child of the individual by blood. A brother or sister of an individual is not, for these purposes, a member of the family.

The IRS also looks to see if your board has adopted a conflict of interest policy to help prevent transactions that benefit the board members personally. An example of a conflict of interest policy is included in the sample bylaws provided in Appendix C.

Compensation. Nonprofit board members normally serve as volunteers without pay. Although paying your board members for their time and service is not illegal, it is frowned upon by the IRS. However, if you as the founder serve both on the board, and the role as the manager of the organization, you may be paid in your staff role as manager. In fact, it is quite common for the founder of a rescue to serve on its board of directors and also as its executive director. The key is that anyone paid not participate in the final discussion and vote on his/her salary. In addition, the board should review "comparability data" showing what the executive directors of other rescues of similar budget size in similar parts of the country are paid to help it determine a reasonable salary. The board minutes should reflect that all of these rules were followed.

Your boards' duties. Best practice rules, such as those of the Better Business Bureau found at www.give.org, provide that not more than one or ten percent (10%) of your board members also be paid staff members. The Better Business Bureau www.give.org rules also provide that the boards' duties include:

- Regular appraisals of the executive director's performance;
- Review and approve the annual budget; and,
- Establishing financial controls to safeguard your group's funds.

Board meetings. The Better Business Bureau nonprofit best practices also recommend a minimum of three (3) board meetings each year. Board meetings may be held face-to-face, or by conference telephone or other means through which all board members may hear each other and participate in the conversation. Boards may only make decisions by written ballot (including an email vote) if the full board agrees on the decision. The rationale is that if there is not full agreement, a meeting at which the issue may be discussed prior to the vote is necessary.

 Appendix D includes a sample agenda for your first board meeting, sample minutes, a guide to drafting minutes, and a handout on basic parliamentary procedure.

6

STRUCTURE FOR SUCCESS

This chapter provides step-by-step instructions on how to set-up your rescue, including the process to incorporate in your state and apply for federal 501(c)(3) tax-exempt status.

START → Select state of incorporation

↓

Draft & file articles of incorporation

↓

Draft Bylaws

↓

Hold first board of directors meeting

↓

Develop 3 year budget

↓

Determine whether to file IRS Form 1023EZ or 1023

↓

Draft & file the IRS Form 1023EZ or 1023

↓

File state fundraising, sales tax, and income/franchise tax registrations

↓

Mark due dates on your calendar for IRS Form 990-series tax return, and renewal of state registrations

↓

Draft & file the IRS Form 1023EZ or 1023

State of incorporation—There are few significant differences between state nonprofit laws. As a result, I recommend that you incorporate in the state in which you will operate.

Articles of incorporation—Most states have fillable forms online. Make sure, however, that you add the IRS required language to qualify as 501(c)(3) tax exempt. Sample articles of incorporation with the IRS language highlighted are included in Appendix C.

Bylaws—Bylaws are the rules for operating your organization, including how often your board of directors meets, the number and titles of officers, and financial controls. See sample bylaws in Appendix C.

First Board Meeting—At your first board meeting you should adopt the bylaws, elect the officers and take other action necessary to delegate operating authority. See sample first board meeting agenda in Appendix D.

Three-year budget—The IRS expects your organization to have a three-year budget listing expected sources of income (donations, grants, in-kind donations of food, etc.) and the expected amount of each, and categories of expenses (facility rent, facility maintenance & utilities, veterinarian costs, food, salaries & benefits, etc.) and the amount of each category of expense. See sample budget in Appendix E.

IRS Form 1023EZ & 1023—Smaller organizations with anticipated gross income of $50,000 or less in each of the first three years may efile Form 1023EZ. Larger organizations must file the longer paper Form 1023. See Form 1023 in Appendix C.

EIN—You will need to obtain an EIN (federal tax identification number also sometimes called an FEIN) prior to filing the Form 1023. Links to the IRS Form 1023EZ and 1023, and the IRS website where you may obtain an EIN, are available on the book website.

State registrations—The registrations required for nonprofit corporations differ by state. Some states require nonprofits to file for exemption from franchise and/or income tax. Many states allow organizations with 501(c)(3) status to apply for exemption from state sales tax. (NOTE: Your 501(c)(3) federal tax-exempt status DOES NOT exempt your group from state sales tax. Most states also require you to register with the state attorney general's office prior to fundraising (sometimes known as "Charity Registration"). A link to state registration requirements and information is available on the book website.

Maintain your exemptions and registrations—To maintain your IRS 501(c)(3) tax-exempt status you must file the appropriate IRS Form 990-series tax return. The form filed—990N, 990EZ, or 990—is based on your gross income for the year. Failure to file the Form 990 on time for three consecutive years results in automatic revocation of your organization's 501(c)(3) status. Many states require annual renewal of your state registrations and exemptions as well. Make sure that you mark the due dates on your calendar and file on time.

Incorporate. Incorporation provides liability protection for your officers, directors, and volunteers. It also provides additional credibility, and a legal entity that may contract for services. Most states have a corporations office, typically under the state's Secretary of State office, and include forms, fees and other information needed to file articles of incorporation on the state corporation commission website.

What must be included in articles of incorporation is governed by each state's laws. However, most states require that you provide:

- a name for your organization
- physical street address for your organization
- a purpose statement
- one or more directors
- whether you will/will not have members
- an individual or corporate registered agent
- an individual serving as the incorporator

 Sample articles of incorporation are included Appendix C.

Name: I recommend that you include the abbreviation for incorporated, "Inc." in your name. By including "Inc." in your name, you are putting everyone on notice that your organization is a corporate entity with the liability and protections that incorporation offers. Some states require that you include "Inc." or "Incorporated" at the end of your name; a few states do not allow you to include this designation in your name (e.g. the state of Washington).

Address: Most states require a street address rather than a P.O. Box on the articles of incorporation.

Purpose: Keep your purpose statement brief and broad. By doing so you decrease the likelihood that you will need to amend the purpose statement in the articles later, requiring another filing with the state. You may define your purpose in more detail in your bylaws. The IRS purpose language also should be included in this section of your articles. [Required IRS purpose language.

> *The corporation is organized and will be operated exclusively for charitable and educational purposes within the meaning of 501(c)(3) of the Internal Revenue code. (All references to sections in these Articles refer to the Internal Revenue code of 1986 as amended or to comparable sections of subsequent internal revenue laws.) In pursuance of these purposes, it shall do all things necessary, proper, and consistent with maintaining tax exempt status under section 501(c)(3).]*

Directors: Many states only require one director to be named; a few states require a minimum of three directors to be named; other states do not require any directors to be named in the formation document. You will need at least three to five directors, however, prior to filing the IRS application for tax-exemption (Form 1023EZ or 1023). Directors are not required to be residents of the state in which you are incorporating; directors may live anywhere, including outside the U.S.

Members: Members are not required. Most animal welfare organizations do not have members.

Registered agent: Most states require that you name a "registered agent", sometimes called a "resident agent". This is the person to whom the state will send any official notices. The most common notice received is notice of the state annual corporate report and its due date. The qualifications to serve as registered agent vary by state. However, typically an individual must be a resident of the state and an officer or director of the corporation. Most states also allow the use of a commercial registered agent—a business incorporated in the state that is qualified to serve as the registered agent. This service typically costs about $100/year.

Incorporator: This is the individual that signs the articles of incorporation and files them in the state. The duties and authority of the incorporator terminate as soon as the board of directors meets for the first time. Generally anyone can serve as the incorporator provided that they are at least 18 years old. They do not need to be a resident of the state in which you are incorporating.

Private benefit: The IRS requires that articles of incorporation for 501(c)(3) groups strictly prohibit any officer, director or member from personal financial gain from the income raised and/or the activities of your organization. [Required IRS private benefit language.

> *The property of this corporation is irrevocably dedicated to charitable and educational purposes and no part of the net income or assets of this corporation shall ever inure to the benefit of any director, officer or member thereof or to the benefit of any private person].*

Dissolution: The IRS requires that 501(c)(3) groups contribute any remaining funds when they dissolve to another 501(c)(3) organization or to the government. [Required IRS dissolution language.

> *Upon the dissolution or winding up of the corporation, its assets remaining after payment, or provision for payment, of all debts and liabilities of this corporation shall be distributed to a nonprofit fund, foundation or corporation which is organized and operated exclusively for charitable and educational purposes and which has established its tax exempt status under Internal Revenue Code section 501(c)(3).]*

Lobbying and political activity: The IRS requires that the articles of incorporation of a 501(c)(3) group include language that limits lobbying activity to the allowable amount, and strictly prohibits political campaign activity. [IRS required lobbying and political activity language.

No substantial part of the activities of this corporation shall consist of carrying on propaganda, or otherwise attempting to influence legislation, and the corporation shall not participate or intervene in any political campaign (including the publishing or distribution of statements) on behalf of any candidate for public office.]

. . . .

TIPS & TOOLS

To find your state's corporation website, search your state's two-letter abbreviation, followed by a space and then "SOS" (secretary of state). For example, to find the Virginia Secretary of State website, I search [VA SOS]. A listing for the state corporation office should result.

. . . .

Draft bylaws. An organization's bylaws provide the rules for how to operate. Having a set of bylaws is generally a requirement of your state's nonprofit laws. Bylaws usually include the duties of the officers and their election process, budget guidelines, and detailed financial control. State laws usually provide minimum requirements. However, your bylaws may impose stricter rules. For example, you typically have the ability to set the minimum number of people that make up a quorum to transact business. If you don't include a quorum provision in your bylaws, the state law provision applies. Some state requirements such as the minimum number of people who must serve on your board of directors cannot be changed by a provision in your bylaws.

 A sample set of bylaws with annotations regarding each provision is included in Appendix C.

OBTAIN 501(C)(3) TAX-EXEMPT STATUS

All groups that raise money must file the appropriate tax return. If your organization has 501(c)(3) status, it may file the IRS 990-series return and be exempt from paying federal income tax. Good deal! However, if your organization is not a registered 501(c)(3), the IRS expects a corporate tax return and taxes paid on your income at the corporate tax rate (currently 33%).

In addition to exemption from paying federal corporate income tax, tax-exempt 501(c)(3) status has other advantages, including allowing your rescue organization to receive tax-deductible donations and apply for private foundation and corporate grants.

IRS Forms 1023-EZ and 1023. There are two IRS application forms for federal tax-exempt status—Form 1023EZ and Form 1023.

Form 1023 is the original, long-form (12+ pages). Organizations anticipating annual gross income of $50,000 or more must use the paper mailed-in Form 1023. The long-form 1023

ᐣᐣ

requires attaching the group's governing documents (articles of incorporation and bylaws), budgets for three years, and a laundry list of other information. The form proves difficult, time consuming, and overwhelming for those not experienced with such forms. The form also comes with an $850 IRS filing fee. IRS review of Form 1023 generally takes six months or more.

Form 1023EZ is a streamlined version of Form 1023. Provided your rescue plans to raise gross income of less than $50,000 during each of the first three years of operation, you likely qualify to file this shorter application. The 1023-EZ, released by the IRS in July 2014, may be completed and filed on-line. The 1023-EZ has a $275 filing fee. IRS review normally takes under 30 days. Users of this government website must register and attest that they've read and understand the eligibility requirements and other rules associated with 501(c)(3) organizations. The 1023-EZ makes the exemption process considerably easier for groups that anticipate raising $50,000 or less during each of their first three years of operation.

 A link to the IRS forms page for the 1023EZ and 1023 is available at the book website. Instructions for completing the forms are available in Appendix C.

What happens if we start small and file the 1023EZ but exceed our wildest expectations?

I'm often asked whether you must file the full 1023 later if you initially filed the IRS Form 1023EZ but have amazing success and exceed the $50,000 maximum gross estimated income allowed to be eligible to use the Form 1023EZ. The answer is no. However, the IRS is auditing a certain percentage of 1023EZ applicants, requesting their organizing documents (articles of incorporation and bylaws), budgets and other documents. In addition, if the IRS audits your organization and finds that you filed IRS Form 1023EZ knowing that your organization was not eligible, your 501(c)(3) tax-exempt status may be revoked.

OBTAIN AN EIN

You will need an EIN (employer identification number also know as a federal tax identification number or FEIN) to apply for IRS 501(c)(3) tax-exempt status. An EIN identifies your new nonprofit corporation to the IRS similar to how a personal social security number (SSN) identifies an individual to the IRS. EINs should be obtained shortly after you incorporate your animal welfare group.

EINs may be obtained online. Search for "IRS EIN ONLINE". A link to the IRS application site for an EIN is available

at the book website. Step-by-step instructions on how to complete the EIN application are included in Appendix C. Your EIN will be provided in a CP575 letter issued online by the IRS. Download it and keep this letter in your permanent records.

HANDLE STATE REGISTRATIONS

Most states require nonprofit groups to register with the state charity agency prior to fundraising. In addition, your group may be eligible to apply for exemption from state sales tax on items purchased in the state for use by your group.

 A directory of each state's registration requirements is available on the book website.

MAINTAIN YOUR TAX-EXEMPTION

It may be hard to believe, but getting federal tax-exempt status may be the easy part. To maintain your federal tax-exempt status, state corporate and fundraising status requires annual filings and renewals. Failure to file means loss of your status.

But aren't nonprofit organizations exempt from filing IRS tax returns?

I'm glad that you asked that. It's true that small nonprofit tax-exempt organizations with gross income of less than $25,000 used to be exempt from filing an IRS tax return. Once tax-exempt, always tax-exempt. That all changed with the passage of the Pension Protection Act of 2006. It's thought that the IRS wanted to weed off its long list of nonprofit organizations that were no longer operating. As a result, even small organizations must now file at least an "e-post-card" also known as the IRS Form 990N. Failure to file the appropriate 990-series tax return on time for three years in a row results in automatic loss of your federal tax-exempt status; this means you have to file the IRS 1023 application all over again to get your tax-exempt status back. Interestingly, the IRS grants new tax-exemptions to about 80,000 organizations each year, and revokes the tax-exempt status of almost 50,000 groups.

ALL ABOUT IRS FORM 990-SERIES

There are three different 990 forms—the 990N, 990EZ and the 990—with the appropriate form based on an organization's gross receipts (total income before any expenses are deducted):

990N	Gross receipts normally ≤ $50,000
990EZ	Gross receipts ≤$200,000 and total assets ≤ $500,000
990	Gross receipts ≥ $200,000 or total assets ≥ $500,000

The IRS 990 return is due on the 15th day of the 5th month after the close of an organization's fiscal year. For example, if your organization operates on a calendar year, January 1—December 31, the IRS Form 990 is due May 15.

ΨΨ

Choosing a Fiscal Year

Most animal welfare organizations follow a calendar fiscal year (January—December). However, you may select any 12-month period, from the first date of one month to the last date of the twelfth month following the first month, for your organization. Some reasons people choose a non-calendar fiscal year are funding cycles (groups funded by a government agency may follow the government agencies fiscal year such as October 1—September 30) or if your group is affiliated with another organization you may want to follow their fiscal year. Fiscal years may be changed by notifying the IRS on Form 1128.

FILING THE 990N *E-POSTCARD*

If your group normally has annual gross income of $50,000 or less, you may complete the online IRS 990N e-postcard. This electronic filing requires only:

- The organization's name
- Any other names your organization uses (DBAs) (Doing Business As)
- The organization's mailing address
- The organization's website address (if you have a website)
- The organization's EIN
- The name and address of a principal officer of the organization (usually the President or CEO)

- Confirmation of your organization's fiscal year
- Confirmation that your organization's annual gross income is still normally less than $50,000
- Confirmation that your organization has not gone out of business

....

990N Based On Average Gross Receipts

The 990N eligibility is based on your average or "normal" gross receipts. The IRS website provides that your group qualifies as normally having $50,000 or less in gross annual income if your group:

- Has been in existence for 1 year or less and received, or donors have pledged to give, $75,000 or less during its first taxable year;
- Has been in existence between 1 and 3 years and averaged $60,000 or less in gross receipts during each of its first two tax years; and
- Is at least 3 years old and averaged $50,000 or less in gross receipts for the immediately preceding 3 tax years (including the year for which calculations are being made).

....

IRS Form 990EZ and 990

Because IRS Forms 990EZ and 990 must be made available to the public (including the forms filed for the most recent three (3) years), your organization's Form 990 should be used to inform the public and prospective funders about the important work your organization is doing. In other words, it's not just a tax return.

Here's how:

- Form 990 requires an organization to report your mission and accomplishments for the year. The information that you present should be consistent with information that you publish in your annual report, brochures, website, and other materials.

- Form 990 requires each organization to allocate its expenses between program, administration, and fundraising expenses. When allocating expenses, you should be consistent and accurate. You should also keep in mind that a higher percentage of program expenses-to-overhead expenses (such as administration and fundraising) is looked at more favorably by the public and prospective funders.

- Keep in mind that donors' names and the amount each contributes is confidential information. You should remove this information from your 990 before making the return available to the public.

....

GuideStar

GuideStar.org is a public website that publishes
information about 501(c)(3) tax-exempt organizations. Once your organization is recognized as tax-
exempt by the IRS you may "adopt" your profile on
GuideStar, updating and adding information about
your activities and board of directors. You may
also include your governing documents (articles of
incorporation, bylaws, tax returns, etc.). GuideStar is
a resource for the public and funders to learn about
nonprofit groups. Using GuideStar provides your
group with credibility and transparency. Federal law
requires your organization to make available to the
public, upon request, your three most recently filed
IRS Forms 990.

....

STATE CORPORATE ANNUAL REPORTS

Once your organization is incorporated, most states require
that a corporate report be filed each year listing the group's
current address, directors and officers. Some states allow
the form to be filed online; others require a paper form be
signed and returned. Most states require an annual fee.
Many states assess a modest penalty for late filing.

Often, failure to file for two or more years will result in the
loss of corporate status. Unless too many years go by, corporate status usually may be restored by filing the late annual

reports and paying the required filing fees and penalties. Due dates for corporate annual reports vary by state. Some are based on an organization's fiscal year; others are based on the date the IRS 990 annual report is due; still others have a unique filing date all their own.

State income and franchise taxes

Some states automatically exempt organizations incorporated within the state as nonprofit corporations from state income tax. Others require a separate application for state income tax exemption. The same applies to state franchise taxes.

Fundraising registration

Most states require nonprofit organizations to register with the state charities division, usually housed within the state attorney general's office, **prior to raising funds from the public**. State laws vary, but many have exceptions for groups that raise less than a specified dollar amount.

Once registered, most states require groups to renew their registration annually. Renewal typically requires filing a report that lists total funds raised, whether any professionals were used to help with fundraising, and the like. Often, there is a renewal fee. Failure to file typically results in fees and penalties.

SALES TAX

In states with a sales tax, organizations with 501(c)(3) status may often (but not always) apply for exemption from paying sales tax on items purchased for use by the organization. Sales tax laws are complex, and vary widely throughout the United States. Some states provide exemption only on certain items. Others provide sales tax exemptions only in very limited cases.

You also should be aware that there are two components to sales tax—the tax you pay when purchasing items; and the tax you must collect when selling items. If your organization plans to sell items to raise funds, such as clothing, animal products and the like, you may need to collect and pay sales tax on the items sold.

Variations in state laws are numerous. Some states allow a certain number of tax-free sale days on which a group is not required to collect and pay sales tax. Other states provide exemptions from sales tax for some items but require sales tax be collected and paid on other items.

10-SECOND TAKEAWAY

1. Incorporation, while not required by law, is highly recommended.

2. To organize properly in IRS lingo means that your formation document (e.g. articles of incorporation) includes all the required IRS language.

3. Obtaining 501(c)(3) status offers myriad benefits on both federal and state levels.

4. Your state has rules, too. Check and follow them!

5. All nonprofit organizations must file an annual IRS 990-series "information" tax return or risk loss of their 501(c)(3) status.

6. States generally require nonprofit corporations to file an annual corporate report, and annual fundraising (charity) renewals.

7. States also may require you to file for exemption from state franchise/income tax and sales tax exemption and/or collection.

7

RAISE SUPPORT

et's face it, caring for animals and managing an organization takes time and money. In this chapter we start with
how to budget and set up your bookkeeping. The second half
of this chapter provides the dos and don'ts on fundraising
legally. You might ask why budgeting comes first? Donors
often want to be sure that your organization has sound
financial practices in place before contributing.

BUDGETING AND BOOKKEEPING

Taking care of the finances involves 5 basic steps:

1. budget
2. track
3. reconcile
4. report
5. review

Step 1: Budget. Managing the finances of your animal rescue doesn't have to be an impossible, thankless job, provided you employ the latest tools and follow some simple guidelines. Here's my 4-step no-fail (okay—no guarantees—but I'm doing my best here) financial management plan.

Get your officers together and develop an annual budget. A simple spreadsheet like the one pictured below works well. First, list each planned fundraising event or income-producing activity down the left column. Then enter how much you hope to raise from each activity to the right of each item. When you list expected income in a budget it should be the total (gross) amount that you expect to raise before expenses are taken out.

INCOME		
Individual donations	$12,000	
Corporate in-kind grants (food)	$5,000	
Adoption fees	$17,000	
TOTAL INCOME		**$34,000**

Next, list your expenses by category, such as the cost of your facility, food, veterinarian expenses and the like.

EXPENSES		
Food	$5,000	
Veterinarian costs	$5,000	
Facility rent & utilities	$24,000	
Insurance	$1,000	
Miscellaneous	$500	
TOTAL EXPENSES		**$35,500**
NET (Carry-over)		**($1,500)**

 A sample budget worksheet is included in Appendix E.

. . . .

Is it o.k. to make a profit?

Absolutely! If you don't bring in more money than you spend it will be hard to keep your organization running. There is no rule or law against carrying over income to start the next year. In fact, many larger nonprofits with paid staff will try to set aside reserve funds in an amount that would cover 6-12 months operating expenses. Larger projects, such as building a new shelter, may require you to set aside funds for several years before the total required amount is raised. Saving funds for future expenses, or a "rainy day", is both legal under IRS fundraising rules and a good way to do business.

. . . .

Step 2. Track. Once your budget is in place you need to keep track of all income and expenses, including attaching invoices and receipts to each transaction. At each board meeting you should provide a budget-to-actual to report on how well you are actually doing compared to your planned budget, modifying the budget (with the approval of the board) as needed to reflect reality.

You can use a simple spreadsheet and make a report such as the one below. However, I recommend using one of the many different online cloud-based accounting software packages. Using cloud-based accounting software allows you to easily track your income and expenses, produce professional reports, and make board access to your financials easier.

Sample Year End Budget-to-Actual Report

	BUDGET January 1—December 31, 2017	ACTUAL-TO-DATE[2] April 1, 2017
INCOME		
Individual donations	$12,000	$2,500
Corporate in-kind grant (food)	$5,000	$1,500
Adoption fees	$17,000	$6,000
TOTAL INCOME	**$34,000**	**$10,000**
EXPENSES		
Food	$5,000	$1,250
Veterinarian costs	$5,000	$1,250
Facility rent & utilities	$24,000	$8,000
Insurance	$1,000	$0
Miscellaneous	$500	$50
TOTAL EXPENSES	**$35,500**	**$10,550**

 A list of cloud-based accounting software is included in Appendix E.

Step 3. Reconcile. It's important to reconcile your books to the bank's records each month within thirty days (30) of when the bank statement is available. Using accounting software makes this task much easier.

Step 4. Report. A full financial report includes the bank balance, reconciliation and budget-to-actual report, and a balance sheet. A reluctance on the part of a treasurer or other officer to make financial records available for review or a failure to routinely report on income and expenses are both bad practices, and may be red flags that the books are not in order.

Step 5. Review. A financial review should be conducted each year. The review may be done internally—until your gross receipts exceed $250,000—by members of your board or other volunteers. The review should be conducted by individuals without bank signature authority, who are outside the day-to-day financial management loop.

Annual Review Guidelines

The Better Business Bureau's Charity Division sets standards for who may conduct the annual financial review based on the gross income of an organization as follows:

GROSS INCOME	REVIEW MAY BE CONDUCTED
Less than $250,000	Internally by volunteers without signature or routine banking authority
$250,000–$499,999	Compilation review (less than a full audit) by an outside certified professional accountant (CPA)
$500,000+	Full audit by outside CPA

The Better Business Bureau's Charity Division rules are all found at give.org.

Step-by-step guidelines on how volunteers can conduct an internal financial review are included in Appendix E.

THEFT & FINANCIAL CONTROLS

Including strong financial policies in your bylaws is critical to your success. Your group needs to operate like a business, including implementing strong financial controls and being transparent about how your income is spent. The most basic financial controls include requiring two people to count cash, two people to sign checks, and two people to reconcile the bank account. All nonprofit groups also should require an annual financial review be conducted.

Theft is a common problem in small nonprofits, likely because the trust level is high and business and financial controls are not in place, or are not followed. You can reduce the risk of theft substantially by following these three simple rules:

1. **Cash controls**—never count cash alone. Two people should always be present to count cash. Cash should be counted on-site where it's collected. A cash tally sheet, signed by the counters, should be used to record the totals. Cash should then be immediately deposited into the bank.

2. **Checks**—two people should be required to sign checks. This requirement should be printed on the organization's checks and strictly adhered to. Never pre-sign blank checks!

3. **Bank statements—two sets of eyes on the bank statements.** A second person, without signature authority, should reconcile bank statements. It's a good idea to require the bank statements, reconciliation reports, deposit slips, and cash tally sheets to be kept together and made available at meetings for review.

....

It's about good business, not trust!

Too often I see groups include sound financial rules in their bylaws, and then fail to enforce the rules as soon as someone complains that getting a second person to count the cash or sign the checks is too hard. "Don't you trust us?" is a common refrain. Trust has nothing to do with it. In the eyes of the IRS and state government, operating an animal rescue is the same as operating a business, only with more scrutiny, because it involves donations. Strong financial controls protect everyone—the group, the public, and the people counting the cash.

....

Audits: When the IRS comes calling

While IRS audits of nonprofit groups are fairly rare, it's a good idea to have some knowledge of what the IRS looks for when it reviews tax-exempt organization returns. The IRS commonly looks at five areas in a nonprofit audit: private benefit (are any of the officers, directors or members getting personal financial benefit from the organization's income);

commercial activities (is the organization working with a for-profit organization in any capacity and providing too much benefit to the for-profit/commercial entity); has the organization changed its activities from when it obtained tax-exempt status; is the organization engaged in too much lobbying activity or prohibited political activity; and the composition and size of the organization's board of directors, including a review of the board's minutes.

Tips when responding to an audit:

1. **Be brief.** Give the auditor only the information requested and the information that they are entitled to; everything that they ask for may not be necessary to the audit. Only provide information for the specific tax year(s) being audited.

2. **Ask for help.** If concerns about how the audit is being handled come up, contact the auditor's supervisor. In addition, hiring an attorney or tax professional to intervene in the audit is often helpful.

3. **Unsatisfactory Results?** Contact the auditor if you cannot understand, or if you disagree with, the examination report. If the result of the audit is unsatisfactory, it can be appealed within the IRS and, if still unsatisfactory, to tax court.

Appendix E includes a fact sheet with more audit dos and don'ts. The book website includes a link to IRS publications on audits

FUNDRAISING DOS AND DON'TS

Organizations provided tax-exemption by the IRS under 501(c)(3) must make sure that all the funds raised are used to promote the organization's tax-exempt purpose. None of the funds may be used primarily to benefit an individual, such as the founder. Understanding what types of expenditures result in "private benefit" can sometimes be hard to understand and put into practice. One common question I get is whether a nonprofit, tax-exempt rescue may spend funds to improve the founder's home, such as by adding a fence or additional kennel space. While these types of expenditures support the mission of operating an animal rescue, they are not allowed if the property is owned by an individual (such as the founder) rather than being owned by the rescue itself. This is because making improvements to the property may increase the property's value. If the property is owned by the rescue that's o.k. But you may not use tax-exempt dollars to benefit and increase the value of an individual who owns the property.

The existence of any private benefit expenditures may result in the loss of an organization's tax-exempt status. This is just one of the key fundraising rules you need to know. My top 6 fundraising dos and don'ts are listed below:

1. **Funds must support a <u>public</u> tax-exempt purpose**

   Prevention of cruelty to animals is recognized as a 501(c)(3) tax-exempt purpose.

2. **No private benefit allowed**

   As discussed above, no part of your activities may directly benefit you or your family rather than serve to further your tax-exempt purpose. For example, you may not expense the entire cost of your home (rent, mortgage) as a cost of your rescue because you house rescue animals. However, you may be able to expense a building or facility used solely for the purpose of your rescue work. You also must be careful when expensing improvements to your property for the benefit of your rescue. However, you may (with your board of director's approval) pay yourself a salary for work in a staff position, such as being the Executive Director of your rescue. Private benefit is a tricky subject. It's always a good idea to seek counsel from an attorney to make sure mistakes are not made.

3. **Know & advise donors about the tax-deduction rules**
   - Voluntary payments to 501(c)(3)s for which the donor receives nothing of value in exchange for the donation/payment are fully tax-deductible.
   - The value of anything substantial (think more than a lapel pin, newsletter or mug) must be subtracted from the payment to determine the tax-deductible portion.
   - The 501(c)(3) is responsible for telling the donor the deductible portion of payments to the organization.

*Adoption fees are typically not tax-deductible if the fee is **required** to be paid in exchange for receiving the companion animal. However, if an adoption fee is voluntary, it may be tax-deductible. Also, if an adopting family pays more than the minimum adoption fee, the amount exceeding the minimum fee may be tax-deductible.*

4. **Raffles, Bingo and other "games of chance" have special rules**
   - Many states, counties and/or cities require you to register before undertaking games of chance.
   - In many places, games of chance are not legal.
   - It's important to check your state and local rules before conducting a raffle or other game of chance as a fundraiser.

5. **Sales tax**
   - Some states provide exemption for items <u>purchased</u> by 501(c)(3) organizations for use by the group; an application to the state tax agency is generally required.
   - Some states require registration, collection and payment of sales tax on items <u>sold</u> by your group to raise funds.

10-SECOND TAKEAWAY

1. Handling your organization's finances carefully is key to success.

2. Always adopt a budget, and report actual income and expenses against the budget, throughout the year.

3. Conduct an annual financial review (aka "audit") each year.

4. Be prepared if the IRS audits your organization by knowing the types of activities the IRS most commonly scrutinizes.

5. The IRS has a strict rule against the founders of a nonprofit receiving any financial or other benefit from the donations raised. All donations must support the tax-exempt mission of the organization and cannot pay, for example, for improvements to the founder's house.

6. Required adoption fees are not usually tax-deductible; it's the organization's responsibility to tell donors what is/is not tax-deductible.

8

INSURANCE & RISK MANAGEMENT

Working with animals can be risky business. As a result, it is strongly recommended that you carry insurance protection for your group.

There are four basic types of insurance that nonprofit organizations typically carry:

1. **General Liability**—to cover accidents and injuries to individuals;
2. **Directors and Officers (D&O)**—to cover the personal liability of officers and directors for their legal responsibilities serving the organization;
3. **Property**—to cover loss of property/assets of the organization, such as damage to your facilities, owned and rented equipment, and the like; and,

4. **Bonding**—to cover loss of funds of the organization to embezzlement and the like.

Insurance is just one way to handle the potential liability of operating an animal rescue. The other key way to limit your risks is to put in place a risk management program, and transfer or place the risks of your activities on another party that is most able to manage the risks when possible. A basic risk-management system can be developed following these simple steps:

1. **Identify the most likely risks**

   Think about the activities your group is planning this year and the most likely risks involved.

2. **Assess the risks and modify as appropriate**

   Decide if an activity is so important to your mission that you must tolerate the risk. Other activities may be modified to reduce the risk, or be eliminated, if the risk outweighs the benefit of continuing the activity.

3. **Control for the risks**

   This means that you avoid risks that are too great to bear, and modify policies, plans, and procedures to reduce risks where you can. Controlling for the risks also includes transferring risks to others where appropriate, including the use of informed consent documents, by contractual agreement, and through insurance.

10-SECOND TAKEAWAY

1. Obtain insurance. Taking care of animals is risky business.
2. Limit risk by establishing a risk management program, transferring the risks of your activities onto another party.

PART III

ALL THE DOG-GONE RULES

There are many local, state and federal laws and regulations dealing with animals and animal welfare including ownership of animals, sterilization and vaccination requirements, transporting animals across state lines, limits on the number of animals allowed on private property, zoning and nuisance laws, tethering restrictions, breed specific laws and animal cruelty laws. Some states distinguish between "shelters", "rescues" and "foster homes" while other state laws are less clear. Fostering arrangements and rescues in general are less regulated than organizations operating as animal shelters. The laws are evolving with new regulations often going into effect after a complaint is filed with government authorities. This section discusses the major types of laws relating to animal welfare groups including property rights (chapter 10), state licensing laws (chapter 11), state health laws (chapter 12), local laws (chapter 13) and liability and breed specific legislation (chapter 14). Appendix A provides a state-by-state guide to the laws existing at the time of this book's publication. With the ever-changing landscape in animal laws you should frequently review the local and state laws that impact your program for changes and updates.

9

WHO OWNS FIDO?

Understanding the legal rights in and to a companion animal is critical. While we often think of our companion animals as "human" and nobody owns a human, legally companion animals are considered "property". As property, one or more people, shelters, rescues or other organizations own Fido. As a result, it is critically important in all situations—when an owner surrenders an animal, when a rescue fosters out an animal, when a shelter places an animal in a forever home—that the ownership of the animal is made clear. For this reason, it's a good idea to put who owns Fido into a written contract.

Putting your intentions in writing and making sure that the writing is clear is critically important. I've been in more than one meeting where people seemed to argue endlessly about where to place the adjective. That said, as an attorney

I also know that ensuring a document can be interpreted in just one way is important. So what should you put in writing? There are four main types of written agreements used by animal rescues—surrender, adoption, foster care, and partnership agreements.

Surrender. When your organization takes in a companion animal make sure the current owners sign over their ownership rights. It's also a good idea to find out about the animal's behavior and medical history. Both the surrender and the animal's history may be included on the Surrender Agreement. *See sample in Appendix B.*

Adoption. Adoption agreements generally transfer ownership from a rescue or shelter to a new forever home. The biggest issue with adoption agreements is "overreaching" meaning that the rescue or shelter tries to maintain too much control over the animal once it is adopted out.

Overreaching can be seen in several ways including:

- Attempts by the rescue to retain some ownership rights
- Provisions allowing rescues to illegally retrieve animals after adoption
- Vaccination and other animal care requirements that exceed state mandated requirements

Retaining ownership. Attempting to retain full or partial ownership of an animal after it is adopted out is a mistake for several reasons. First, you want the adopter to make a life-time commitment to the animal. If the adopter can easily return the animal you are sending the wrong message. Second, because animals are "property" under the law, being fuzzy about how you use the word "adoption" and attempting to share ownership of the animal simply opens your organization up to disputes. Third, if your rescue maintains ownership of the animal you are opening yourself up to continued liability for the animal. For example, if the animal becomes dangerous you may be subject to liability for injuries caused by the animal when it is not under your care and control. If the animal is not properly cared for, your organization may be liable for animal cruelty charges. If you require visitation or inspections after placement and one of your inspectors is injured, your organization may be liable for claims due to the injuries.

Retrieving animals after adoption. Courts are unlikely to uphold any provision that allows a rescue to go onto an adoptive family's property to retrieve an animal, even if the adoptive family is violating rules for the care of the animal that you included in the adoption agreement. While the intent of such provisions may be good –the care and welfare of the animal—courts are far more likely to side with the property and privacy rights of the people living at the residence over upholding rights of your rescue to ensure the well-being of the animal.

Animal care requirements. Animal care requirements in adoption agreements should be limited to state-required vaccines such as rabies and spay/neuter requirements; all other medical care should be left to the discretion of the adopter's veterinarian with input from the adoptive family. While you may think mandating specific vaccines and medical care makes sense, the needs of each animal are unique and based on factors including where the animal lives, the animal's specific immune system and underlying diseases or conditions, and other exposures and factors. One size does not fit all and providing medical advice should be left to trained professionals.

 The sample Adoption Agreement in Appendix B provides clear transfer of the animal (and liability relating to the animal) from the rescue to the adopter, and includes the expected level of care and responsibility involved when adopting an animal without going beyond what is typically legally enforceable.

Foster care. When you place animals into foster homes the details of the fostering arrangement should be in writing, making clear that the rescue organization holds ownership rights to the animal. Both the duties and responsibilities of the fostering individual or family and the duties and responsibilities of your rescue organization should be listed. The agreement also needs to clearly state which party, foster or organization, is liable for possible claims including if the animal becomes dangerous. You will want to provide adequate oversight of your foster families because as the owner of the animal, you cannot sign away all liability to the foster family. *See sample Foster Agreement in Appendix B.*

Shelter/Rescue Partnership agreements. Sometimes rescues work under contract with shelters to take in animals. These agreements may be written so that the animal remains the property of the shelter, or ownership may be transferred to the rescue. Make sure your intentions and all the details regarding ownership, costs, animal care, animal return and surrender, fostering, adoption and the like are clearly set forth in the document. *See sample Shelter/Rescue Partnership Agreement in Appendix B.*

Disputes and Dog fights. Nobody wins when contract disputes arise, especially if the disputes go to court. (O.K., maybe the lawyers win.) Generally, attorneys apply state civil, property, and contract law to resolve "dog fights" over ownership rights and other disputes involving companion animals. The cases below are examples of how some disputes were resolved in court.

Foster refuses to surrender

A case in the State of Washington involved a rescue that asked a caretaker to return Chance, the black lab he was fostering, because the caretaker refused to take Chance to adoption events. The foster contract included a provision that allowed the rescue organization the right to break into the caretaker's home to retrieve the dog. After the rescue filed a civil lawsuit seeking the return of Chance, the caretaker returned Chance to the rescue group. As a result, the court did not rule on whether the provision allowing the rescue group to retrieve the dog was valid. It is likely, however, that the court would find that the caretaker had a greater right to peaceful enjoyment of his home than the rescue group had to break in and retrieve the animal.[2]

 This case points out the importance of writing contracts with valid provisions that do not exceed a rescue group's rights.

Breeder Ownership dispute

A buyer purchased a Newfoundland named Sage from a breeder for $1000. The sales contract provided that if the buyer could no longer take care of Sage, he would return the dog to the breeder and would not try to resell or re-home the dog. After Sage attacked another dog, the buyer's friend attempted to return Sage to the breeder. It so happened that the breeder was busy that day handling the emergency delivery of a litter of puppies and could not pick up Sage. The buyer then sold Sage to another dog breeder. The court found that the original breeder had not given up her contract rights to the dog and that Sage must be returned to the original breeder and owner. In this case it was relevant that the breeder who purchased Sage from the original buyer knew that the original breeder was not giving up her contractual ownership rights, and also that the original breeder had good reason not to pick up Sage when first asked due to the emergency puppy delivery.[3]

 This case makes clear the importance of always asking when an animal is surrendered whether the owner ever

ᵞ⊱

*signed any type of agreement with respect to the animal,
including a contract from the breeder, rescue or other organization or person.*

Pet Flipping

Pet flipping occurs when someone finds a pet for sale or
adoption online and then re-sells the animal.[4] It is a good
idea to include a "no pet-flipping" clause in your agreements.

For example, a woman in Hawaii adopted a 10-year-old
Jack Russell for $85 from the Hawaii Humane Society and
then immediately relisted the dog for sale on Craigslist
for $200. Because the Humane Society adoption contract
did not include a no-flipping provision, the Humane Society had no claim against the woman who resold the dog.
While tracking and enforcing a no-flipping clause may be
difficult, including a no-flipping clause in your agreement
at a minimum educates adopters that the intent is to place
the animal in a forever home and may slow the practice of
pet-flipping.[5]

Animal property rights versus adequate care

What happens when an owner's property rights in an animal are contested based on the owner providing inadequate
care of the animal? This was the case when an animal rescue
hired an animal transport organization that used a vehicle
in poor condition. After being tipped off, the state dog law
enforcement officials intercepted the transport vehicle, took
the dogs, and placed them with the Pennsylvania Society

for the Prevention of Cruelty to Animals. The rescue that owned the dogs filed a lawsuit claiming that they were being deprived of their ownership rights to the dogs. The court agreed finding that while the rescue had made a bad decision in using the transportation company, there was no evidence that the rescue could not provide proper care for the dogs and therefore the dogs were returned to the rescue.[6]

 This case shows that animal cruelty prevention laws may trump property rights if it was shown that the rescue could not adequately take care of the dogs. As a result, rescues must be familiar with and abide by animal welfare laws.

10-SECOND TAKEAWAY

1. Companion animals are considered "property" thus, it is critical to understand the legal rights associated with owning them.

2. Intentions regarding ownership, liability and animal care requirements should be put in writing to ensure they are clear to all parties.

3. When using contracts, they should have valid provisions that do not exceed the animal welfare group's rights.

4. Be familiar with and abide by animal welfare laws.

10

STATE LICENSING LAWS

Many states require animal welfare organizations to be licensed. Licensing usually requires an application, fee, and annual renewals. States also often require inspections to ensure facilities are safe and animals are treated humanely. Following is a brief survey of licensing requirements.

WHAT GROUPS ARE SUBJECT TO LICENSING?

Some states require licenses only for breeders and the operators of commercial kennels. However, other states define the word "kennel" broadly to require any organization that keeps or transfers a specified number of animals a year as a "kennel." For example, Pennsylvania passed a law in 2008 requiring any "establishment in or through which at least 26 dogs are kept or transferred in a calendar year..." to apply for a kennel license.[7] Pennsylvania categorizes kennels by type—research, boarding, commercial, private, pet shop, rescue and nonprofit kennels, with the licensing fee based on the type of kennel along with the number of dogs kept and/or transferred over the year.

Similarly, Colorado's Pet Animal Care and Facilities Act (PACFA)[8] requires a license for any place that shelters, trades or transfers "pet animals." PACFA impacts a wide variety of facilities and organizations including pet shops, breeders, shelters, and rescues. The Colorado law includes rescues that do not have their own facilities but that "accepts pet animals for the purpose of finding permanent adoptive homes for animals... us[ing] a system of fostering in private homes...." While each foster home is not required to have a license, the rescue is responsible to ensure that each foster home meets all PACFA standards and must provide to Colorado upon request a list of the foster homes.

Many states treat rescues and shelters the same without recognizing the differences in the types of organizations. For example, in Wisconsin both shelters and animal rescues that take in 25 dogs or more per year must be licensed regardless if the dogs are kept in a central facility or cared for in a network of foster homes. All shelter facilities and foster homes are subject to inspection and must provide a veterinary certificate and vaccination record whenever animals are adopted out or sold.[9]

Similarly, rescues and fosters in Georgia are subject to inspections by the Department of Agriculture and each pays licensing fees based on the total number of animals the facility is capable of holding.[10] All facilities also must ensure that they meet local zoning ordinances, and abide by the Georgia Animal Protection Act[11] to be licensed.

10-SECOND TAKEAWAY

1. Research and abide by state licensing laws.
2. Every state has different requirements for licensing including fees, license types, and inspection requirements.

11

STATE ANIMAL HEALTH LAWS

STERILIZATION

A majority of states have spay and neuter requirements. These laws are in place to help curb pet over population and decrease the number of homeless animals. Laws vary by state but often require that a shelter or rescue either have a licensed veterinarian sterilize the animals prior to adopting them out, or require adopters to sign an agreement to have the animal sterilized within 90 days and pay a deposit to the shelter or rescue which will be refunded once the adopter brings in proof that the sterilization procedure has been completed. See for example the Colorado Pet Animal Care Facilities Act.[12] The law is similar in Texas requiring the releasing agency to have the animals sterilized or have the adopters sign an agreement that they will sterilize an adult animal within 30 days after adoption.[13]

A state-by-state list of sterilization laws is included in Appendix A.

VACCINATION

Most states also require all "animal custodians" to have the animals they keep vaccinated against rabies. The terms used in the state laws (e.g. "animal custodian") and how each term is defined varies by the state. For example, in Texas, the term animal custodian refers to "[a] person or agency which feeds, shelters, harbors, owns, has possession or control of, or has the responsibility to control an animal."[14] This definition is written broadly to include not just dog owners and shelters, but also rescue organizations and foster care providers.

 A state-by-state list of vaccination laws is included in Appendix A.

TRANSFER AND TRANSPORT LAWS

As the number of groups transporting animals across state lines has increased, the number of states passing laws regulating the transfer and transport of animals across state lines also is increasing. For example, Connecticut passed a law in 2011 that tracks the number of animals imported into the state. The law also is intended to confirm that the animals brought in from out of state are healthy.[15] Connecticut requires a health certificate for a rescue to bring an animal into the state and a 10-day notice before bringing the animal into the state. After arriving in state the animal must be seen by a licensed veterinarian within 48 hours, and must receive follow-up examinations every 90 days until the animal is adopted out or sold. There are fines for failing to comply.

Massachusetts issued an emergency order in 2005 that requires imported animals to have a health certificate from the place of origin and then be quarantined for 48 hours upon arriving in the state. After quarantine the animals must be examined by a veterinarian and declared in good health before they can be released to a foster or adoptive home.[16] The Emergency Order is not yet codified into law.

The bottom line—if you plan to start an animal welfare group that transports animals across state lines make sure that the animals have a health certificate, proof of rabies vaccinations, and you are aware of the appropriate state transport laws.

 A state-by-state list of state transport laws is found in Appendix A.

TETHERING

Many states have tethering laws. Tethering is a practice of chaining or fastening a dog to a stationary object, such as a tree, fence, dog house, or stake. Some states have anti-tethering laws that limit the amount of time and the type of conditions under which a dog may be tethered. In Texas, for example, you may not leave a dog unattended or to unreasonably tether or restrain a dog between 10 p.m. and 6 a.m.[17] The Texas law also disallows tethering an animal outside when the temperature is below 32 degrees Fahrenheit, when a heat advisory has been declared, and when there is a hurricane, tornado or tropical storm warning.

Delaware permits tethering a dog provided the tether does not get entangled with other objects or touch other dogs. The tether must be at least 10 feet long and be made of material that is unlikely to be severed by chewing.[18] California law starts by prohibiting tethering and then listing certain exceptions when tethering is allowed.[19] Colorado prohibits tethering except when grooming a cat or dog.[20]

 A state-by-state list of tethering laws is found in Appendix A.

ANIMAL CRUELTY LAWS

Some state laws provide that a person convicted of animal cruelty must pay for the costs of medical and other care incurred by an animal welfare organization that are needed to rehabilitate the animal. For example, Washington's animal anti-cruelty statute says:

In addition to fines and court costs, the defendant, only if convicted or in agreement, shall be liable for reasonable costs incurred pursuant to this chapter by law enforcement agencies, animal care and control agencies, or authorized private or public entities involved with the care of the animals. Reasonable costs include expenses of the investigation, and the animal's care, euthanization, or adoption. [21]

An Ohio court upheld a decision to grant a local humane society, various rescue groups, and individual volunteers the right to collect reimbursement costs for caring and providing for the welfare of over one hundred companion animals from a kennel operator found guilty of animal cruelty.[22] In an Alaska case an equine rescue was able to collect restitution from a defendant after they took in over 130 animals that were ill and had been taken care of inadequately.[23]

 A state-by-state list of animal cruelty laws is found in Appendix A.

10-SECOND TAKEAWAY

1. Research and abide by animal health laws. (See appendix A)

2. Sterilization laws are in place to help curb pet homelessness and over population.

3. Most states require pets to be vaccinated for rabies.

4. Animals being transported across state lines need heath certificates, proof of rabies vaccinations and other documents based on individual state requirements.

5. A person convicted of animal cruelty may be required to pay for medical and other care costs incurred by an animal welfare organization.

12

LOCAL ANIMAL LAWS

Your city and county also may have laws relating to the care of animals, including setting pet limits, zoning rules, nuisance ordinances, and sometimes breed specific rules. As a result, before you start a rescue, shelter, foster or other animal welfare program, you are encouraged to check for all applicable state and local licensing requirements.

PET LIMIT LAWS

Limits on the number of animals a person may keep on their property are often set by local cities and counties. These laws are intended to reduce animal hoarding, and help reduce the noise and smells in neighborhoods and communities. Many locations limit the number of pets to three or four. However, some states allow foster homes to have more, such as Colorado that allows up to eight dogs or cats at a time in a foster home.

ZONING RULES

Zoning laws may impact the number of animals allowed on property. Land zoned "agricultural", for example, often allows more animals than land zoned "residential". Check your zoning before setting up a kennel, rescue or other animal welfare organization to make sure what you have in mind does not violate the local laws.

NUISANCE LAWS

Nuisance laws allow people to bring a claim and request for action ("redress") if they believe another person's use of his/her land is interfering with the complainant's use or enjoyment of their property. Claims may be brought if a landowner believes that the noise and/or smells from a rescue that has an excessive number of animals on their property interferes with their sleep, use of their property or other reason.

Beware of zoning changes. If your area is changed from agricultural to residential, complaints may soon follow if you house animals. In Iowa, a landowner had been operating a rescue for many years, housing as many as 40 dogs. When the zoning in her area was changed from agricultural to residential a nuisance complaint was brought. The neighbors said that barking of the dogs could be heard through closed doors and windows at night and that the smell of the urine and waste coming from the rescue property could not be avoided. The court found that the rescue was a nuisance and that no more than five dogs could be kept on the property despite the fact that the rescue owner took in unwanted dogs, fed and housed them, did her best to pick up the dogs' waste, and was permitted by law to have the animals in her home when she started the rescue.

BREED SPECIFIC LEGISLATION (BSL)

Some states and localities prohibit the keeping of specific breeds of animals that are considered dangerous. Pit bulls are an example of a breed frequently outlawed. The Denver, Colorado code states, "[i]t shall be unlawful for any person to own, possess, keep, exercise control over, maintain, harbor, transport, or sell within the city any pit bull." The Denver law includes "American Pit Bull Terriers, American Staffordshire Terrier, Staffordshire Bull Terrier, or any dog that displays a majority of the physical traits of those breeds" in its prohibition.[24] Private animal welfare groups that are registered and licensed by the city may temporarily hold a pit bull until they are able to hand over the pit bull to the city's municipal animal shelter or, if the city shelter grants permission, to destroy the pit bull.[25]

Some breed restriction laws have strict rules requiring licensing, fees, secured enclosures, microchipping, muzzles and insurance policies.[26] The laws sometimes have exceptions for dogs traveling through the city, dogs licensed and living in the city prior to the legislation, or for dogs in exhibitions.

Groups are working to change breed specific laws to be breed-neutral, favoring laws that hold all dog owners liable if their dog attacks and injures someone, regardless of the breed.[27]

10-SECOND TAKEAWAY

1. Research and abide by city and county animal laws.

2. Pet limit and zoning rules impact the number of animals allowed on a person's property.

3. Nuisance claims may be filed if a landowner believes the noise and/or smells from a rescue interferes with their sleep or use of their property or other reason.

4. Some states and localities have laws that are breed specific. These laws may prohibit the keeping of specific breeds or specific licensing requirements related to the specific breed.

13

DOG BITES AND
OTHER STRICT LIABILITY

There is always a risk of liability whenever working with animals and the public, regardless of the animal or breed or the care taken to meet local and state laws. For example, a rescue operating in Indianapolis took care to meet all local requirements including having a six foot reinforced fence around her outdoor enclosure. Nevertheless, one dog got out of the enclosure and was found running, lunging, barking and aggressively growling. The rescue was found in violation of having a menacing dog at large in the city.[28] Until that point the rescue had been appropriated successfully, including adopting out 190 dogs. The court held the rescue owner strictly liable, regardless of her past history and good intentions, resulting in the rescue dissolving with the rescue owner no longer permitted to own or keep more than two dogs.

At least 36 states and the District of Columbia impose strict liability in dog bite cases. Most of these laws will apply to rescues and shelters while the dog is kept by the shelter or rescue. Liability gets fuzzier after an animal is adopted out. For example, in a Connecticut case a rescue dog attacked another dog after it was adopted out and while it was being walked off leash. The owner of the dog attacked brought a law suit claiming that the rescue should have known and warned the adopting family about the dog's dangerous and aggressive tendencies. The court found that the rescue was not negligent and therefore was not liable for not warning of the dog's dangerous propensities.[29]

Even though liability was not found in this case, the rescue still had to cover the costs of defending itself in the lawsuit and the possible loss of its reputation in the community. For these reasons it is important that rescues have insurance to cover potential claims and liabilities, and follow a strong code of ethics to limit exposure to claims and maintain its good standing in the community.

10-SECOND TAKEAWAY

1. Even after researching and abiding by all state and local laws there remains a risk of liability when working with animals and the public.

2. Even if an animal welfare group is not found liable in a law suit, the financial costs and reputation loss of such a suit can be debilitating for an organization.

3. Rescues should carry insurance and follow a strong code of ethics to cover potential claims and liabilities.

14

DOG BONES & OTHER TREATS

Having gotten this far in the book you may now be wondering whether you really have the time, energy and know-how to set-up your animal welfare organization, to maintain the federal and state registrations, to raise funds and volunteer help, and to take care of the animals and all the other details associated with an animal welfare organization. You're a dog-, cat-, you-name-the-animal-person...not a lawyer. I get it. That's why I wrote this book and founded myRENOSI™ (myrenosi.com). This book, its appendices full of tools and templates, and the companion website are intended to give you a good overview and a running start. However, if you are still feeling overwhelmed, myRENOSI™ is here to help you get your rescue started, and handle the annual federal and state tax and registration requirements, so you can go back to doing what you love—taking care of the animals.

FORTY-TWO QUICK TIPS AND TAKEAWAYS

1. Pet ownership is growing exponentially throughout the world.
2. Over 7 million pets enter shelters every year.
3. Roughly half of all rescued animals are given new homes.
4. Approximately half of all rescued animals are euthanized.
5. There is a growing need for rescue organizations.
6. Animal "pounds" began in colonial times to collect stray animals and return them to their owners for a fee.
7. Publicly (tax) funded "pounds", later called "shelters" relied on euthanasia due to limited funds and facilities.
8. Privately funded shelters began in 1866 with the ASPCA.
9. Animal shelters, rescues and sanctuaries come in a wide variety of types, distinguished by the animals accepted, community served, and work conducted.
10. Most shelters and rescues are started and managed by people passionate about animals who need tools, tips and resources to help them successfully set-up, maintain and operate their animal welfare organizations. Incorporation, while not required by law, is highly recommended.
11. To organize properly in IRS lingo means that your formation document (e.g. articles of incorporation) includes all the required IRS language.
12. Obtaining 501(c)(3) status offers myriad benefits on both federal and state levels.
13. Your state has rules, too. Check and follow them!

14. All nonprofit organizations must file an annual IRS 990-series "information" tax return or risk loss of their 501(c)(3) status.

15. States generally require nonprofit corporations to file an annual corporate report, and annual fundraising (charity) renewals.

16. States also may require you to file for exemption from state franchise/income tax and sales tax exemption and/or collection.

17. Handling your organization's finances carefully is key to success.

18. Always adopt a budget, and report actual income and expenses against the budget, throughout the year.

19. Conduct an annual financial review (aka "audit") each year.

20. Required adoption fees are not usually tax-deductible; it's the organization's role to tell donors what is/is not tax-deductible.

21. Be prepared if the IRS audits your organization by knowing the types of activities the IRS most commonly scrutinizes.

22. Don't meet to meet. Give your board policy-level items to discuss.

23. Board minutes should be brief, listing only the actions taken.

24. Volunteers often have limits on their time. Provide a variety of volunteer opportunities and let your volunteers know how much time each opportunity involves.

25. Obtain insurance. Taking care of animals is risky business.

26. Legally companion animals are considered "property" meaning property laws apply.

27. Put all your intentions regarding ownership, liability and animal care requirements in writing.

28. Be careful not to exceed what's allowed under the law when drafting your contracts.

29. Be familiar with and abide by animal welfare laws.

30. Every state has different requirements for licensing including fees, license types, and inspection requirements.

31. Research and abide by animal health laws. (See appendix A)

32. Sterilization laws are in place to help curb pet homelessness and over population.

33. Most states require pets to be vaccinated for rabies.

34. Animals being transported across state lines need heath certificates, proof of rabies vaccinations and other documents based on individual state requirements.

35. A person convicted of animal cruelty may be required to pay for medical and other care costs incurred by an animal welfare organization.

36. Research and abide by city and county animal laws.

37. Pet limit and zoning rules impact the number of animals allowed on a person's property.

38. Nuisance claims may be filed if a landowner believes the noise and/or smells from a rescue interferes with their sleep or use of their property or other reason.

39. Some states and localities have breed specific laws, although there is a movement to do away with such laws.
40. There is always a risk of liability when working with animals and the public, even if you follow all the laws.
41. The financial costs and reputation loss of lawsuits may be debilitating for an organization, even if you are cleared of any wrongdoing.
42. Rescues should carry insurance and follow a strong code of ethics to cover potential claims and liabilities.

END NOTES

Chapter 2

1   Lila Miller, Animal Sheltering in the United States: Yesterday, Today, and Tomorrow, Veterinary Medicine, Oct. 1, 2007, accessed at http://veterinarymedicine.dvm360.com/animal-sheltering-united-states-yesterday-today-and-tomorrow?id=&pageID=1&sk=&date=

Chapter 9

2   Adam Lynn, Lakewood animal rescue group sues to get dog returned, The Columbian, Oct. 7, 2013, accessed at http://www.columbian.com/news/2013/oct/07/lakewood-rescue-group-sues-for-dog/

3   Wiederhold v. Derench, 2003 Conn. Super. LEXIS 1795, Conn. Super. Ct. June 17, 2003.

4   (Brad Tuttle, 'Pet flipping' is Now a Thing, Time, (July 16, 2013), available at http://business.time.com/2013/07/16/pet-flipping-is-now-a-thing/).

5   Manolo Morales, Craigslist ad sparks public outrage, disappointment, (June 24, 2014), available at http://khon2.com/2014/06/24/craigslist-dog-ad- sparks-public-outrage-disappointment/).

6   (Sixth Angel Shepherd Rescue, Inc. v. Bengal, 448 Fed. Appx. 252 (3d Cir. Pa. 2011)).

Chapter 10

7   See Pennsylvania passed Act 119 at http://www.
    agriculture.state.pa.us/portal/server.pt/gateway/
    PTARGS_0_2_24476_10297_0_43/AgWebsite/ProgramDetail.
    aspx? palid=62&).

8   (PACFA), (C.R.S. §§ 35-80-101 et seq.),

9   (W.S.A. §173.41).

10 See Animal Protection FAQs, Georgia Department of
    Agriculture, available at http://www.agr.georgia.gov/animal-
    protection-faqs.aspx).

11 (O.C.G.A. § 4-11-1)

Chapter 11

12 (C.R.S. 35-80-106.4).

13 See Texas statutes §§ 828.001—828.00.

14 (§169.22(6)).

15 (Janice Podsada, Rescue Groups Decry New Animal Importa-
    tion Law, The Hartford Courant, (July 14, 2011), available
    at http://articles.courant.com/2011-07-14/business/hc-dog-
    rescue-bill-protest- 20110714_1_animal-rescue-rescue-groups-
    susan-linker).

16 See, Emergency Order 1-AHO-05, (May 26, 2005), available
    at http://www.mass.gov/eea/agencies/agr/animal-health/
    shelter-and-rescue/).

17 See Texas Health and Safety Code § 821.077.

18 See, 9 Del. Code § 904(d)(4)).

19 See, California Health and Safety Code § 122335).

20 (8 C.C.R. 1201-11(18.00)(I)).

21 (Wash. Rev. Code § 16.52.200(6)).

22 (Lay v. Chamberlain, 2000 Ohio App. LEXIS 5783, (Ohio Ct. App., Madison County Dec. 11, 2000)).

23 (See Mahan v. State, 51 P.3d 962, 968-69, (Alaska App. 2002)).

Chapter 12

24 (See, § 8-55(b)).

25 See, § 8-55 (c)(3)).

26 (See, Aurora, Colorado ordinance § 14-75; Louisville, Colorado ordinance § 6.12.160; Commerce City, Colorado ordinance § 4-2011).

27 (See(Maryland Passes Breed Neutral Dog Bite Liability Legislation, Reverses Tracey v. Solesky Decision, The Humane Society of the United States, (April 3, 2014), http://www. humanesociety.org/news/press_releases/2014/04/md_neu-tral_dog_bite_law_040314.html? credit=web_id80919688).

Chapter 13

28 (See Francis v. City of Indianapolis, 2011 Ind. App. Unpub. LEXIS 1605, 1 (Ind. Ct. App. 2011))

29 (Dutka v. Cassady, 2012 Conn. Super. LEXIS 1901).

STATE BY
STATE LAWS

ALABAMA

Law	Requirements	Reference
Exotic pets	This Alabama statute makes it unlawful to hunt or kill any species of nonindigenous animals for a fee or for recreation. This section does not apply to feral swine, nuisance animals, or to any nonindigenous animal lawfully brought into this state prior to 2006.	Ala. Code § 9- 11-501 to 505 (1975)
	This set of laws authorizes all cities and towns to regulate animals and animal related conditions that pose a threat to the public health.	Ala. Code 5 § 11- 47-130 to 132 (1975)
	This Alabama law provides that the Commissioner of Conservation and Natural Resources may, by regulation, prohibit the importation of any animal when such importation is not in the best interest of the state. However, this does not apply to those animals used for display purposes at circuses, carnivals, zoos, and other shows or exhibits. Importing a prohibited animal into the state is a Class C misdemeanor with a fine of $1,000 - 5,000, or jail for 30 days, or both.	Ala. Code § 9- 2-13 (1975)
	This set of Alabama laws relates to the possession of captive wildlife. The Commissioner of Conservation and Natural Resources may issue an annual permit to possess wildlife for public exhibition to a person qualified by education or experience in the care and treatment of wildlife at a cost of $25.00. Violation of any provision of the article results in a fine of not more than $500.00, imprisonment for not more than three months, or both. Notably, the provisions of the article do not apply to any municipal, county, state or other publicly owned zoo or wildlife exhibit, privately owned traveling zoo or circus or pet shop.	Ala. Code § 9- 11-320 to 328 (1975)
Sterilization	Dogs and cats must be sterilized before adoption, or adopters must enter into a sterilization agreement.	Ala. Code § 3-9-2 (1975)

Law	Requirements	Reference
Vaccination	Cats – within 3 months of age vaccinate for rabies and possess certificate evidencing the same.	
Tethering	NONE	
Parked vehicles	NONE	
Leash	All cities and towns of this state shall have the power to regulate and prevent the running of dogs at large on the streets.	Ala. Code § 11-47- 110 (1975)
Leash – wildlife management region	No dog shall be permitted, except on leash, within any wildlife management area except per state rule; the owner of any dog at large within any wildlife management area shall be guilty of a misdemeanor.	Ala. Code § 9-11-305 (1975)
Chasing wildlife	No dog shall be permitted except on leash within any wildlife management area except in accordance with the rules and regulations promulgated by the commissioner of conservation and natural resources, and whoever shall be the owner of any dog at large within any wildlife management area shall be guilty of a misdemeanor. Dogs found in violation of this statute will be impounded until either redeemed by the owner or destroyed (in accordance with the provisions of 9-11-306).	Ala. Code §§ 9- 11-30, 9- 11-306
Strict liability	The owner of any dog, that causes a bite or injury, in any place the victim has a legal right to be, is liable for actual expenses, except in cases of provocation or if the owner proves that s/he had no knowledge of any circumstances indicating dog was vicious, dangerous or mischievous.	Ala. Code §§3-6- 1, 3-6- 3
Dog Bites	If owner proves that s/he had no knowledge of any circumstances indicating dog was vicious, dangerous or mischievous, then s/he is only liable for actual expenses.	Ala. Code §§3-6- 1, 3-6- 3

Law	Requirements	Reference
Dangerous dogs	A person who keeps a dangerous or vicious animal of any kind, and through his negligent management of the animal allows it to break free, is liable to any person damaged personally or in his property as a result.	Ala. Code § 3-1-3 (1975) Note: the phrase/ terms "dangerous or vicious animal" is not defined in the law
Breed Specific	Most cities ban: Pit bulls, Rottweilers and wolf hybrids declared "potentially dangerous". See city website for more information.	
Cruelty	The act of cruelty to animals, particularly domesticated dogs and cats, is defined as: "Overloads, overdrives, deprives of necessary sustenance or shelter, unnecessarily or cruelly beats, injures, mutilates or causes the same to be done; intentionally tortures any dog or cat or skins a domestic dog or cat or offers for sale or exchange or offers to buy to exchange the fur, hide, or pelt of a domestic dog or cat." Cruelty to a dog or cat is a Class A Misdemeanor, punishable with a fine of up to $1,000 and/or imprisonment up to 6 months. Intentionally torturing a dog or cat is a Class C Felony punishable with a fine of up to $5,000 and/or imprisonment up to 10 years. Person convicted could also be made to pay for the cost of care of the animal. Exceptions are made for research, protection of life or property, training, or shooting a dog or cat for urinating or defecating on property. Animals can also be seized by animal control officers.	Ala. Code § 13A-11-14 (1977)
Minimum age sale of puppies	NONE	

Alaska

Law	Requirements	Reference
Exotic Pets	NONE	
Sterilization	NONE	
Vaccination	NONE	
Tethering	NONE	
Parked Vehicles	NONE	
Leash	NONE	
Leash – wildlife management region	NONE	
Chasing Wildlife	A state park officer may seize a dog or other pet running at large in a state park and may destroy the dog or other pet if it is mad, vicious, or harassing wildlife.	Alaska Stat. § 03.55.030
Strict Liability	NONE	
Dog Bites	NONE	
Dangerous Dog	Any dog which when unprovoked has ever bitten or attacked a human being.	Alaska Stat. § 03.55.020
	Any person may lawfully kill any vicious or mad dog running at large.	Alaska Stat. § 03.55.010
Breed specific	Pit bulls and Rottweilers declared "vicious". See city website for more information.	

Law	Requirements	Reference
Cruelty	Cruelty to animals is defined as "Knowingly inflict[ing] severe physical pain or suffering; or with criminal negligence fails to care for an animal and causes its death or severe pain or prolonged suffering". It is a Class A Misdemeanor, with sentencing provisions including a fine of up to $5,000, imprisonment up to 1 year, community service and restitution. Exceptions are made for farming, hunting, research, training and veterinary care.	Alaska Stat. § 11.61.140
Minimum age sale of puppies	NONE	

Arizona

Law	Requirements	Reference
Exotic Pets	NONE	
Sterilization	Dogs and cats must be sterilized before adoption.	Ariz. Rev. Stat. § 11-1022
Vaccination	NONE	
Tethering	NONE	
Parked Vehicles	Unattended and confined in a motor vehicle and physical injury to or death of the animal is likely to result. A peace officer, animal control enforcement agent or animal control enforcement deputy may use reasonable force reasonable force to open a vehicle to rescue an animal.	Ariz. Rev. Stat. § 13-2910
Leash	County board of supervisors may, for unincorporated areas of the county, prohibit dogs running at large, except dogs used for control of livestock or while being used or trained for hunting, by ordinance.	Ariz. Rev. Stat. § 11-1005
	The common council shall also have power within the limits of the town incorporated under A.R.S. § 9-101 to regulate, restrain and prohibit the running at large of dogs.	Ariz. Rev. Stat. § 9-240
Leash— wildlife management region	No person in charge of any dog shall permit such dog in a public park or upon any public school property unless the dog is physically restrained by a leash, enclosed in a car, cage or similar enclosure or being exhibited or trained at a recognized kennel club event, public school or park sponsored event.	Ariz. Rev. Stat. § 11- 1012
Chasing Wildlife	It is a misdemeanor to take big game (except bear or mountain lion) with the aid of dogs.	Ariz. Rev. Stat. § 17- 309

Law	Requirements	Reference
Strict Liability	The owner of any dog, that causes a bite in a public place, or private place where a person has legal right to be, including dog owner's property. Except in cases of provocation or dog used in military or police work if defending itself from a harassing or provoking act and dog is used in military or police work if dog was assisting in apprehending a suspect, investigation of a crime, execution of a warrant, or defense of a person.	Ariz. Rev. Stat. §§11-1025, 11-1027
Dog Bites	Dog used in military or police work if dog was assisting in apprehending a suspect, investigation of a crime, execution of a warrant, or defense of a person.	Ariz. Rev. Stat. §§11-1025, 11-1027
Dangerous Dog	Class 2 Misdemeanor Owner strictly liable for damage/injury to persons or property.	Ariz. Rev. Stat. §§11-1019, 11-1025
Breed specific	NONE	
Cruelty	Animal cruelty is defined as: "Intentionally, knowingly or recklessly subjects any animal to cruel neglect or abandonment, failing to provide necessary medical attention to prevent protracted suffering, causes unnecessary physical injury, kills any animal without the legal privilege or consent of the owner, leaves an animal unattended and confined in a motor vehicle and injury or death is a likely result." There are also special provisions for harming service animals, including allowing or having another animal harm or interfere with a service animal. Intentional, knowingly or recklessly subjecting an animal to cruel treatment is a Class A Misdemeanor, punishable by a fine up to $2,500 and/or imprisonment for 6 months.	Ariz. Rev. Stat. §13-2910

Law	Requirements	Reference
	Intentionally subjecting an animal to cruel neglect, mistreatment, or killing or harming a service animal is a Class 6 Felony punishable by a fine of up to $150,000 and/or imprisonment of up to 1.5 years. Sentences can also include community service, no animal ownership for 3 years, and restitution. Exceptions are made for hunting, poisoning rodents or dogs killing or wounding livestock.	
Minimum age sale of puppies	Not less than eight weeks' old Class 1 misdemeanor	Ariz. Rev. Stat. § 44- 1799.04

ARKANSAS

Law	Requirements	Reference
Exotic Pets	This Arkansas statute outlines the procedure for vaccination of wolf-hybrid dogs, including procedures for handling bites by these canines.	Ark. Code Ann. §20-19-406
	This chapter of Arkansas laws concerns the regulation of wolves and wolfdog hybrids kept as companion animals. Under the law, a "wolf-dog hybrid" means any animal which is publicly acknowledged by its owner as being the offspring of a wolf and domestic dog; however, no animal may be judged to be a wolf or wolf-dog hybrid based strictly on its appearance. The specific rabies vaccination requirements for wolf-dog hybrids are detailed as well as confinement requirements (i.e., specific fence dimensions). If a wolf or wolf-dog hybrid bites a person or injures or destroys another animal while out of its confined area, the person responsible for the adequate confinement of the animal upon conviction shall be guilty of a Class A misdemeanor.	Ark. Code Ann. §20-19-401 – 408
	This Arkansas subchapter concerns the ownership and possession of large carnivores. Under the law, a large carnivore is defined as a bear, lion, or tiger. A person may possess a large carnivore only if he or she was in possession of the large carnivore on or before August 12, 2005 and the person applies for and is granted a permit for personal possession for each large carnivore not more than one hundred eighty (180) days after August 12, 2005. Except for these "grandfathered" possessors and other entities (zoos, USDA permittees, veterinary hospitals, etc.) it is illegal for anyone to own, possess, breed, or transfer ownership of a large carnivore.	Ark. Code Ann. §20-19-501 – 511

Law	Requirements	Reference
	This new 2013 Act prohibits the importing, possession, selling, or breeding of apes, baboons, and macaques. It is unlawful under the act for a person to allow a member of the public to come into direct contact with a primate. Further, a person cannot tether a primate outdoors or allow a primate to run at-large. The section does not apply to accredited AZA institutions, AWA regulated research facilities, wildlife sanctuaries, temporary holding facilities, licensed veterinarians providing treatment, law enforcement officers, circuses holding AWA Class C licenses as provided, and those temporarily in the state. The act has a grandfathering provision that allows a person at least 18 years of age to continue to possess the restricted primate if within 180 days after the effective date of the act the person registers the animal per § 20-19-605 and follows other listed requirements.	Ark. Code Ann. §20-19-601 -610
Sterilization	Dogs and cats must be sterilized before adoption.	Ark. Code Ann. §20-19-103
Vaccination	Four (4) months of age or older	Ark. Code R. §007.15.1-I to II
Tethering	NONE	
Parked Vehicles	NONE	
Leash	Municipal corporations shall have the power to prevent the running at large of dogs, and injuries and annoyances therefrom, and to authorize the destruction of them, when at large contrary to any prohibition to that effect.	Ark. Code Ann. §14-54 1102
Leash— wildlife management region	NONE	

Law	Requirements	Reference
Chasing Wildlife	Recreational hunting is good for wildlife management. There was a statute that prohibited dogs from running at large to protect wildlife, but it was repealed in 1999. Now, there is a statute that punishes (fines and fires) state employees who try to enforce the statute prohibiting dogs from running at large.	Ark. Code Ann. §15-41-302
Strict Liability	NONE	
Dog Bites	NONE	
Dangerous Dog	NONE	
Breed specific	Most cities restrict or ban pit bulls and some other breeds. See city website for more detailed information.	
Cruelty	The crime of cruelty to animals is defined as: "Knowingly abandons any animal, subjects it to cruel mistreatment or cruel neglect, or kills or injures an animal without the owner's consent." Cruelty to animals is a Class A Misdemeanor punishable with a fine up to $1,000 and/or imprisonment up to 1 year, cost of care for the animal, and counseling. Exemptions are made for hunting and protection of livestock.	Ark. Code Ann. §5-62-101
Minimum age sale of puppies	NONE	

STATE BY STATE LAWS · 111

CALIFORNIA

Law	Requirements	Reference
Exotic Pets	This California law provides that no person may perform, or otherwise procure or arrange for the performance of, surgical claw removal, declawing, onychectomy, or tendonectomy on any cat that is a member of an exotic or native wild cat species, and shall not otherwise alter such a cat's toes, claws, or paws to prevent the normal function of the cat's toes, claws, or paws. Violation results in a misdemeanor punishable by imprisonment for up to one year and/or a fine of up to $10,000.	Cal. Penal Code §597.6
	These California laws relate to the importation of certain animal's parts for commercial purposes. Under the law, it is unlawful to import into this state for commercial purposes, to possess with intent to sell, or to sell within the state, the dead body, or any part or product thereof, of any polar bear leopard, ocelot, tiger, cheetah, jaguar, sable antelope, wolf (Canis lupus), zebra, whale, cobra, python, sea turtle, colobus monkey, kangaroo, vicuna, sea otter, free-roaming feral horse, dolphin or porpoise (Delphinidae), Spanish lynx, or elephant. Starting in 2015, it shall be unlawful to import into this state for commercial purposes, to possess with intent to sell, or to sell within the state, the dead body, or any part or product thereof, of any crocodile or alligator. Section 653p makes it unlawful to possess with the intent to sell any part or dead body of any species on the federal endangered species list or species covered under the MMPA. Section 653q makes it illegal to import for commercial purposes, to possess with intent to sell, or to sell within the state, the dead body, or any part or product thereof, of any seal.	Cal. Penal Code §653o - 653r

Law	Requirements	Reference
	This California set of law relates to the importation of "wild animals" (defined as any animal of the class Aves (birds) or class Mammalia (mammals) that either is not normally domesticated in this state or not native to this state). The violation of any provision of this chapter shall be a misdemeanor. The department may issue a permit to import a wild animal provided that a determination is made that public health or safety will not be endangered.	Cal. Health & Safety Code § 121775 – 121870
	This statute enumerates the fully protected mammals in the state of California. These animals may not be taken or possessed at any time. The statute also specifically states that permits or licenses to take these animals will not be issued, with a possible exception in the case of necessary scientific research.	Cal. Fish & G. Code § 4700
	The California Legislature adopted this act based on a finding that wild animals are captured for importation and resold in California and that some populations of wild animals are being depleted, that many animals die in captivity or transit, and that some keepers of wild animals lack sufficient knowledge or facilities for the proper care of wild animals. It was the intention of the Legislature to regulate the importation, transportation, and possession of wild animals to protect the native wildlife and agricultural interests against damage from the existence at large of certain wild animals, and to protect the public health and safety in this state. The act defines "wild animal" and classifies them by species. Among other things, the act also includes inspection and permit provisions that govern the treatment of wild animals and the actions that may be taken where they are concerned.	Cal. Fish & G. Code §2116 2203

Law	Requirements	Reference
Sterilization	Dogs and cats must be "spayed or neutered" before adoption.	Cal. Food & Agric. Code §§30503, 31751.3
Vaccination	NONE	
Tethering	No person shall tether, fasten, chain, tie, or restrain a dog to any dog house, tree, fence, or other stationary object. A person may temporarily tether a dog "no longer than is necessary for the person to complete a temporary task. Infraction or misdemeanor. Animal control may issue a warning to a person who violates this chapter, requiring the owner to correct the violation, in lieu of an infraction or misdemeanor, unless the violation endangers the health or safety of the animal, or the animal has been wounded as a result of the activity.	Cal. Health & Safety Code §122335
Parked Vehicles	First conviction: fine not exceeding $100 per animal. If the animal suffers great bodily injury, a fine not exceeding $500, imprisonment in a county jail not exceeding 6 months, or by both. Any subsequent violation of this section, regardless of injury to the regardless of injury to the animal, punishable by a fine not exceeding $500, imprisonment in a county jail not exceeding six months, or by both. Peace officer, humane officer, or animal control officer is authorized to take all steps all steps that are that are reasonably necessary for the removal of an animal from a motor vehicle. Must leave written notice bearing his or her name and office, and the address of the location where the animal can be claimed.	Cal. Penal Code §597.7
Leash	NONE	
Leash— wildlife management region	NONE	

Law	Requirements	Reference
Chasing Wildlife	It is unlawful to permit or allow any dog to pursue any big game mammal during the closed season on such mammal, to pursue any fully protected, rare, or endangered mammal at any time, or to pursue any mammal in a game refuge or ecological reserve if hunting within such refuge or ecological reserve is unlawful. Any employee of the fish and game department may capture or dispatch a dog causing injury to wildlife without liability.	Cal. Fish & G. Code §3960
Strict Liability	The owner of any dog that causes a bite in any Public place, Or Private place where person has legal right to be, including dog owner's property. Provocation exception, the dog is used in military or police work if defending itself from a harassing or provoking act, or Contributory negligence (See Johnson v. McMahan, 68 Cal.App.4th 173, 176 (1998). Other exceptions are the person injured was trespassing (not lawfully on owner's property), dog used in military or police work if dog was assisting in apprehending a suspect, in the investigation of a crime, in the execution of a warrant, or in the defense of a person.	Cal. Civ. Code §3342
Dog Bites	Person injured was trespassing (not lawfully on owner's property) Dog used in military or police work if dog was assisting in apprehending a suspect, in the investigation of a crime, in the execution of a warrant, or in the defense of a person.	Assumption of the risk (See Johnson v. McMahan, 68 Cal. App. 4th 173, 176 (1998))

Law	Requirements	Reference
Dangerous Dog	Any dog which, when unprovoked and off owner's property, on two separate occasions within the prior 36- month period, engages in any behavior that requires a defensive action by any person to prevent bodily injury Any dog which, when unprovoked, bites a person causing a less severe injury Any dog which, when unprovoked and off owner's property, on two separate occasions within the prior 36- month period, has killed, seriously bitten, inflicted injury, or otherwise caused injury attacking a domestic animal.	Cal. Food & Agric. Code §31602
	Must be licensed and vaccinated Must be registered City or county may charge a registration fee Must be kept indoors or in a securely fenced yard May leave the owner's residence if the dog is restrained by a substantial leash Must notify the animal control department of changes in dog's situation in writing within two working days after the changes.	West's Ann. Cal. Food & Agric. Code §31641 & Cal. Food & Agric. Code §31643
	Any violation involving a potentially dangerous dog shall be punished by a fine not to exceed $500 Any violation involving a vicious dog shall be punished by a fine not to exceed $1,000 Owner of a vicious dog may be prohibited by the city or county from owning, possessing, controlling, or having custody of any dog for a period of up to three years.	Cal. Food & Agric. Code §§31646, 31662
Breed specific	Mandatory sterilization for pit bulls. See city website for more detailed information.	

Law	Requirements	Reference
Cruelty	Cruelty to animals is defined as "Maliciously and intentionally mains, mutilates, tortures, or wounds a living animal, or maliciously and intentionally kills an animal; or overdrives, overloads, drives when overloaded, overworks, tortures, torments, deprives of necessary sustenance, drink, or shelter, cruelly beats, mutilates, or cruelly kills any animal or causes or procures any animal to be so treated." Animals shall be seized and impounded and ownership forfeited. These crimes may be charged as either a misdemeanor or felony, with punishment of a fine up to $20,000 and/or imprisonment up to 1 year. If a defendant is granted probation for a conviction, the defendant must pay for and successfully complete counseling as determined by the court. It is also a misdemeanor to "Carry or causes to be carried in or upon any vehicle or otherwise any domestic animal in a cruel or inhumane manner." Exemptions are made for farming, hunting and research.	Cal. Penal Code §596-597
Minimum age sale of puppies	Must be at least eight weeks old.	Cal. Penal Code §597z; Cal. Health & Safety Code §122045 – 122315

COLORADO

Law	Requirements	Reference
Exotic Pets	This Colorado statute authorized the commissioner of the department of agriculture to appoint and convene an advisory group to study the behavior of hybrid canids (wolf hybrids) and felines, including a review of any incidents involving property damage and personal injury caused by such animals. The department was to present its findings and proposals for legislation in January of 1998.	Colo. Rev. Stat. Ann. §35-81-101 to 102
Sterilization	Dogs and cats must be sterilized before adoption, or adopters must enter into a sterilization agreement.	Colo. Rev. Stat. §35-80-106.4
Vaccination	NONE	
Tethering	NONE	
Parked Vehicles	NONE	
Leash	It is unlawful for any owner of any dog, cat, other pet animal, or other mammal which has not been inoculated as required by the order of the county board of health or board of health of a health department to allow it to run at large. The health department or health officer may capture and impound any such dog, cat, other pet animal, or other mammal found running at large and dispose of such animal in accordance with local program policy.	Colo. Rev. Stat. Ann. § 25-4-610
Leash— wildlife management region	NONE	
Chasing Wildlife	The division may bring a civil action against the owner of any dog inflicting death or injury to any big game and to small game, birds, and mammals for the value of each game animal injured or killed.	Colo. Rev. Stat. § 33 3-106

Law	Requirements	Reference
Strict Liability	The owner of any dog, that causes a bite, injury or death, in any public or private place where a person has legal right to be, including dog owner's property, except in cases of provocation. Other exceptions are, person injured unlawfully on public or private property; person injured on property of dog owner if there is a "no trespassing" or "beware of dog" sign; if dog is performing duties for peace officer or military personnel; if person injured is a veterinary health care worker, dog groomer, humane agency staff person, professional dog handler, trainer, or dog show judge performing his or her duties; or if dog is working as a hunting, herding, farm or ranch dog, or predator control dog on the property of or under the control of its owner.	Colo. Rev. Stat. §13-21-124
Dog Bites	Person injured unlawfully on public or private property; Person injured on property of dog owner if there is a "no trespassing" or "beware of dog" sign; If dog is performing duties for peace officer or military personnel; If person injured is a veterinary health care worker, dog groomer, humane agency staff person, professional dog handler, trainer, or dog show judge performing his or her duties; or If dog is working as a hunting, herding, farm or ranch dog, or predator control dog on the property of or under the control of its owner.	Colo. Rev. Stat. § 13-21-124
Dangerous Dog	Engages in or is trained for animal fighting Inflicts bodily or serious bodily injury or death of person or domestic animal Demonstrates tendencies that would cause a reasonable person to believe that the dog may inflict bodily or serious bodily injury upon or cause the death of any person or domestic animal.	Colo. Rev. Stat. Ann. § 18-9-204.5(2)(b)
	A person or a personal representative of a person who suffers serious bodily injury or death from being bitten by a dog while lawfully on public or private property shall be entitled to bring a civil action to recover economic damages against the dog owner.	Colo. Rev. Stat. Ann. § 13-21-124

Law	Requirements	Reference
	Ownership of a dangerous dog can be punished by a class 1 misdemeanor to a class 5 felony Restitution may be ordered for the injured or dead domestic animal, for the property damage caused by the dog, and for title 16 provisions that govern restitution.	Colo. Rev. Stat. Ann. § 18-9-204.5(e) and (f)
Breed specific	Some cities ban pit bulls while others ban all fighting breeds. See city website for more detailed information.	
Cruelty	Animal cruelty is defined as: "Knowingly, recklessly or with criminal negligence overdrives, overloads, over-works, torments, deprives of necessary sustenance, unnecessarily or cruelly beats, allows to be housed in a manner that results in chronic or repeated serious physical harm, carries or confines in or upon any vehicles in a cruel or reckless manner, or otherwise mistreats or neglects any animal, or causes or pro-cures it to be done, or, having the charge or custody of any animal, fails to provide it with proper food, drink, or protection from the weather, consistent with the species, breed, and type of animal involved, or abandons an animal" or "recklessly or with criminal negligence tortures, needlessly mutilates, or needlessly kills an animal." Conviction of Cruelty to Animals is a Class 1 Misdemeanor with a minimum fine of $400, maximum fine of $5000. In addition to any other fine, a surcharge of up to $400 shall be paid to the county where the violation occurred to be put into the Animal Cruelty Prevention fund. A subsequent conviction of Cruelty to Animals carries of minimum fine of $1000, maximum fine of $5000 and a minimum of 90 days' imprisonment or home detention, maximum imprisonment of 18 months. Anger Management or other psychological treatment as defined by the court is required, cost of care may also be assessed. Aggravated Cruelty is: "knowingly tortures, needlessly mutilates, or need-lessly kills an animal."	Colo. Rev. Stat. 18-9-202

Law	Requirements	Reference
	A conviction of Aggravated Animal Cruelty is a Class 6 Felony with a maximum fine of up to $100,000 and imprisonment for up to 18 months, minimum of 90 days in prison or in-home detention. Subsequent conviction of Aggravated Animal Cruelty is a Class 5 Felony with a maximum fine of $100,000 and imprisonment for up to 3 years. Exemptions are made for farming, draft or pack animals, rodeos, veterinary care, research, hunting and trapping.	
Minimum age sale of puppies	Minimum of eight weeks old.	Colo. Rev. Stat. § 35-80-108

CONNECTICUT

Law	Requirements	Reference
Exotic Pets	These Connecticut states reflect the state's laws on the keeping of wild animals. Under § 26-40a, no person shall possess a potentially dangerous animal, which includes wildlife such as the lion, leopard, cheetah, jaguar, ocelot, jaguarondi cat, puma, lynx, bobcat, wolf, coyote, all species of bears, gorilla, chimpanzee and orangutan. The Department of Environmental Protection shall issue a bill to the owner or person in illegal possession of such potentially dangerous animal for all costs of seizure, care, maintenance, relocation or disposal of such animal. Additionally, any person who violates any provision of this section shall be assessed a civil penalty not to exceed $2000, and is guilty of a class A misdemeanor. Under § 26-55, no person shall import or introduce into the state, possess or let loose, any live fish, wild bird, wild mammal, reptile, amphibian or invertebrate unless such person has obtained a permit. Again, a violator is responsible for expenses from the seizure, maintenance, and relocation of the illegally imported animal. The penalty includes a civil fine up to $1000 and results in a class C misdemeanor.	Conn. Gen. Stat. Ann. §§ 26-1, 26-40a, 26-54, 26-55, 26-61
Sterilization	Dogs and cats must be "spayed or neutered" before adoption, or the adopter must pay for a sterilization voucher.	Conn. Gen. Stat. § 22-380f
Vaccination	Cats: Three (3) months of age or older.	Conn. Gen. Stat. Ann. § 22-339b
Tethering	No person shall tether a dog to a stationary object or to a mobile device, including, but not limited to, a trolley or pulley by means of: 1. A tether that does not allow such dog to walk at least eight feet, excluding the length of such dog as measured from the tip of such dog's nose to the base of such dog's tail, in any one direction,	Conn. Gen. Stat § 22-350a

Law	Requirements	Reference
	2. a tether that does not have swivels on both ends to prevent twisting and tangling, unless a person is in the presence of such dog, 3. a coat hanger, choke collar, prong-type collar, head halter or any other collar, halter or device that is not specifically designed or properly fitted for the restraint of such dog, 4. a tether that has weights attached or that contains metal chain links more than one quarter of an inch thick, or 5. a tether that allows such dog to reach an object or hazard, including, but not limited to, a window sill, edge of a pool, fence, public road or highway, porch or terrace railing that poses a risk of injury or strangulation to such dog if such dog walks into or jumps over such object or hazard, unless a person is in the presence of such dog. Also prohibits tethering dog outdoors to a stationery object or to a mobile device (i.e., trolley or pulley) when a weather advisory or warning is issued by authorities, or when outdoor conditions (extreme heat, cold, wind, rain, snow or hail) pose an adverse risk to the health or safety of particular dog unless tethering is for a duration of no longer than fifteen minutes.	
Parked Vehicles	NONE	
Leash	No owner or keeper of any dog shall allow such dog to roam at large upon the land of another and not under control of the owner or keeper or the agent of the owner or keeper, nor allow such dog to roam at large on any portion of any public highway and not attended or under control of such owner or keeper or his agent, provided nothing in this subsection shall be construed to limit or prohibit the use of hunting dogs during the open hunting or training season. Violation of any provision of this subsection shall be an infraction.	Conn. Gen. Stat. Ann. § 22-364
	A municipality shall have the power to regulate and prohibit the going at large of dogs and other animals in the streets and public places of the municipality.	Conn. Gen. Stat. Ann. § 7-148(c) (7)(D)

Law	Requirements	Reference
Leash—wildlife management region	NONE	
Chasing Wildlife	No person shall allow his dog to enter any state wildlife refuge or closed area. Such person shall be fined not more than $100.	Conn. Gen. Stat. § 26-107
Strict Liability	The owner of any dog that causes any damage to a person or property, presumably in any place, except in cases of provocation- the victim was teasing, tormenting or abusing the dog. Other exceptions are person injured was trespassing or committing other tort.	Conn. Gen. Stat. §22-357
Dog Bites	Any damage to person or property. Presumably any place. Provocation - victim was teasing, tormenting or abusing the dog. Person injured was trespassing or committing other tort.	Conn. Gen. Stat. §22- 357
Dangerous Dog	NONE	
Breed specific	NONE	
Cruelty	Animal Cruelty is defined as: "Overdrives, overworks, tortures, deprives of necessary sustenance, mutilates or cruelly beats or kills or unjustifiably injures any animal, or who, having impounded or confined any animal, fails to give such animal proper care or neglects to cage or restrain any such animal from doing injury to itself or to another animal or fails to supply any such animal with wholesome air, food and water, or unjustifiably administers any poisonous or noxious drug or substance to any domestic animal or, having charge or custody of any animal, inflicts cruelty upon it or fails to provide it with proper food, drink or protection from the weather or abandons it or carries it or causes it to be carried in a cruel manner, or fights with or baits, harasses or worries any animal for the purpose of making it perform for amusement, diversion or exhibition."	Conn. Gen. Stat. §Section 53-247

Law	Requirements	Reference
	Cruelty to animals can be prosecuted as either a misdemeanor or felony with a fine up to $1000 and/or imprisonment up to 1 year. Intentionally and maliciously torturing or injuring an animal can be prosecuted as either a misdemeanor or felony with a fine up to $5000 and/or imprisonment up to 5 years. Additional sentencing provisions include counseling and participation in animal cruelty prevention and education programs as conditions of probation. Exemptions are made for farming, hunting, research and veterinary care.	
Minimum age sale of puppies	Minimum age of eight weeks unless such dog or cat is transported with its dam for import or export. Minimum age of eight weeks for sale, offer for sale, adoption, or transfer within the state.	Conn. Gen. Stat. § 22-354

DISTRICT OF COLUMBIA

Law	Requirements	Reference
Exotic Pets	Among other things covered under the law, this D.C. law prohibits the importation into the District, possession, display, offering for sale, trading, bartering, exchanging, or adopting, or giving as a household pet any living member of the animal kingdom including those born or raised in captivity, except the following: domestic dogs (excluding hybrids with wolves, coyotes, or jackals), domestic cats (excluding hybrids with ocelots or margays), domesticated rodents and rabbits, captive-bred species of common cage birds, nonpoisonous snakes, fish, and turtles, traditionally kept in the home for pleasure rather than for commercial purposes, and racing pigeons (when kept in compliance with permit requirements).	D.C. Code § 8-1808.
Sterilization	Animals must be "spayed or neutered" prior to adoption.	D.C. Code § 8-1807
Vaccination	Pursuant to rules issued by the Mayor, an owner of a cat over the age of 4 months shall have that cat vaccinated against rabies.	D.C. Code § 8-1803
Tethering	"Cruelly chains" means attaching an animal to a stationary object or a pulley by means of a chain, rope, tether, leash, cable, or similar restraint under circumstances that may endanger its health, safety, or wellbeing. Cruelly chains include a tether that: Causes the animal to choke Does not permit the animal to reach food, water, shade, dry ground Does not permit the animal to escape harm. Imprisonment up to 180 days and/or fine up to $250.	D.C. Code § 22.1001
Parked Vehicles	NONE	

Law	Requirements	Reference
Leash	The Council of the District of Columbia is hereby authorized and empowered to make and modify, and the Mayor of the District of Columbia is hereby authorized and empowered to enforce, regulations in and for the District of Columbia to regulate the keeping and leashing of dogs and to regulate or prohibit the running at large of dogs.	D.C. Code § 1-303.41
	If any owner or possessor of a female dog shall permit her to go at large in the District of Columbia while in heat, he shall, upon conviction thereof, be punished by a fine not exceeding $20.	D.C. Code § 22-1311
Leash— wildlife management region	NONE	
Chasing Wildlife	NONE	
Strict Liability	The owner of any dog that causes any injury, presumably in any place.	D.C. Code ST §8-1808 DC ST §8-1812
Dog Bites	Dogs at large only. Any injury. Presumably any place.	D.C. Code §§8-1808, 8-1812
Dangerous Dog	Without provocation, causes a serious injury to a person or domestic animal; or Without provocation, engages in behavior described in paragraph (4) (A)(i) after dog is determined to be a potentially dangerous dog.	D.C. Code § 8-1901(1)(A)
	Without provocation, chases or menaces a person or domestic animal in an aggressive manner, causing an injury to a person or domestic animal that is less severe than a serious injury in a menacing manner, approaches without provocation any person or	D.C. Code § 8-1901(4)(A

Law	Requirements	Reference
	domestic animal as if to attack, or has demonstrated a propensity to attack without provocation or otherwise to endanger the safety of human beings or domestic animals.	
	Must register the dangerous or potentially danger-ous dog Must leash a potentially dangerous dog if outside proper enclosure Must keep a dangerous dog exclusively on the owner's property except for medical treatment or examination Must notify the mayor within 24 hours if there has been a change in circumstances with a potentially dangerous dog or dangerous dog Must comply with special security requirements the Mayor may establish Owner of a potentially dangerous dog must be 18 years old Potentially dangerous dog must be spayed or neu-tered A valid license must be issued for a potentially dangerous dog A potentially dangerous dog must have current vaccinations A potentially dangerous dog must have a proper enclosure A potentially dangerous dog must be microchipped Must have permission of property owner or homeowner's association to keep a potentially dangerous dog or a dangerous dog on the property Owner of a danger-ous dog must post a sign.	D.C. Code §§ 8-1903, 8-1904, 8-1905
	The Mayor may humanely destroy a dog if: (1) The dog has been determined to be a threat to public safety if it is returned to the owner; (2) The owner fails to comply with the registration requirements of § 8-1904, the requirements of § 8-1905, or any special security or care requirements established by the Mayor; (3) The owner fails to reimburse the animal control agency for the costs and expenses of the dog's impoundment as required by § 8- 1902(d) (2); or (4) The owner forfeits the dog for humane destruction.	DC ST § 8-1903

Law	Requirements	Reference
Breed specific	The act imposed restrictions on pit bulls and Rottweilers.	Act 11-257 (1996)
Cruelty	Cruelty to animals is defined as: "Knowingly over-drives, overloads, drives when overloaded, overworks, tortures, torments, deprives of necessary sustenance, cruelly chains, cruelly beats or mutilates, any animal, or knowingly causes or procures any animal to be so treated, and whoever, having the charge or custody of any animal, either as owner or otherwise, knowingly inflicts unnecessary cruelty upon the same, or unnecessarily fails to provide the same with proper food, drink, air, light, space, veterinary care, shelter, or protection from the weather." Serious bodily injury is defined as: "bodily injury that involves a substantial risk of death, unconsciousness, extreme physical pain, protracted and obvious disfigurement, mutilation, or protracted loss or impairment of the function of a bodily member or organ." Cruelty to animals is not classified in the statute, but carries a fine up to $250 and/or imprisonment up to 180 days. Cruelty to animals resulting in serious bodily injury or death is a Felony with a fine of up to $25,000 and/or imprisonment up to 5 years. Exemptions are made for research.	D.C. Code §22-1001
Minimum age sale of puppies	NONE	

DELAWARE

Law	Requirements	Reference
Exotic Pets	This Delaware law requires a permit to possess, sell, or import any nonnative wild animal. No such permits will be granted for non-native venomous snakes.	Del. Code Ann. tit. 3, § 7201 - 7203
Sterilization	Dogs and cats must be "spayed or neutered" before adoption.	Del. Code Ann. tit. 3, § 8220
Vaccination	Cats- Six (6) months of age or older.	Del. Code Ann. tit. 3, §§ 7201 – 7203, 8204
Tethering	Law addresses the design of a tether: Outdoor dog houses: tethers shall be attached so that dog cannot become entangled with other objects or come into physical contact with other dogs. Tether shall be 6 feet long or at least 3 times the length of the dog. Must allow the dog convenient access to dog house and to food and water.	Del. Code Ann. tit. 9, § 904
Parked Vehicles	Confining an animal unattended in a standing or parked motor vehicle in which the temperature is either so high or so low as to endanger the health or safety of the animal. A law enforcement officer, animal control officer, animal cruelty investigator, or firefighter who has probable cause probable cause to believe that an animal is confined in a motor vehicle under conditions that are likely to cause suffering, injury, or death to the animal may use reasonable force to remove the animal left in the vehicle in violation of this provision. A person removing an animal under this section shall use reasonable means to contact the owner. If the person is unable to contact the owner, the person may take the animal to an animal shelter and must leave written notice bearing his or her name and office, and the address of the location where the animal can be claimed.	Del. Code Ann. tit. 11, § 1325(b) (6)

Law	Requirements	Reference
Leash	No dog shall be permitted to run at large at any time, unless the dog is accompanied by the owner or custodian and under the owner's or custodian's reasonable control and is licensed in accordance with county ordinances, except that a person who is an occupant of a farm or property containing 20 acres or more on which there are no more than 3 resident dwelling units may permit a dog to run at large between October 1 and the last day of February, next following.	Del. Code Ann. tit. 9, § 908
Leash–wildlife management region	Unlawful to allow any dog in the designated swimming or sunbathing area of a state coastal beach strand at any time between May 1 and September 30 (except for law enforcement dogs or guide dogs for the blind). Violators are guilty of a violation with fine of $25 - $50. For each subsequent offense, fine of $50 - $100.	Del. Code Ann. tit. 7, § 1702
Chasing Wildlife	All state lands, except as otherwise provided, and state, county and municipal parks in Delaware shall be state game refuges and no person shall hunt upon said lands and parks or kill or injure any game therein at any time of the year.	Del. Code Ann. tit. 7, § 736
Strict Liability	The owner of any dog that causes any injury death or loss to person or property, presumably in any place, except in cases of provocation where the victim was teasing, tormenting or abusing the dog. Other exceptions are, the person injured was committing a trespass or criminal offense on owner's property, or was committing a criminal offense against any person.	Del. Code Ann. tit. 9, § 913
Dog Bites	Any injury, death or loss to person or property. Presumably any place. Provocation - victim was teasing, tormenting or abusing the dog. Person injured was committing a trespass or criminal offense on owner's property, or was committing a criminal offense against any person.	Del. Code Ann. tit. 9, § 913

Law	Requirements	Reference
Dangerous Dog	Was declared potentially dangerous dog and was kept or maintained in violation of statutory requirements for owning a potentially dangerous dog Killed or inflicted physical injury or serious physical injury upon a human being Killed or inflicted serious physical injury upon a domestic animal Was subject to, or was used to facilitate animal cruelty or animal fighting as alleged in a criminal complaint or charge.	Del. Code Ann. tit. 9, §§ 920(3), 925
	Attacked or inflicted physical injury upon a human being Attacked or inflicted serious physical injury upon a domestic animal Chased or pursued a person upon the streets, sidewalks or any public or private property, other than the dog owner's property, in an apparent attitude of attack on 2 separate occasions within a 12- month period.	Del. Code Ann. tit. 9, §§ 920(9), 926
	Any dog or other animal which had been declared dangerous or potentially dangerous Any dog or other animal which had been trained for animal fighting, or that has been used primarily or occasionally for animal fighting Any dog or other animal which had been intentionally trained so as to increase its viciousness, dangerousness or potential for unprovoked attacks upon human beings or other animals Any dog or other animal which had an individualized and known propensity, tendency or disposition, specific to the individual dog, for viciousness, dangerousness or unprovoked attacks upon human beings or other animals.	Del. Code Ann. tit. 11, § 1327
	If the dog is classified as dangerous, the Panel may order the dog euthanized. If an owner cannot be found within 5 days, the Animal Control can destroy the dog. Mandatory destruction of the declared dangerous dog if the dog kills, attacks or inflicts physical injury or serious physical injury, without provocation upon a human being or domestic animal.	Del. Code Ann. tit. 9, §§ 928 & 9, 924

Law	Requirements	Reference
Breed specific	Pit bulled declared "dangerous" in the city of Bridgeville. See city website for more information.	Town of Bridgeville, Section: 84-10
Cruelty	Cruelty to animals is defined as: "Intentionally or recklessly subjects an animal to cruel mistreatment, cruel neglect, kills or injures an animal without the owner's consent, cruelly or unnecessarily kills or injures any animal." Cruelty to animals is a Class A Misdemeanor with a $1000 fine, possible imprisonment for up to 1 year, forfeiture of any and all animals (unless 25% or more income is provided from animals), and no animal ownership for 5 years. Intentional cruelty is a Class F Felony with a $5000 fine, possibly imprisonment up to 3 years, forfeiture of any and all animals (unless 25% or more income is provided from animals), and no animal ownership for 15 years. Exemptions are made for farming, hunting, protection of life or property, research and veterinary care.	Del. Code Ann. tit. 11, § 1325
Minimum age sale of puppies	NONE	

FLORIDA

Law	Requirements	Reference
Exotic Pets	This set of laws explains the powers and duties of the Department of Agriculture & Consumer Services in enforcing the Animal Industry laws (Chapter 585). Any person or officer that is charged with a duty under the animal Industry laws may be compelled to perform the same by mandamus, injunction, or other court-ordered remedy. Department employees are authorized to enter any premises in the state for the purposes of carrying out their duties under the Animal Industry laws and it is illegal for any person to interfere with the discharge of those duties.	Fla. Stat. Ann. § 585.001 -585.008
	This set of laws addresses the role of the Department of Agriculture & Consumer Services, Division of Animal Industry in the prevention, control, or eradication of any contagious, infectious, or communicable disease among domestic or wild animals. The Department is authorized to regulate the importation, transportation, transfer of ownership, and maintenance of animals; establish quarantine areas; and inspect, test, treat, condemn, and destroy animals and animal housing facilities as necessary for the eradication of communicable diseases or the detection of harmful biological and chemical residues in food animals. The laws also direct the Department to develop a list of dangerous transmissible diseases. All veterinarians and animal owners are required to report suspected and confirmed cases of dangerous transmissible diseases to the State Veterinarian; failure to do so is a felony of the second degree.	Fla. Stat. Ann. § 585.01 -585.69

Law	Requirements	Reference
	This set of laws authorizes the establishment of the Office of Agricultural Law Enforcement within the Department of Agriculture & Consumer Services for the enforcement of laws relating to wild or domesticated animals or animal products. Law enforcement officers employed by the Department have statewide jurisdiction and have full law enforcement powers granted to other peace officers of the state, including the authority to make arrests, carry firearms, serve court process, and seize contraband and the proceeds of illegal activities. It is a misdemeanor of the second degree to threaten, interfere with, or impersonate an enforcement officer or other employee of the Department.	Fla. Stat. Ann. § 570.065; 570.15; 570.051
	These Florida statutes define endangered and threatened species and provide the State's intent to protect these species. Under statute, the intentional killing or wounding of a listed species incurs a third degree felony. Interestingly, the state has a reward program for the arrest and conviction of those who violate state endangered species laws.	Fla. Stat. Ann. § 379.2291 -231
	This law makes it illegal to exhibit any deformed, mutilated or disfigured animal for compensation.	Fla. Stat. Ann. § 877.16
	This set of laws describes the scope and methods of enforcement of the state's fish and wildlife laws.	Fla. Stat. Ann. § 379.33 -379.343
	These Florida laws concern the keeping and taking of captive wildlife. Places where wildlife is held in captivity are subject to inspection by the officers of the state commission at any time. The commission shall promulgate rules defining Class I, Class II, and Class III types of wildlife. A companion statutory section provides that, in order to assure humane treatment of captive wildlife, no person, firm, corporation or association shall be in possession of captive wildlife for public display unless a permit has been obtained. The cost of the permit depends on whether the species fall into Class I, II, or III).	Fla. Stat. Ann. § 379.231 -504

Law	Requirements	Reference
Sterilization	Dogs and cats must be sterilized before adoption, or adopters must enter into a sterilization agreement.	Fla. Stat. § 823.15
Vaccination	Cats: Four (4) months of age or older.	Fla. Stat. §828.30; Fla. Stat. Ann. §828.30
Tethering	NONE	
Parked Vehicles	NONE	
Leash	NONE	
Leash– wildlife management region	NONE	
Chasing Wildlife	No person shall knowingly or negligently allow any dog to pursue or molest any wildlife during any period in which the taking of such wildlife by the use of dogs is prohibited. No person shall knowingly allow a dog under their care to enter or remain upon a critical wildlife area during any period in which public access is prohibited by the order establishing such area.	Fla. Admin. Code R. 68A-15.004 and 68A-19.005
Strict Liability	The owner of any dog that causes a bite, in any public place, or private place where person has legal right to be, including dog owner's property. Other exceptions are, contributory negligence, display of "Bad Dog" sign on owner premises.	Fla. Stat. § 767.04
Dog Bites	Any dog. Public place, or private place where person has legal right to be, including dog owner's property. Other exceptions; contributory negligence display of "Bad Dog" sign on owner premises.	Fla. Stat. § 767.04

Law	Requirements	Reference
Dangerous Dog	Must be registered and may have to pay a registration fee. Owner must be 18 year of age. Dog must have current rabies vaccinations. Must confine dog in a proper enclosure. Must post a warning sign. Must identify the dog with a tattoo or microchip. Must notify the proper authorities if the dog's circumstances change. Must provide the proper authorities with a new owner's information if the dog is sold. Must not permit the dog to be outside the proper enclosure unless the dog is muzzled and restrained by a leash; unless the dog is exercised in a securely fenced or enclosed area; or unless the dog is safely and securely restrained in a vehicle.	Fla. Stat. Ann. § 767.12
Breed specific	Pit bulls are banned in Miami-Dade County. See city website for more information.	Fla. Admin. Code R. 5-17.6b
Cruelty	Cruelty to animals is defined as: "Overloads, overdrives, torments, deprives of necessary sustenance or shelter, or unnecessarily mutilates, or kills any animal, or causes the same to be done, or carries in or upon any vehicle, or otherwise, any animal in a cruel or inhumane manner". This is a 1st Degree Misdemeanor with a fine up to $5000 and/or imprisonment up to 1 year. Intentional Animal Cruelty is defined as: "commits an act to any animal which results in the cruel death, or excessive or repeated infliction of unnecessary pain or suffering." This is a 3rd Degree Felony with a fine up to $10,000 and/or imprisonment up to 5 years. Intentional Cruelty with "knowing and intentional torture or torment of an animal that injures, mutilates, or kills the animal" carries a minimum fine of $2500 and completion of a psychological or anger management treatment program. A second conviction of the same carries a minimum fine of $5,000 and minimum 6 months' incarceration, with no parole or early release available. Exemptions are made for veterinary care.	Fla. Stat. §828.12 et seq.
Minimum age sale of puppies	Not less than eight weeks old.	Fla. Stat. §828.29

ΨΨ

GEORGIA

Law	Requirements	Reference
Exotic Pets	These Georgia wildlife provisions embody the General Assembly's finding that it is in the public interest to ensure the public health, safety, and welfare by strictly regulating in this state the importation, transportation, sale, transfer, and possession of certain wild animals. Animals such as kangaroos, certain non-human primates, wolves, bears, big cats, hippopotamus, and crocodile, among others, are considered to be inherently dangerous to human beings and are subject to the license or permit and insurance requirements outlined in the laws. The section also details specifications for the humane handling, care, confinement and transportation of certain wild animals.	Ga. Code Ann. § 27-5-1 to 12
Sterilization	Dogs and cats must be sterilized before adoption, or adopters must enter into a sterilization agreement.	Ga. Code Ann. § 4-14-3
Vaccination	NONE	
Tethering	NONE	
Parked Vehicles	NONE	
Leash	NONE	
Leash— wildlife management region	NONE	
Chasing Wildlife	Owners are responsible for their dogs and any damage they may do to wildlife other than raccoon, fox, opossum or bobcat. It is unlawful to hunt deer with dogs.	No statutory citation
Strict Liability	Vicious or dangerous animals who are at large due to owner's negligence. Places include, anywhere but dog owner's property (dog must be "at large"). Provocation exception.	Ga. Code Ann. §51-2-7

Law	Requirements	Reference
Dog Bites	Vicious or dangerous animals who are at large due to owner's negligence. Places include, anywhere but dog owner's property (dog must be "at large"). Provocation exception.	Ga. Code Ann. § 51-2-7
Dangerous Dog	Owner must be 18 years old. Owner of a dangerous or vicious dog must have a certificate; only one certificate per domicile. No certificate of registration shall be issued to any person who has been convicted of two or more violations of article 2. Owner must notify the dog control officer within 24 hours if the dog is loose, has attacked, or has died. Dog must remain on the premises unless the dog is on a leash and is under the immediate physical control of a capable person; the dog is in a closed or locked crate or cage; or the dog is working or training as a hunting, herding, or predator control dog. Owner must register the dog in new jurisdiction if the owner moves.	Ga. Code Ann. §§ 4-8-27, 4-8-28, 4-8-29
Breed specific	Some cities ban pit bulls. Declare pit bulls and other breeds such as; Rottweilers, Doberman pinschers and German shepherds declared "potentially dangerous". See city website for more detailed information.	
Cruelty	Animal Cruelty is defined as: "causes death or unjustifiable physical pain or suffering to any animal by an act, an omission, or willful neglect. Willful neglect means the intentional withholding of food and water required by an animal to prevent starvation or dehydration." This is a misdemeanor with a fine up to $1000 and/or imprisonment for up to 1 year. A second or subsequent conviction carries of fine of up to $5000 and imprisonment for up to 1 year. A second or subsequent conviction which resulted in the death of an animal will be a misdemeanor of "a high and aggravated nature" with imprisonment for a minimum 3 months, maximum 12 months and/or a fine up to $10,000. Aggravated Cruelty is defined as: "knowingly and maliciously causes death or physical harm to an animal by rendering a part of such	Georgia Code Ann. §16-12-4

Law	Requirements	Reference
	animal's body useless or by seriously disfiguring such animal." This carries imprisonment of minimum 1 year, maximum 5 years, and/or a fine up to $15,000. Exemptions are made for agricultural, animal husbandry, butchering, food processing, marketing, scientific, research, medical, zoological, exhibition, competitive, hunting, trapping, fishing, wildlife management, or pest control practices or the authorized practice of veterinary medicine.	
Minimum age sale of puppies	Puppies must be a minimum age of eight weeks prior to sale.	Ga Comp. R. & Regs. 40-13-13-.04

HAWAII

Law	Requirements	Reference
Exotic Pets	These laws concern the importation of animals, plants, and microorganisms into the State of Hawaii.	Haw. Rev Stat. § 150A-5 -15
Sterilization	No statewide sterilization requirements for adoption. However, municipalities may require that dogs and cats be neutered prior to adoption.	
Vaccination	Regulations relating to importing cats and rabies vaccinations.	Haw. Admin. Rules § 4-29-8
Tethering	A person commits the offense of cruelty to animals in the second degree if the person intentionally, knowingly, or recklessly tethers, fastens, ties, or restrains a dog to a doghouse, tree, fence, or any other stationary object by means of a choke collar, pinch collar, or prong collar. Misdemeanor offense results in forfeiture of animal and reimbursement for costs incurred for care of animal.	Haw. Rev. Stat. § 711-1109
Parked Vehicles	NONE	
Leash	It shall be unlawful for the owner of any female dog, licensed or unlicensed, to permit it to run at large while the dog is in the copulating season.	Haw. Rev. Stat. § 143-14
Leash— wildlife management region	NONE	
Chasing Wildlife	On any game management area, public hunting area, or forest reserve or other lands under the jurisdiction of the department, predators (dogs or cats) deemed harmful to wildlife by the department may be destroyed by any means deemed necessary by the department. Signs shall be posted at the entrance to these areas alerting owners to such predator destruction programs.	Haw. Rev. Stat. § 183D-65

Law	Requirements	Reference
Strict Liability	The owner of any animal, that causes any personal or property damage, in any place. Exceptions - Provocation -victim teased, tormented, or abused the dog. Person injured was trespassing. Other justification.	HI ST 663- 9 and 663-9.1
Dog Bites	Any animal. Any personal or property damage. Any place. Exceptions - Provocation -victim teased, tormented, or abused the dog. Person injured was trespassing. Other justification.	Haw. Rev. Stat. § 663- 9 to 663-9.1
Dangerous Dog	NONE	
Breed specific	NONE	
Cruelty	Animal Cruelty is defined as: "intentionally, knowingly, or recklessly: Overdrives, overloads, tortures, torments, cruelly beats or starves any animal, deprives a pet animal of necessary sustenance, mutilates, poisons, or kills without need any animal other than insects, vermin, or other pests, keeps, uses, or in any way is connected with fighting or baiting any bull, bear, dog, cock, or other animal, carries or causes to be carried, in or upon any vehicle or other conveyance, any animal in a cruel or inhumane manner; or assists another in the commission of any act of cruelty to any animal." This is a Misdemeanor punishable with a fine up to $2000 and/or imprisonment up to 1 year. Exemptions are made for scientific research and veterinary practices.	Haw. Rev. Stat. §711-1109
Minimum age sale of puppies	NONE	

IDAHO

Law	Requirements	Reference
Exotic Pets	In Idaho, all apes and other nonhuman primates are classified as "deleterious exotic animals," which are dangerous to the environment, livestock, agriculture, or wildlife of the state. According to Idaho's legislature, it is in the public interest to strictly regulate the importation and possession of those animals.	Idaho Code Ann. § 25-3901 -3905
	This section comprises Idaho's captive wildlife provisions. Under the law, no person shall engage in any propagation or hold in captivity any species of big game animal found wild in this state, unless the person has been issued a license or permit by the director. All other species of mammals, birds or reptiles that are found in the wild in this state and are not species of special concern or threatened and endangered species, may be held in captivity without permit so long as the possessor retains proof that such wildlife was lawfully obtained. The laws concerning commercial wildlife farms are also included in this section. Additionally, there is also a section on the transition of wolves from federal to state management (§ 36-715).	Idaho Code Ann. § 36-701 to 716
Sterilization	NONE	
Vaccination	NONE	
Tethering	NONE	
Parked Vehicles	NONE	
Leash	NONE	
Leash— wildlife management region	NONE	

Law	Requirements	Reference
Chasing Wildlife	No person may allow a dog to take, chase, pursue, or kill any big game animal. Any dog found running at large and which is actively tracking, pursuing, harassing, attacking or killing deer or any other big game animal may be destroyed without criminal or civil liability by the director, or any peace officer, or other persons authorized to enforce the Idaho fish and game laws.	ID ST § 36-1101
Strict Liability	NONE	
Dog Bites	NONE	
Dangerous Dog	Any dog which, when not physically provoked, physically attacks, wounds, bites or otherwise injures any person who is not trespassing.	Idaho Code Ann. § 25-2805
	Must keep inside secure enclosure. If outside of secure enclosure, dog must be restrained by a chain sufficient to control the vicious dog.	Idaho Code Ann. § 25-2805
	For a second or subsequent violation of this subsection, the court may, in the interest of public safety, order the owner to have the vicious dog destroyed or may direct the appropriate authorities to destroy the dog.	Idaho Code Ann. § 25-2805
	Misdemeanor if persons guilty of a violation of section 25-2805 and in addition to any liability as provided in section 25-2806, Idaho Code.	Idaho Code Ann. § 25-2805
Breed specific	Some cities ban: pit bulls; declares presa canarios, cane corsos, Russian wolfhounds, wolf hybrids and mountain dogs "vicious". See city website for more detailed information.	

Law	Requirements	Reference
Cruelty	Animal Cruelty is defined as: "The intentional and malicious infliction of pain, physical suffering, injury or death upon an animal; To maliciously kill, maim, wound, overdrive, overload, drive when overloaded, overwork, torture, torment, deprive of necessary sustenance, drink or shelter, cruelly beat, mutilate or cruelly kill an animal; To subject an animal to needless suffering, inflict unnecessary cruelty, drive, ride or otherwise use an animal when same is unfit; To abandon an animal; To negligently confine an animal in unsanitary conditions or to negligently house an animal in inadequate facilities; to negligently fail to provide sustenance, water or shelter to an animal" This is a Misdemeanor. The first conviction of Animal Cruelty is punishable by a fine of $100 to $5000 and/or imprisonment up to 6 months. The second conviction within 10 years of the first is punishable by a fine of $200 to $7000 and/or imprisonment up to 9 months. The third conviction within 15 years of the first is punishable by a fine of $500 to $9000 and/or imprisonment up to 12 months. Exemptions are made for normal veterinary practices, humane slaughter, professionally recognized research facilities, humane destruction of an injured or diseased animal beyond recovery, accepted practices of animal identification and husbandry, killing an animal posing a threat to any person or property, killing a vicious animal by animal control officers, veterinarians or law enforcement officers, predatory animals and vermin, exhibitions, competitions, activities, practices or procedures normally or commonly considered acceptable.	Idaho Code Ann. § 25-3501
Minimum age sale of puppies	NONE	

ILLINOIS

Law	Requirements	Reference
Exotic Pets	This Illinois law states that no person shall have a right of property in, keep, harbor, care for, act as custodian of or maintain in his or her possession any dangerous animal or primate except at a properly maintained zoological park, federally licensed exhibit, circus, college or university, scientific institution, research laboratory, veterinary hospital, hound running area, or animal refuge in an escape-proof enclosure. A "dangerous animal" is defined as a lion, tiger, leopard, ocelot, jaguar, cheetah, margay, mountain lion, lynx, bobcat, jaguarondi, bear, hyena, wolf or coyote. This Section does not prohibit a person who had lawful possession of a primate before January 1, 2011, from continuing to possess that primate if the person registers the animal by providing written notification to the local animal control administrator on or before April 1, 2011. Violation is a Class C misdemeanor.	720 Ill. Comp. Stat. §5/48-10
	(Repealed 2011). This Illinois statute provides that any person who imports into Illinois wild or semi-domestic mammals from other states or foreign countries for the purpose of providing hunting with bow and arrow or gun with or without dogs must obtain an exotic game hunting area permit. Certain specifications are outlined in the statute, including the requirement that the area be at least 640 contiguous acres and a certification that the animals are disease-free.	520 Ill. Comp. Stat. § 5/3.34 (repealed 2011)

Law	Requirements	Reference
	This collection of statutes provides that the title of all wild birds and mammals rests with the state. A new section in 2011 vests the Department of Natural Resources with the ability to control the possession and release of species deemed exotic or invasive. Other sections concern the possession of certain wild birds and animals. Possession of any listed wild bird or its parts (including the eagle) is illegal under the statute, except for the bona fide scientific or zoological exhibition.	520 Ill. Comp. Stat. §5/2.1 to 2.5a; 520 I.L.C.S. §5/2.36a
Sterilization	Dogs and cats must be "rendered incapable of reproduction" before adoption, or persons wishing to adopt "prior to the surgical procedures" must enter into a sterilization agreement.	510 Ill. Comp. Stat. §5/11
Vaccination	NONE	
Tethering	70/3 (b) To lawfully tether a dog outdoors, an owner must ensure that the dog: (1) does not suffer from a condition that is known, by that person, to be exacerbated by tethering; (2) is tethered in a manner that will prevent it from becoming entangled with other tethered dogs; (3) is not tethered with a lead that (i) exceeds one-eighth of the dog's body weight or (ii) is a tow chain or a log chain; (4) is tethered with a lead that measures, when rounded to the nearest whole foot, at least 10 feet in length; (5) is tethered with a properly fitting harness or collar other than the lead or a pinch, prong, or choke-type collar; and (6) is not tethered in a manner that will allow it to reach within the property of another person, a public walkway, or a road. (e) A person convicted of violating subsection (b) of this Section is guilty of a Class B misdemeanor.	510 Ill. Comp. Stat. §70/3
Parked Vehicles	Confine any animal in a motor vehicle in such a manner that places it in a life or health threatening situation by exposure to a prolonged period of extreme heat or cold, without proper ventilation or other protection from such heat or cold. A person	510 Ill. Comp. Stat. §70/7.1

ᐱᐤ

Law	Requirements	Reference
	convicted of violating this Section is guilty of a Class C misdemeanor. A second or subsequent violation is a Class B misdemeanor. An animal control officer, law enforcement officer, or Department investigator has authority to enter such motor vehicle by any reasonable means under the circumstances after making a reasonable effort to locate the owner or other person responsible.	
Leash	The corporate authorities of each municipality may regulate and prohibit the running at large of dogs. The county board of each county may regulate and prohibit the running at large of dogs in unincorporated areas of the county which have been subdivided for residence purposes. To prevent the spread of rabies, the Department of Agriculture shall act to prevent its spread among dogs and other animals. The Department may order that all dogs be kept muzzled and restrained by leash. The Department may determine the area of the locality in which, and the period of time during which, such orders shall be effective.	65 Ill. Comp. Stat. §5/11-20-9 55 Ill. Comp. Stat. §5/5-1071 510 Ill. Comp. Stat. §5/14
Leash— wildlife management region	NONE	
Chasing Wildlife	It is unlawful for a person to enter a Wildlife Habitat Management Area Refuge Safety Zone with a dog.	520 Ill. Comp. Stat. §20/19
Strict Liability	Any animal. Any injury or attack. Any place where victim has legal right to be. Exceptions: Provocation and person injured was not peacefully conducting him or herself.	510 Ill. Comp. Stat. §5/16
Dog Bites	Any animal. Any injury or attack. Any place where victim has legal right to be. Exceptions: Provocation and person injured was not peacefully conducting him or herself.	510 Ill. Comp. Stat. §5/16

Law	Requirements	Reference
Dangerous Dog	Dangerous dog ownership conditions: Owner must pay a $50 public safety fine. Dog must be spayed or neutered and microchipped. One or more of the following: Evaluation of the dog by a certified applied behaviorist or direct supervision by an adult 18 years of age or older whenever the animal is on public premises. Dog may be ordered to be muzzled whenever on public premises.	510 Ill. Comp. Stat. §5/15.1(d)
	Vicious dog ownership conditions: Owner must pay $100 public safety fine. Dog must be spayed or neutered and microchipped. Dog is subject to an Enclosure. Failure to comply with the above requirements means the animal control agency will impound the dog and the owner will pay a $500 fine plus impoundment fees. Vicious dogs are only allowed outside of their enclosures for veterinarian visits, court, or natural disasters. In which case, the dog must be muzzled, leashed, and under the owner's control.	510 ILCS §5/15
Breed specific	Some cities ban pit bulls and Rottweilers. See city website for more information.	
Cruelty	Owner's Duties are defined as: "provide for each of his animals: sufficient quantity of good quality, wholesome food and water; adequate shelter and protection from the weather; veterinary care when needed to prevent suffering; and humane care and treatment." Conviction is a Class B Misdemeanor, with a second conviction a Class 4 Felony with each day that the violation continues being a separate offense. In addition to other penalties provided by law, the person may be required to undergo psychological evaluation and treatment.	510 Ill. Comp. Stat. §70/3

Law	Requirements	Reference
	Cruel Treatment is defined as: "No person or owner may beat, cruelly treat, torment, starve, overwork or otherwise abuse any animal. No owner may abandon any animal where it may become a public charge or may suffer injury, hunger or exposure." Conviction is a Class a Misdemeanor, a subsequent conviction is a Class 4 felony. In addition to other penalties provided by law, the person may be required to undergo psychological evaluation and treatment.	510 Ill. Comp. Stat. §70/3.01
Minimum age sale of puppies	Minimum age is eight weeks.	225 Ill. Comp. Stat. § 605/2.2

INDIANA

Law	Requirements	Reference
Exotic Pets	This Indiana statute provides the definition of an exotic mammal, which does not include a feral cat or dog.	Ind. Code §14-8-2-87
	This set of Indiana laws concerns the keeping of protected and dangerous wild animals. Under the law, a person must obtain a permit to possess these classes of animals. A permit may be suspended if an emergency exists (e.g., the animal is in peril or the animal is in a position to harm another animal).	Ind. Code §14-22-26-1 to 6
	In Indiana, a person needs a permit to import live fish or any living wild animal into the state for release. A permit may be granted only upon proof that the animals are free of a communicable disease, will not become a nuisance, and will not cause damage to a native wild or domestic species.	Ind. Code §14-22-25-1, -4
Sterilization	No statewide sterilization requirements for adoption. Municipalities may require that dogs and cats be spayed or neutered before adoption.	Ind. Code §5-30
Vaccination	Cats: Three (3) months of age and older.	345 IAC 1-5-2
Tethering	"Neglect" means restraining an animal for more than a brief period in a manner that endangers the animal's life or health by the use of a rope, chain, or tether that: is too heavy causes the animal to choke, is less than 3x the length of the animal, seriously endangers the animal's life or health.	Ind. Code § 35-46-3-.05
Parked Vehicles	NONE	
Leash	NONE	
Leash— wildlife management region	NONE	

Law	Requirements	Reference
Chasing Wildlife	An individual may not take or chase, with or without dogs, a wild animal without having a license except under certain conditions.	Ind. Code § 14- 22-11-1
Strict Liability	The owner of any dog that causes a bite, person is in a location where required to be to discharge a duty imposed by the: laws of Indiana; laws of the United States; or postal regulations of the United States. Exceptions: Person injured was not peacefully conducting him or herself.	Ind. Code §15-20-1-3
Dog Bites	Person is in a location where required to be to discharge a duty imposed by the: laws of Indiana; laws of the United States; or postal regulations of the United States. Exceptions: Person injured was not peacefully conducting him or herself.	Ind. Code §15-20-1-3
Dangerous Dog	NONE	
Breed specific	Some cities ban and restrict pit bulls. See city website for more detailed information.	
Cruelty	Animal Cruelty is defined as: "Intentionally beating a vertebrate animal." This, along with removal of a dog's vocal cords, are considered Animal Cruelty and are Class A Misdemeanors with a fine up to $5000 and/or imprisonment up to 1 year. A second conviction of Animal Cruelty or intentional torture and mutilation of a vertebrate animal is a Class C Felony with a fine up to $10,000 and/or an addition 1 1/2 years' imprisonment. Exemptions are made for fishing, hunting, trapping, veterinary practice, farm management, humane slaughter, research, training or discipline of a vertebrate animal, protection of person or property, and prolonged suffering of the animal.	Ind. Code §35-46-3-13
Minimum age sale of puppies	Must be at least eight weeks old.	Ind. Code § 15-17-18-10

IOWA

Law	Requirements	Reference
Exotic Pets	This Iowa set of laws concerns the keeping of dangerous wild animals. Except as otherwise provided in this chapter, a person shall not own or possess a dangerous wild animal or cause or allow a dangerous wild animal owned by a person or in the person's possession to breed. Further, a person shall not transport a dangerous wild animal into this state. There is a grandfather provision that allows a person who owns or possesses a dangerous wild animal on July 1, 2007 to continue to own or possess the dangerous wild animal subject the provisions of the laws. A person owning or possessing a dangerous wild animal who violates a provision of this chapter is subject to a civil penalty of not less than two hundred dollars and not more than two thousand dollars for each dangerous wild animal involved in the violation.	Iowa Code Ann. § 717F.1 -13
Sterilization	Dogs and cats must be sterilized before adoption, or adopters must enter into a sterilization agreement.	Iowa Code § 162.20).
Vaccination	NONE	
Tethering	NONE	
Parked Vehicles	NONE	
Leash	A dog shall be apprehended and impounded by a local board of health or law enforcement official if the dog is running at large and the dog is not wearing a valid rabies vaccination tag or a rabies vaccination certificate is not presented to the local board of health or law enforcement official.	Iowa Code Ann. § 351.37
	If local board of health declares a Quarantine due to rabies, any person owning or having a dog in the person's possession in the quarantined area shall keep such animal securely enclosed or on a leash for the duration of the quarantine period.	Iowa Code Ann. § 351.40

Law	Requirements	Reference
Leash— wildlife management region	NONE	
Chasing Wildlife	It is unlawful to hunt, pursue, kill, trap or take any wild animal, bird or game on designated wildlife refuge areas.	No statutory citation
Strict Liability	The owner of any dog that causes damages done by the dog if dog caught in the act of worrying, maiming, or killing a domestic animal, or the dog is attacking or attempting to bite a person, presumably in any place. Exception: Dog affected with hydrophobia, party damaged is doing an unlawful act, directly contributing to the injury, dog not caught in the act of worrying, maiming, or killing a domestic animal, or dog was not attacking or attempting to bite a person.	Iowa Code Ann. § 351.28
Dog Bites	All damages done by the dog if dog caught in the act of worrying, maiming, or killing a domestic animal, or the dog is attacking or attempting to bite a person. Exception: Dog affected with hydrophobia, party damaged is doing an unlawful act, directly contributing to the injury, dog not caught in the act of worrying, maiming, or killing a domestic animal, or dog was not attacking or attempting to bite a person.	Iowa Code Ann. § 351.28
Dangerous Dog	NONE	
Breed specific	Many cities ban pit bulls. See city website for more detailed information.	

Law	Requirements	Reference
Cruelty	Animal abuse is defined as: "intentionally injures, maims, disfigures, or destroys an animal owned by another person, in any manner, including intentionally poisoning the animal." This is an Aggravated Misdemeanor with a fine of $500 to $5000 and/or imprisonment up to 2 years. Animal Neglect is defined as: "fails to supply the animal during confinement with a sufficient quantity of food or water; fails to provide a confined dog or cat with adequate shelter; or tortures, deprives of necessary sustenance, mutilates, beats, or kills an animal by any means which causes unjustified pain, distress, or suffering." Negligent animal neglect is a Simple Misdemeanor which carries a fine of $50 to $500 and/or imprisonment up to 30 days. Intentional Neglect is a Serious Misdemeanor with a fine of $250 to $1500 and/or imprisonment up to 1 year. Animal Torture is defined as: "regardless of whether the person is the owner of the animal, if the person inflicts upon the animal severe physical pain with a depraved or sadistic intent to cause prolonged suffering or death." This is an Aggravated Misdemeanor with a fine of $500 to $5000 and/or imprisonment up to 2 years and psychological treatment. A second conviction of Animal Torture is a Class D Felony with a fine of $500 to $7500 and/or imprisonment up to 5 years and psychological treatment. Exemptions are made for owner's consent (except torture), carrying out an order of the court, veterinary practice, hunting, trapping, fishing, protecting person or property, destroying a diseased or injured animal to a degree that would cause severe or prolonged suffering.	Iowa Code Ann. § 717B.1
Minimum age sale of puppies	NONE	

KANSAS

Law	Requirements	Reference
Exotic Pets	This set of Kansas statutes comprises the state's dangerous regulated animals act. Under the Act, a "dangerous regulated animal" means a live or slaughtered parts of lions, tigers, leopards, jaguars, cheetahs and mountain lions, or any hybrid thereof; bears or any hybrid thereof; and all nonnative, venomous snakes. Except as provided in this section, it is unlawful for a person to possess, slaughter, sell, purchase or otherwise acquire a dangerous regulated animal.	Kan. Stat. Ann. §32-1301 to 1312
Sterilization	Dogs and cats must be sterilized before adoption, or adopters must enter into a sterilization agreement.	Kan. Stat. Ann. § 47-1731
Vaccination	NONE	
Tethering	NONE	
Parked Vehicles	NONE	
Leash	NONE	
Leash – wildlife management region	NONE	
Chasing Wildlife	NONE	
Strict Liability	NONE	
Dog Bites	NONE	
Dangerous Dog	NONE	
Breed specific	Many cities ban pit bulls and other breeds. See city website for more detailed information	

Law	Requirements	Reference
Cruelty	Animal Cruelty is defined as: "Intentionally killing, injuring, maiming, torturing or mutilating any animal; abandoning or leaving any animal in any place without making provisions for its proper care; having physical custody of any animal and failing to provide such food, potable water, protection from the elements, opportunity for exercise and other care as is needed for the health or well-being of such kind of animal; or intentionally using a wire, pole, stick, rope or any other object to cause an equine to lose its balance or fall, for the purpose of sport or entertainment." This is a Class A Nonperson Misdemeanor with a fine up to $2500 and/or imprisonment up to 1 year. Exemptions are made for veterinary practice, bona fide research, hunting, fishing, trapping, rodeo, diseased or disabled animal beyond recovery by proper authority or vet, protection of person or property, use of a tranquilizer gun on a vicious animal, laying an equine down for medical or ID purposes.	Kan. Stat. Ann. § 21-4310
Minimum age sale of puppies	Unless the puppy is eight weeks' old AND weaned. "Weaned" means that an animal has become accustomed to taking solid food and has done so, without nursing, for a period of at least five days.	Kan. Admin. Regs. §9-25-12

KENTUCKY

Law	Requirements	Reference
Exotic Pets	This Kentucky statue authorizes counties and cities to regulate or prohibit the holding of inherently dangerous wildlife. For example, the Department of Fish and Wildlife Resources has identified some of the following animals as being dangerous: African buffalo, Hippopotamus, Hyenas, Old world badger, Lions, jaguars, leopards, or tigers, Clouded leopard, Cheetah, Elephants, Rhinoceroses, Gorillas, Baboons, drills, or mandrills, Crocodiles, Alligators or caimans, certain snakes, Gila monsters or beaded lizards, Komodo dragon, Wolverine, Bears, Wolf, mountain lion.	Ky. Rev. Stat. Ann. § 65.877
	This law states that any person who displays, handles or uses any kind of reptile in connection with any religious service or gathering shall be fined not less than fifty dollars ($50) nor more than one hundred dollars ($100).	Ky. Rev. Stat. Ann. § 437.060
Sterilization	No statewide sterilization requirements for adoption. Local ordinances may contain requirements, for example: "No unclaimed dog or cat or other animal shall be released for adoption unless the new owner agrees to subject the animal to the spay-neuter program sponsored by the Daviess County Fiscal Court and the payment of any and all applicable fees required thereof."	Owensboro, Kentucky Code of Ordinances § Sec. 4-17).
Vaccination	Cats: Must be vaccinated against rabies by the age of four (4) months.	Ky. Rev. Stat. Ann. § 258.015
Tethering	NONE	
Parked Vehicles	NONE	

Law	Requirements	Reference
Leash	Every female dog in heat shall be confined in a building or secure enclosure in such a manner that the female dog cannot come in contact with a male dog except for a planned breeding.	Ky. Rev. Stat. Ann. § 258.255
	Any peace officer or animal control officer may seize or destroy any dog found running at large between the hours of sunset and sunrise and unaccompanied and not under the control of its owner or handler.	Ky. Rev. Stat. Ann. § 258.265
Leash– wildlife management region	NONE	
Chasing Wildlife	NONE	
Strict Liability	The owner of any dog that causes any damage to a person, livestock, or other property, presumably any place.	Ky. Rev. Stat. Ann. §258.235(4)
Dog Bites	Any damage to a person, livestock, or other property. Presumably any place.	Ky. Rev. Stat. Ann. §258.235(4)
Dangerous Dog	Dog must be confined in a locked enclosure or a locked kennel run with a secured top. Dog may leave the enclosure only to visit the veterinarian or to be turned in to an animal shelter. The dog must be muzzled when leaving the enclosure.	Ky. Rev. Stat. Ann. § 258.235
	Any person violating or failing or refusing to comply with KRS § 258.235, except KRS 258.235(5)(a), shall, upon conviction, be fined between $5 -$100, or be imprisoned in the county jail between 5 to 60 days, or both. Any person violating KRS 258.235(5)(a) shall be punished by a fine between $50 to $200, or by imprisonment in the county jail between 10 to 60 days, or both.	Ky. Rev. Stat. Ann. §258.990(b)

Law	Requirements	Reference
Breed specific	Many cities ban pit bulls and other breeds. See city's website for more detailed information.	
Cruelty	Cruelty to animals (in the Second Degree) is defined as: "intentionally or wantonly subjects any animal to or causes cruel or injurious mistreatment through abandonment, participates other than as provided in KRS 525.125 in causing it to fight for pleasure or profit, (including, but not limited to being a spectator or vendor at such an event) mutilation, beating, torturing, tormenting, failing to provide adequate food, drink, space, or health care, or by any other means; or subjects any animal in his custody to cruel neglect; or kills any animal." (Note: KRS 525.125 specifies anyone owning the animal or organizing an animal fight is guilty of a Class D Felony and is called Cruelty to Animals in the First Degree.) This is a Class A Misdemeanor with a fine up to $500 and/or imprisonment up to 1 year. Torture of a Dog or Cat is defined as: "intentional infliction of or subjection to extreme physical pain or injury, motivated by an intent to increase or prolong the pain of the animal." The first offense is a Class A Misdemeanor with a fine up to $500 and/or imprisonment up to 1 year. The second or subsequent offense is a Class D Felony with a fine of $1000 to $10,000 and/or imprisonment from 1 to 5 years. When convicted of a felony, at least 1-year imprisonment is mandatory. Exemptions are made for hunting, fishing, trapping, processing for food or other commercial product, humane purposes.	Ky. Rev. Stat. Ann. §525.130 Ky. Rev. Stat. Ann. §525.135
Minimum age sale of puppies	NONE	

LOUISIANA

Law	Requirements	Reference
Exotic Pets	This Louisiana law states that no person shall have a cause of action against any nonprofit organization which operates or maintains a tax exempt animal sanctuary for any injury, death, loss, or damage in connection with the Chimp Haven Festival, Dixie Chimps art contest, Les Boutiques de Noel, SciPort and Chimp Haven events, Run Wild and Have a Field Day, Eye-20 Art Show Gala, Krewe of Barkus and Meow Paws parade, Krewe of Centaur parade, Krewe of Highland parade, garden tour, ChimpStock, and any other educational and public awareness activities in which the organization sponsors or participates, unless the loss or damage was caused by the deliberate and wanton act or gross negligence of the organization or any officer, employee, or volunteer thereof.	La. Rev. Stat. Ann. §9:2796.2
Sterilization	Dogs and cats must be sterilized before adoption, or adopters must enter into a sterilization agreement.	La. Rev. Stat. Ann. § 3:2472
Vaccination	Cats: At three months of age.	La. Admin. Code tit. 51, III, § 103
Tethering	It shall be unlawful to tie, tether, or restrain any animal in a manner that is inhumane, cruel, or detrimental to its welfare.	La. Rev. Stat. Ann. §14:102.26
Parked Vehicles	NONE	
Leash	No person shall suffer or permit any dog in his possession, or kept by him about his premises, to run at large on any unenclosed land, or trespass upon any enclosed or unenclosed lands of another.	La. Rev. Stat. Ann. §3:2771
Leash— wildlife management region	NONE	

Law	Requirements	Reference
Chasing Wildlife	Pets must be caged or leashed.	No statutory citation
Strict Liability	The owner of any animal that causes any damages for injuries to persons or property that owner could have prevented and that were not provoked by victim. Exception: Provocation and owner could not have prevented damage.	LA C.C. Art. §2321
Dog Bites	Any damages for injuries to persons or property that owner could have prevented and that were not provoked by victim. Exception: Provocation and owner could not have prevented damage.	LA C.C. Art. §2321
Dangerous Dog	Dog must be properly restrained or confined. Dog must be kept indoors or in a secure enclosure. Dog must be leashed when off owner's property. Dog must be licensed, vaccinated, and registered. Municipality or parish may charge a dangerous dog fee. Owner must post warning signs. Owner must notify the animal control agency about a change in the dog's circumstances.	La. Rev. Stat. Ann. §§14: 102.14, 102.17
Breed specific	Many cities ban and/or restrict pit bulls and other breed. See city website for more detailed information.	
Cruelty	Cruelty to animals is defined as: "intentionally or with criminal negligence Overdrives, overloads, drives when overloaded, or overworks a living animal; torments, cruelly beats, or unjustifiably injures any living animal; unjustifiably fails to provide it with proper food, proper drink, proper shelter; abandons any animal; Carries, or causes to be carried, a living animal in or upon a vehicle or otherwise, in a cruel or inhumane manner; unjustifiably administers any poisonous or noxious drug or substance to any domestic animal; injures any animal belonging to another person without legal privilege or consent of the owner; mistreats any living animal; causes or procures to be done by any person any act enumerated."	LA Rev. Stat. Ann. §14.102

Law	Requirements	Reference
	This is Simple Animal Cruelty with a fine up to $1000 and/or imprisonment up to 6 months. In addition, 5 8-hour days of court approved community service is required. Aggravated Animal Cruelty is when one tortures, maims, or mutilates, tampers with livestock, or causes or procures another to do such. This carries a fine of $5000 to $25,000 and/or imprisoned for 1 to 10 years. Exemptions are made for lawful hunting and trapping, herding of domestic animals, veterinary practice, scientific and medical research.	
Minimum age sale of puppies	NONE	

MAINE

Law	Requirements	Reference
Exotic Pets	This Maine statute outlines the requirements that apply to wolf hybrid kennels. A person who operates a wolf hybrid kennel must register with the department. The offspring of a wolf hybrid must be permanently identified prior to transferring ownership or care of the animal. Failure to comply with the provisions of this section results in a civil violation with a forfeiture not to exceed $1,000. (For other exotic pet laws in Maine, see Chapter 730-A. Breeding, Sale and Transportation of Small Mammals).	Me. Rev. Stat. Ann. tit. 7 § 3931-B (§ 3931-B. Repealed. Laws 2011, c. 100, § 13, eff. May 19, 2011)
	These Maine statutes prohibit keeping wildlife in captivity, importing, breeding or releasing wildlife into the wild, with exceptions for a person holding a license. Taking reptiles, amphibians, and certain non-marine invertebrates from the wild is also prohibited without a license. Provisions for the disposition of wolf hybrids are included. Penalties for violations incur fines that range from $100 to $500. Three or more such violations are considered to be a Class E criminal offense.	Me. Rev. Stat. Ann. tit. 12 § 12151 – 12161
	This chapter concerns the sale and importation of juvenile ferrets.	Me. Rev. Stat. Ann. tit. 7 § 3970- A to 3970-B
Sterilization	Dogs and cats must be "spayed or neutered" before adoption, or adopters must enter into a sterilization agreement.	Me. Rev. Stat. Ann. tit. 7 § 3939-A).
Vaccination	Cats: An owner or keeper of a cat over three (3) months of age must have that cat vaccinated against rabies.	Me. Rev. Stat. Ann. tit. 7 § 3916
Tethering	Unlawful to tie, tether or restrain any animal in a manner that is inhumane or detrimental to its welfare. Civil violation: forfeiture up to $100.	Me. Rev. Stat. Ann. tit. 7 § 3972

Law	Requirements	Reference
Parked Vehicles	Animal's safety, health or well-being appears to be in immediate danger from heat, cold or lack of adequate ventilation and the conditions could reasonably be expected to cause extreme suffering or death.	Me. Rev. Stat. Ann. tit. 7 § 4019
Leash	It is unlawful for any dog, licensed or unlicensed, to be at large, except when used for hunting. The owner or keeper of any dog found at large is subject to the penalties provided in this chapter.	Me. Rev. Stat. Ann. tit. 7 §3901
	Municipalities shall control dogs running at large.	Me. Rev. Stat. Ann. tit. 7 § 3948
Leash— wildlife management region	NONE	
Chasing Wildlife	A person shall not trap, hunt, or possess any animal taken from a wildlife sanctuary. Doing so is a civil violation punishable by a fine (first offense).	Me. Rev. Stat. Ann. tit. 12 § 12707
Strict Liability	The owner of any dog that causes damage to a person or property, in any place but the owner's property. Exceptions: Fault of the person injured may reduce damages if his or her fault exceeds owner's fault.	Me. Rev. Stat. Ann. tit. 7§ 3961
Dog Bites	Any damage to person or property. Exceptions: Fault of the person injured may reduce damages if his or her fault exceeds owner's fault.	Me. Rev. Stat. Ann. tit. 7 §3961
Dangerous Dog	The dog must be confined in a secure enclosure. The court shall specify the length of the period of confinement and may order permanent confinement. The dog must be muzzled and leashed when off premises. Court may order the owner to provide an animal control officer with photographs and descriptions of the dog. Court may order the dog tattooed or microchipped. Court may order other dogs confined or kept on owner's premises.	Me. Rev. Stat. Ann. tit. 7 §3952
Breed specific	NONE	

Law	Requirements	Reference
Cruelty	Animal Cruelty is defined as: "Kills or attempts to kill any animal without the consent of the owner, or in a manner which does not produce instantaneous death, injures, overworks, tortures, torments, abandons or cruelly beats or intentionally mutilates an animal; gives drugs to an animal with an intent to harm the animal; gives poison or alcohol to an animal; or exposes a poison with intent that it be taken by an animal, deprives an animal that the person owns or possesses of necessary sustenance, necessary medical attention, proper shelter, protection from the weather or humanely clean conditions, commits bestiality." Cruelty to Animals is a Class D crime, carrying a fine of $500 to $2500 and/or imprisonment up to 1 year. In addition, the court may prohibit the person from owning or possessing animals and to pay for the care, housing and veterinary care of the animal. Aggravated Animal Cruelty is defined as: "in a manner manifesting a depraved indifference to animal life or suffering, intentionally, knowingly or recklessly causes extreme physical pain, kills or physically tortures an animal." A second or similar conviction of Cruelty to Animals, or Aggravated Animal Cruelty is a Class C crime, carrying a fine of $1000 to $10,000 and/or imprisonment up to 5 years. In addition, the court will prohibit the person from owning or possessing animals and may order to pay for the care, housing and veterinary care of the animal. Psychological or other treatment or counseling may also be required. Exemptions are made for pest control, research, veterinary care, hunting and animal husbandry.	Me. Rev. Stat. Ann. tit. 7 §1031
Minimum age sale of puppies	Until completion of seventh week of life.	ME ADC 01- 001 CMR Ch. 701, §I(N)

MARYLAND

Law	Requirements	Reference
Exotic Pets	This chapter of Maryland laws declares that it is in the public interest to ensure public health and safety by strictly regulating the possession, breeding, and importation of certain animals that pose risks to humans. Certain animals such as domestic dogs, cats, and ferrets; animal used for agricultural, scientific, or education purposes; and animals used for public exhibitions are excluded from the provisions of this section. Any person who imports, transports, sells, transfers, breeds, raises, keeps, or possesses any animal which is prohibited under regulations promulgated by the Secretary is guilty of a misdemeanor and on conviction is subject to a fine not exceeding $500, or imprisonment not exceeding 1 year, or both.	Md. Code Ann., Health -Gen. § 18-217 -222
	Under this Maryland law, a person may not import into the State, offer for sale, trade, barter, possess, breed, or exchange the following species of animals: foxes, skunks, raccoons, bears, caimans, alligators, crocodiles, wildcats, wolves, nonhuman primates, and venomous snakes. Animal sanctuaries, AWA licensed facilities, those holding valid permits from the Department of Natural Resources, and veterinarians are exempted. This section does not prohibit a person who had lawful possession of an animal listed above on or before May 31, 2006, from continuing to possess that animal if the person provided written notification to the local animal control authority on or before August 1, 2006. Violation results in a fine and seizure of the animal(s).	Md. Code Ann., Crim. Law § 10-621
	This Maryland statute states that it is in the state's public interest to preserve native species by strictly regulating the possession, importation, exportation, breeding, raising, protection, rehabilitation, hunting, killing, trapping, capture, purchase, or sale of certain wildlife which pose a possibility of harm to native wildlife.	Md. Code Ann., Nat. Res. § 10-901 -911

Law	Requirements	Reference
Sterilization	No statewide sterilization requirements for adoption, but local ordinances may contain requirements, for example: "No statewide, local ordinances may contain requirements, for example: "Within a period to be specified by the Administrator, depending on the age, sex, health, and species of the animal, an adopted animal shall be spayed or neutered by a licensed veterinarian at the expense of the adopter."	Howard County, Maryland Code of Ordinances §17.311
Vaccination	Cats: Four months or older.	Md. Code Ann., Health -Gen. § 18-318
Tethering	A person may not leave a dog outside and unattended by use of a restraint that unreasonably limits the movement of the dog; Or one that uses a collar that: is made primarily of metal is not at least as large as the circumference of the dog's neck plus 1 inch that restricts the access of the dog to suitable and sufficient clean water or appropriate shelter in unsafe or unsanitary conditions that causes injury to the dog. Misdemeanor subject to imprisonment not exceeding 90 days or a fine not exceeding $1,000 or both.	Md. Code Ann., Crim. Law § 10- 623
Parked Vehicles	Standing or parked motor vehicle in a manner that endangers the health or safety of the cat or dog. May use reasonable force to remove from a motor vehicle a cat or dog left in the vehicle in violation of the provisions if person is: A law enforcement officer, a local or state public safety employee, a local or state animal control officer. An officer of a prevention of cruelty to animals authorized to make arrests. A volunteer or professional of a fire and rescue service.	Md. Code Ann., Transp. §21-1004.1
Leash	See various individual county provisions regarding dogs at large in Maryland's Local Government Code.	
Leash– wildlife management region	See various individual county provisions regarding dogs at large in Maryland's Local Government Code.	

Law	Requirements	Reference
Chasing Wildlife	Natural Resources police officer may kill dog destroying game birds or mammals. A Natural Resources police officer or any law enforcement officer shall and any other person may destroy any cat found hunting any game bird or mammal or protected bird or mammal. Entry into refuge (a) A person may not enter in any manner on any State wildlife refuge without the consent of the Department or person in charge of the area of land or water. (b)(1) A person may not allow any dog, domestic stock, or poultry to enter in any manner on any State-owned wildlife refuge. (2) The Department may grant a special written permit, subject to revocation at any time, to any person regularly residing on lands included within any wildlife refuge to have any trap, dog, or gun on the refuge. However, the trap, dog, or gun may not be used in hunting wildlife unless done under special permit from the Department for propagating purposes. (3) Where any portion of a State wildlife refuge is used for a State park, entry by any person within the refuge area for recreational pursuits may not be restricted on the portion used as a State park as long as the person does not carry any firearm or trap nor permit any dog to disturb or chase wildlife. (c) The Department by written permission may grant to any responsible person the right to hunt for vermin and use any dog and gun in connection with hunting on State wildlife refuges. The Department also may grant permission to hunt wildlife to be used for propagation purposes. CREDIT(S) Acts 1973, 1st Sp. Sess., c. 4, § 1; Acts 1990, c. 6, § 2.	Md. Code Ann., Nat. Res. §§ 10- 413, 10-807
Strict Liability	NONE	
Dog Bites	NONE	

Law	Requirements	Reference
Dangerous Dog	Dog owner may not leave a dangerous dog unattended on the owner's real property unless the dog is confined indoors; in a securely enclosed and locked pen; or in another structure designed to restrain the dog. Dog must be muzzled and leashed when off owner's property. If the owner wishes to sell the dog, the owner must give notice to potential owner of the dog's dangerous or potentially dangerous behavior. The owner must also notify the authority that made the determination of the sale.	Md. Code Ann., Crim. Law § 10-619
	A person who violates this section is guilty of a misdemeanor and on conviction is subject to a fine not exceeding $2,500.	Md. Code Ann., Crim. Law § 10-619
Breed specific	Some cities ban or declare pit bulls dangerous. See city website for more detailed information.	
Cruelty	Cruelty or Neglect of an Animal is defined as: "overdrive or overload an animal; deprive an animal of necessary sustenance; cause or procure such actions; if an animal is in a person's charge or custody they may not inflict unnecessary suffering or pain on the animal or unnecessarily fail to provide the animal with nutritious food in sufficient quantity, necessary veterinary care, proper drink, air, space, shelter, or protection from the weather." This is a Misdemeanor with a fine up to $1000 and/or imprisonment for up to 90 days. Aggravated Cruelty to Animals is defined as: "intentionally mutilate, torture, cruelly beat, or cruelly kill an animal; cause, procure, or authorize such action; or except in the case of self-defense, intentionally inflict bodily harm, permanent disability, or death on an animal owned or used by a law enforcement unit." This is a Felony which carries a fine of up to $5000 and/or imprisonment up to 3 years. Exemptions are made for veterinary and husbandry practices, research; food processing, pest elimination, training, and hunting as long as the person uses the most humane method reasonably available; normal human activities in which pain to animals is incidental and unavoidable.	Md. Code Ann., Crim. Law § 10-601

Law	Requirements	Reference
Minimum age sale of puppies	Minimum of eight weeks old.	Md. Code Ann., Crim. Law § 10-613

MASSACHUSETTS

Law	Requirements	Reference
Exotic Pets	Massachusetts bans private possession of exotic pets, and requires licenses for those who deal and propagate wild species for other reasons. The Massachusetts director of the Division of Fisheries and Wildlife also issues a list of exempted species for which no permit is needed.	Mass. Gen. Laws Ann. ch. 131 § 23
	Massachusetts bans hybrid animals, those offspring of mating between a domestic animal and its wild counterpart, usually wolves and dogs. No individual may possess or own a hybrid as a pet.	Mass. Gen. Laws Ann. ch. 131 § 77A
Sterilization	Dogs and cats must be spayed or neutered prior to adoption, or the adopter may enter into a written agreement and pay a deposit.	Mass. Gen. Laws Ann. ch. 140 § 139A.
Vaccination	Cats: Six months of age or older.	Mass. Gen. Laws Ann. ch. 140 §145B; Mass. Gen. Laws Ann. ch. 140 § 145B
Tethering	No person owning or keeping a dog shall chain or tether a dog to a stationary object including, but not limited to, a structure, dog house, pole or tree for longer than 24 consecutive hours. The tether used must not allow the dog to leave the owner's, guardian's or keeper's property. Tether must be designed for dogs (no logging chains or other lines or devices not designed for tethering dogs). No chain or tether shall weigh more than 1/8 of the dog's body weight. No dog under the age of 6 months shall be tethered outside for any length of time. A trolley system or a tether attached to a pulley in a cable run is allowed provided listed conditions are met. No person owning or keeping a dog shall subject the dog to cruel conditions or inhumane chaining or the tethering at any time (i.e., exposure to filth, taunting or harassing tethered dog, or subjecting dog to dangerous conditions like animal attacks).	Mass. Gen. Laws Ann. ch. 140 § 174E

Law	Requirements	Reference
Parked Vehicles	NONE	
Leash	A person owning, keeping or possessing a dog shall not allow, permit or consent to such dog chasing, hunting, molesting, attacking or killing a deer. The director is hereby authorized to issue an order to restrain all dogs from running at large in any city or town where, in his opinion, such a restraining order is necessary to prevent dogs from chasing, hunting, molesting, attacking or killing deer.	Mass. Gen. Laws Ann. ch. 131 § 82
	The mayor, aldermen or board of selectmen may order that all dogs shall be restrained from running at large during such times as shall be prescribed by the order.	Mass. Gen. Laws Ann. ch. 140 § 167
Leash— wildlife management region	Whoever is the owner or keeper of a dog shall restrain said dog by a chain or leash when in an officially designated public highway rest area. Whoever violates the provisions of this section shall be punished by a fine of not more than fifty dollars.	Mass. Gen. Laws Ann. ch. 140 § 174B
Chasing Wildlife	It shall be unlawful to pursue or hunt bear or bobcat with the aid of a dog. Dogs may not run at large chasing deer.	Mass. Gen. Laws Ann. ch. 131 § § 21A, 82
Strict Liability	The owner of any dog that cause any damage to person or property, presumably in any place. Exceptions: Person injured was teasing, tormenting or abusing dog. Person injured was committing a trespass or other tort.	Mass. Gen. Laws Ann. ch. 140 § 155
Dog Bites	Any damage to person or property. Exceptions: Person injured was teasing, tormenting or abusing dog. Person injured was committing a trespass or other tort.	Mass. Gen. Laws Ann. ch. 140 § 155

Law	Requirements	Reference
Dangerous Dog	If the hearing authority deems a dog a dangerous dog, the hearing authority shall order 1 or more of the following: The dog be humanely Restrained. The dog be confined to the premises of the owner. The dog be muzzled and leashed when not on owner's premises. The owner provides proof of insurance. The owner provides the licensing authority or animal control information by which the dog can be identified. The dog to be sterilized or euthanized. Ownership of the dog may not be transferred unless potential owner is aware of dog's dangerousness. No person over the age of 17 who has actual knowledge that a dog has been deemed dangerous shall permit a child under the age of 17 to own, possess or have the care or custody of such dog.	Mass. Gen. Laws Ann. ch. 140 § 157
Breed specific	Boston restricts pit bulls.	Mass. Gen. Laws Ann. ch. § 16-1.9e
Cruelty	Cruelty to animals is defined as: "overdrives, over-loads, drives when overloaded, overworks, tortures, torments, deprives of necessary sustenance, cruelly beats, mutilates or kills an animal, or causes or pro-cures such; and whoever uses in a cruel or inhuman manner in a race, game, or contest, or in training therefor, as lure or bait a live animal; inflicts unnecessary cruelty upon it, or unnecessarily fails to provide it with proper food, drink, shelter, sanitary environment, or protection from the weather, or cruelly drives or works it when unfit for labor, or willfully abandons it, or carries it or causes it to be carried in or upon a vehicle, or otherwise, in an unnecessarily cruel or inhuman; or knowingly and willfully authorizes or permits it to be subjected to unnecessary torture, suffering or cruelty of any kind." This is a Misdemeanor with a fine up to $1000 and/or imprisonment up to 90 days.	Mass. Gen. Laws Ann. ch. §272-77

Law	Requirements	Reference
Minimum age sale of puppies	Minimum of eight weeks' old including acquire, offer for sale, or display by regulation. Cannot import under eight weeks by statute.	Mass. Gen. Laws Ann. ch. 129 § 39G, also by Admin. Regulation 330 CMR 12.05

MICHIGAN

Law	Requirements	Reference
Exotic Pets	Michigan completely prohibits the importation into the state of "any species having the potential to spread serious diseases or parasites, to cause serious physical harm, or to otherwise endanger native wildlife, human life, livestock, domestic animals, or property." For other wild or exotic animals, Michigan regulates various aspects of their importation, such as requiring physical exams by vets, negative disease tests, and proper animal care and restraint. (See also link to Chapter 287. Animal Industry - Large Carnivore Act; link to Wolf-dog Cross Act). This Michigan statute provides the requirements for ownership of wolfdog hybrids in the state.	Mich. Comp. Laws Ann. § 287.731
	Under this Michigan statute, a local unit is empowered to adopt an ordinance governing wolf-dog crosses that is more restrictive than this act, provided it fulfills the requirements of this act in addition to any other requirements governing a wolf-dog cross under state and federal law.	Mich. Comp. Laws Ann. § 287.1004 Mich. Comp. Laws Ann. § 287.1021
Sterilization	Dogs, cats, and ferrets must be "altered" before adoption, or adopters must enter into an agreement that the animal will be altered.	Mich. Comp. Laws Ann. § 287.338a
Vaccination	NONE	
Tethering	An owner, possessor, or person having custody shall not tether a dog unless the tether is at least 3 times the length of the dog and is attached to a harness or nonchoke collar designed for tethering.	Mich. Comp. Laws § 750.50
Parked Vehicles	NONE	

Law	Requirements	Reference
Leash	It shall be unlawful for any owner to allow any dog, except working dogs such as leader dogs, guard dogs, farm dogs, hunting dogs, and other such dogs, when accompanied by their owner or his authorized agent, while actively engaged in activities for which such dogs are trained, to stray unless held properly in leash.	Mich. Comp. Laws Ann. § 287.262
Leash—wildlife management region	NONE	
Chasing Wildlife	A person shall not take, release, transport, sell, buy, or have in his or her possession game or any protected animal, whether living or dead, or parts of any game or protected animal, from this state or from outside of this state. "Take" includes chasing, pursuing, or harassing with dogs.	Mich. Comp. Laws Ann. § 324.40106
Strict Liability	The owner of any dog that causes a bite in any public place, or private place where a person has the legal right to be, including the owner's property. Exception: Trespass- person injured was not lawfully on property.	Mich. Comp. Laws Ann. § 287.351
Dog Bites	Any dog. Bite. Public place, or private place where a person has the legal right to be, including the owner's property. Exception: Trespass- person injured was not lawfully on property.	Mich. Comp. Laws Ann. § 287.351
Dangerous Dog	If the court or magistrate finds that an animal is a dangerous animal but has not caused serious injury or death to a person, the court or magistrate shall order the owner of that animal to do 1 or more of the following: Have the dog tattooed Take specific steps, such as escape proof fencing or enclosure, including a top or roof, to ensure that the animal cannot escape or nonauthorized individuals cannot enter the premises. Have the animal sterilized. Obtain and maintain liability insurance coverage sufficient to protect the public from any damage or harm caused by the animal. Take any other action appropriate to protect the public.	Mich. Comp. Laws Ann. § 287.322

Law	Requirements	Reference
Breed specific	Many cities ban, restrict or declare pit bulls dangerous. See city website for more information.	
Cruelty	Animal Cruelty is defined as: "Fail to provide an animal with adequate care; Cruelly drive, work, or beat an animal. Carry or cause to be carried in or upon a vehicle or otherwise any live animal having the feet or legs tied together. Carry or cause to be carried a live animal in or upon a vehicle or otherwise without providing a secure space, rack, car, crate, or cage in which all animals may stand, turn around, and lie down during transportation, or while awaiting slaughter. Abandon an animal or cause an animal to be abandoned, in any place, without making provisions for the animal's adequate care, unless premises are temporarily vacated for the protection of human life during a disaster. Willfully or negligently allow any animal, including one who is aged, diseased, maimed, hopelessly sick, disabled, or nonambulatory to suffer unnecessary neglect, torture, or pain. Tether a dog unless the tether is at least 3 times the length of the dog as measured from the tip of its nose to the base of its tail and is attached to a harness or nonchoke collar designed for tethering." The first offense of such is a Misdemeanor with a fine up to $1000 and/or imprisonment up to 93 days and/or community service for not more than 200 hours. The second offense of such is a Felony with a fine up to $2000 and/or imprisonment up to 2 years and/or community service for not more than 300 hours. The third or subsequent offence of such is a Felony with a fine up to $5000 and/or imprisonment up to 4 years and/or community service for not more than 500 hours. In all of the above, the convicted shall pay for the prosecution of his case and may be required to forfeit the animal(s) in his charge and may prohibit the ownership of animals for a period of time or permanently for a second conviction. Exemptions are made for fishing, hunting, trapping, wildlife control, horse racing, operation of a zoological park or aquarium, pest or rodent control, farming, husbandry, and research.	MCL § 750.50

Law	Requirements	Reference
Minimum age sale of puppies	Not less than 8 weeks old; also Import or cause to be imported into this state, or offer for sale or resale, a dog or cat unless the dog or cat Has deciduous (baby) teeth visibly present.	Mich. Comp. Laws Ann. § 287.335a

MINNESOTA

Law	Requirements	Reference
Exotic Pets	In Minnesota, a person may not possess wildlife in captivity for public exhibition purposes without a permit. The commissioner may issue a permit to an applicant qualified by education or experience in the care and treatment of wildlife. A permit shall include a condition that allows an enforcement officer to enter and inspect the facilities where the wildlife covered by the permit are held in captivity. A violation may result in the attorney general bringing an abatement action.	Minn. Stat. Ann. § 97A.041
	This Minnesota law defines "regulated animal" to mean all members of the Felidae family except the domestic cat, bears, and all non-human primates. Unless a person possessed a regulated animal on or before January 1, 2005, and came into compliance with AWA regulations, possession of the above-mentioned regulated animals is unlawful. A person who lawfully possessed a regulated animal before that date, must comply with registration, microchipping, fee, and inspection requirements.	Minn. Stat. Ann. § 346.155
Sterilization	NONE	
Vaccination	NONE	
Tethering	NONE	
Parked Vehicles	Unattended in a standing or parked motor vehicle in a manner that endangers the dog's or cat's health or safety.	Minn. Stat. Ann. § 346.57
Leash	Any person may seize, impound, or restrain any unlicensed dog which the person may find running at large. The fact that a dog is without a license attached to a collar shall be presumptive evidence that the dog is unlicensed. The sheriff and sheriff's deputies or other police officer shall seize, impound or restrain any dog for which no license has been issued and for which one is required.	Minn. Stat. Ann. § 347.14

Law	Requirements	Reference
	The electors of a town, at their annual town meeting, may let the town board pass an ordinance for licensing dogs and cats and regulating their presence, keeping, and running at large in the town.	Minn. Stat. Ann. § 365.10
Leash— wildlife management region	NONE	
Chasing Wildlife	The owner of a dog that kills or pursues a big game animal is guilty of a petty misdemeanor and is subject to a civil penalty of up to $ 500 for each violation.	Minn. Stat. Ann. § 97A.321
Strict Liability	The owner of any dog that cause any injury or attack, in any place where the victim has legal right to be, except in cases of provocation. Other exceptions: Person injured was not acting peaceably. Person injured was not in a place where s/he had a legal right to be.	Minn. Stat. Ann. § 347.22
Dog Bites	Any injury or attack. Exception: Provocation. Person injured was not acting peaceably. Person injured was not in a place where s/he had a legal right to be.	Minn. Stat. Ann. § 347.22
Dangerous Dog	Must implant a microchip in the dog. Any statutory or home rule charter city, or any county, may regulate potentially dangerous and dangerous dogs. Must have a surety bond issued of at least $300,000, payable, or a policy of liability insurance of at least $300,000. Must be kept in a proper enclosure. Must pay a registration fee of up to $500. Must display a warning sign. Must wear an identifiable tag.	Minn. Stat. Ann. § 347.515 Minn. Stat. Ann. § 347.53 Minn. Stat. Ann. § 347.51
	Must disclose, if the dangerous dog owner rents property, to the landlord that the person owns a dangerous dog that will reside at the property. If the dog is outside the proper enclosure, the dog must be muzzled and restrained by a substantial chain or	Minn. Stat. Ann. § 347.52

Law	Requirements	Reference
	leash and under the physical restraint of a responsible person. Must register the dog annually until the dog is deceased. If the dog is removed from the jurisdiction, it must be registered as a dangerous dog in its new jurisdiction. Must notify animal control if there is a change in the dog's circumstances. Must notify the new owner that the animal control authority has identified the dog as dangerous.	
Breed specific	NONE	
Cruelty	Animal Cruelty is defined as: "No person shall overdrive, overload, torture, cruelly beat, neglect, or unjustifiably injure, maim, mutilate, or kill any animal, or cruelly work any animal when it is unfit for labor, or instigate or in any way further any act of cruelty to any animal or animals, or any act tending to produce cruelty to animals." Cruelty to animals is a Misdemeanor with a fine up to $700 and/or imprisonment up to 90 days. A second or subsequent conviction of cruelty to animals in a Gross Misdemeanor with a fine up to $3000 and/or imprisonment up to 1 year. Intentional cruelty to a companion or pet animal resulting in substantial bodily harm is punishable by a fine up to $3000 and/or imprisonment up to 1 year; a second or subsequent conviction of such is punishable by fine up to $5000 and/or imprisonment up to 2 years. Intentional cruelty to a companion or pet animal resulting in death or great bodily harm is punishable with a fine up to $5000 and/or imprisonment up to 2 years; a conviction of such that was done to threaten, intimidate or terrorize another person is punishable with a fine up to $10,000 and/or imprisonment up to 4 years. In addition, the convicted may have a probation period where they may not own, have custody or control of any companion or pet animal, if they maintain custody of companion animals they may have periodic visits from an animal control officer, may be required to perform community service, or complete	Minn. Stat. Ann. § 343.20

Law	Requirements	Reference
	psychological, behavioral or other treatment. There are no named exemptions.	
Minimum age sale of puppies	Must be eight weeks of age.	Minn. Stat. Ann. § § 347.59

MISSISSIPPI

Law	Requirements	Reference
Exotic Pets	This Mississippi chapter states that it is in the public interest to ensure the public health, safety and welfare by strictly regulating the importation, sale, transfer and possession of those wild animals inherently dangerous to humans. Several species are listed under this section as inherently dangerous to humans, including non-human primates, wolves, bears, hyenas, big cats, and hippopotamus, among others. It is unlawful for a person to import, transfer, sell, purchase or possess any wild animal classified inherently dangerous by law or regulation unless that person holds a permit. Those persons who were in possession of such animals on or before May 1, 1997 were able to continue possession provided that they complied with the permit process. Prior to the issuance of a permit, the applicant must have provided proof of liability insurance in the amount of $100,000.00 for each wild animal up to a maximum of $1,000,000.00.	Miss. Code Ann. § 49-8-1 to 49-8-19
Sterilization	NONE	
Vaccination	Cats: Three months old.	Miss. Code Ann. § 41-53-1
Tethering	NONE	
Parked Vehicles	NONE	
Leash	The governing authorities of municipalities shall have the power to prevent or regulate the running at large of animals of all kinds, and to cause such as may be running at large to be impounded and sold to discharge the costs and penalties provided for the violation of such regulations and the expense of impounding and keeping and selling the same.	Miss. Code Ann. § 21-19-9
Leash— wildlife management region	NONE	

Law	Requirements	Reference
Chasing Wildlife	No wildlife shall be pursued, taken, killed, possessed or disposed of except in the manner, to the extent and at the time or times permitted by such rules and regulations; and any pursuit, taking, killing, possession or disposition thereof, except as permitted by such rules and regulations, are hereby prohibited. Any person violating this section shall be guilty of a misdemeanor except that any person violating any of the rules and regulations pertaining to record keeping requirements imposed on licensed fur buyers and fur dealers shall be guilty of an infraction and shall be fined not less than ten dollars nor more than one hundred dollars. At least one case has held this statute to be applicable to dogs chasing deer.	No statutory citation
Strict Liability	NONE	
Dog Bites	NONE	
Dangerous Dog	NONE	
Breed specific	Many cities ban or restrict pit bulls and other large breeds. See city website for more detailed information.	
Cruelty	Animal cruelty is defined as: "override, overdrive, overload, torture, torment, unjustifiably injure, deprive of necessary sustenance, food, or drink; or cruelly beat or needlessly mutilate." Cruelty to animals is a Misdemeanor with a fine up to $1000 or imprisonment up to 6 months. Malicious injury to dogs is defined as: "maliciously, either out of a spirit of revenge or wanton cruelty, or who shall mischievously kill, maim or wound, or injure any dog." This is a Misdemeanor with a fine up to $1000 or imprisonment up to 6 months, and restitution to the owner of the dog to include replacement, veterinary fees, special supplies and loss of income. There are no exemptions listed.	Miss. Code Ann. § 97-41-1
Minimum age sale of puppies	NONE	

MISSOURI

Law	Requirements	Reference
Exotic Pets	The "Large Carnivore Act" pertains to large cats and bears that are nonnative to Missouri and held in captivity. The Act prohibits ownership, possession, breeding, and transportation of large carnivores (with exceptions). The Act creates civil and criminal liability for persons who own or possess a large carnivore. Violations may result in misdemeanor or felony convictions, community service work, the loss of privileges to own or possess any animal, and forfeiture of a large carnivore.	Mo. Rev. Stat. § 578.600 - 578.625
	This Missouri law states that no person may keep any lion, tiger, leopard, ocelot, jaguar, cheetah, margay, mountain lion, Canada lynx, bobcat, jaguarondi, hyena, wolf, bear, nonhuman primate, coyote, any deadly, dangerous, or poisonous reptile, or any deadly or dangerous reptile over eight feet long, in any place other than a properly maintained zoological park, circus, scientific, or educational institution, research laboratory, veterinary hospital, or animal refuge, unless such person has registered such animals with the local law enforcement agency in the county in which the animal is kept. Violation is a class C misdemeanor.	Mo. Rev. Stat. § 578.023
	This set of statutes authorizes municipal governments to regulate animals and animal-related nuisances.	Mo. Rev. Stat. §§ 77.590, 79.110, 80.090, 82.300
Sterilization	Dogs and cats must be sterilized before adoption, or adopters must enter into a sterilization agreement.	Mo. Rev. Stat. § 273.403-05
Vaccination	NONE	
Tethering	NONE	
Parked Vehicles	NONE	

186 · APPENDIX A

Law	Requirements	Reference
Leash	The board of aldermen may also tax, regulate and restrain and prohibit the running at large of dogs, and provide for their destruction when at large contrary to ordinance, and impose penalties on the owners or keepers thereof.	Mo. Rev. Stat. § 79.400 The Board of Trustees is granted a similar power under Mo. Rev. Stat. § 80.090
Leash—wildlife management region	NONE	
Chasing Wildlife	No wildlife shall be pursued, taken, killed, possessed or disposed of except in the manner, to the extent and at the time or times permitted by such rules and regulations; and any pursuit, taking, killing, possession or disposition thereof, except as permitted by such rules and regulations, are hereby prohibited. Any person violating this section shall be guilty of a misdemeanor except that any person violating any of the rules and regulations pertaining to record keeping requirements imposed on licensed fur buyers and fur dealers shall be guilty of an infraction and shall be fined not less than ten dollars nor more than one hundred dollars. At least one case has held this statute to be applicable to dogs chasing deer.	Mo. Rev. Stat. § 252.040
Strict Liability	The owner of any dog that causes a bite to person or damage to property or livestock, in any public place, or private place where person has legal right to be, including dog owner's property except in cases of provocation and contributory fault.	Mo. Rev. Stat. § 273.036
Dog Bites	Any dog. Bite to person or damage to property or livestock. In any public place, or private place where person has legal right to be, including dog owner's property except in cases of provocation and contributory fault.	Mo. Rev. Stat. § 273.036

Law	Requirements	Reference
Dangerous Dog	NONE	
Breed specific	Many cities ban, restrict or declare pit bulls and other breed as vicious or dangerous. See city website for more information.	
Cruelty	Cruelty to animals is defined as: "Intentionally or purposely kills an animal; purposely or intentionally causes injury or suffering to an animal; or having ownership or custody of an animal knowingly fails to provide adequate care or adequate control." "Willfully" is the key which distinguishes animal abuse from animal neglect. Animal neglect and abandonment is a Class C Misdemeanor with a fine up to $500 and/or imprisonment up to 15 days. Animal abuse is a Class A Misdemeanor with a fine up to $1000 and/or imprisonment up to 1 year. A second or subsequent conviction, or if the abuse includes "torture or mutilation, or both, consciously inflicted while the animal was alive" is a Class D Felony with a fine up to $500 and/or imprisonment up to 5 years. Exemptions are made for care or treatment by a licensed veterinarian, bona fide scientific experiments, hunting, fishing, trapping, zoological parks, rodeo practices, humane killing, animal husbandry, killing an animal that is attacking or injuring another person while outside the owner's property, pests, and field trials, training and hunting practices for hunting dogs.	Mo. Rev. Stat. § 578.005
Minimum age sale of puppies	Must be eight weeks and has been weaned.	Mo. Code Regs. Ann., tit. 2, §30-9.020 (See subsection 14(E) ("Miscellaneous")

MONTANA

Law	Requirements	Reference
Exotic Pets	This set of Montana laws covers both "roadside menagerie" (any place where one or more wild animals are kept in captivity for the evident purpose of exhibition or attracting trade, excluding an educational institution or a traveling theatrical exhibition or circus based outside of Montana) and "wild animal menagerie" (any place where one or more bears or large cats, including cougars, lions, tigers, jaguars, leopards, pumas, cheetahs, ocelots, and hybrids of those large cats are kept in captivity for use other than public exhibition). The latter definition seems to cover the keeping of those listed species as exotic pets. Under the section, it is unlawful for any person to operate a roadside menagerie or wild animal menagerie without a permit. The annual permit fee for five or less animals is $10. The annual permit fee for more than five animals is $25.	Mon. Code Ann. §87-4-801 to 87-4-808
	These Montana statutes control the importation, introduction, and transplantation of exotic wildlife into the state. The importation of any wildlife is prohibited unless the species poses no threat of harm to native wildlife and plants or to agricultural production and that the introduction has significant public benefits. Violations may result in a fine or imprisonment.	Mon. Code Ann. §87-5-701 to 87-5-725
	In Montana, a person may not operate an alternative livestock ranch without a license. Such ranches are defined as enclosed land upon which animals such as privately owned caribou, white-tailed deer, etc, are kept for purposes of obtaining, rearing in captivity, keeping, or selling. The rancher has reporting requirements. Failure to comply with provisions of the act may result in revocation of the license.	Mon. Code Ann. §87-4-401 to 87-4-433
Sterilization	Dogs and cats must be "spayed or neutered" before adoption, or adopters must enter into a sterilization agreement.	Mon. Code Ann. §7-23-4202

Law	Requirements	Reference
Vaccination	NONE	
Tethering	NONE	
Parked Vehicles	NONE	
Leash	A dog found running at large without a valid current dog license tag issued by the authority of a county or municipal corporation may be seized and impounded by any sheriff, deputy sheriff, police officer, game warden, county poundmaster, or other law enforcement officer.	Mon. Code Ann. § 7-23-102 Also see (§7-23-4101 - Control of animals running at large and §7-23-2108 - County Control of Dogs).
Leash—wild-life management region	NONE	
Chasing Wildlife	Except when using dogs to chase stock-killing predators, a person may not chase with a dog any of the game or fur-bearing animals as defined by the fish and game laws of this state. Anyone authorized to enforce Montana game laws may kill such a dog. The owner may be guilty of a misdemeanor.	Mon. Code Ann. § 87-3-124
Strict Liability	The owner of any dog located with an incorporated city or town that cause a bite to any person, in any public place located within an incorporated city or town, or private place where person has the legal right to be, including dog owner's property, located within an incorporated city or town, except in cases of provocation and person bitten was in a place where s/he did not have a legal right to be, person bitten was outside of an incorporated city or town.	Mon. Code Ann. § 27-1-715

Law	Requirements	Reference
Dog Bites	Any dog located within an incorporated city or town. Exception: Provocation. Person bitten was in a place where s/he did not have a legal right to be. Person bitten was outside of an incorporated city or town.	Mon. Code Ann. § 27-1-715
Dangerous Dog	Places this power with the state's counties.	
Breed specific	Some cities ban pit bulls and wolf hybrids and require mandatory insurance on other breeds. See cites website for more detailed information.	
Cruelty	Cruelty to animals is defined as: "overworking, beating, tormenting, injuring, or killing any animal; carrying or confining any animal in a cruel manner; failing to provide an animal in the person's custody with: food and water of sufficient quantity and quality to sustain the animal's normal health; minimum protection for the animal from adverse weather conditions, with consideration given to the species; or in cases of immediate, obvious, serious illness or injury, licensed veterinary or other appropriate medical care; abandoning any helpless animal or abandoning any animal on any highway, railroad, or in any other place where it may suffer injury, hunger, or exposure or become a public charge; or promoting, sponsoring, conducting, or participating in an animal race of more than 2 miles, except a sanctioned endurance race." Cruelty to animals is punishable with a fine up to $1000 and/or imprisonment up to 1 year. In the instance where more than one animal is involved, but less than 10, each animal affected can result in an addition charge of cruelty to animals.	Mon. Code Ann. § 45-8-211
Minimum age sale of puppies	NONE	

NEBRASKA

Law	Requirements	Reference
Exotic Pets	This set of Nebraska laws provides that no person shall keep in captivity any wild bird or mammal that is either in need of conservation or listed as an endangered or threatened species. Further, no person shall keep in captivity in this state any wolf, any skunk, or any member of the families Felidae (except the domestic cat) and Ursidae (the bear family). Any person legally holding in captivity, on March 1, 1986, any such animal subject to the prohibition shall be allowed to keep the animal for the duration of its life. The section also outlines the legal requirements for obtaining and maintaining captive wildlife. (See also Chapter 37. Game and Parks. Article 2. Game Law General Provisions).	Neb. Rev. St. § 37-477 to 37-482
	These statutes comprise the definitional section of Nebraska's wildlife code. Among the definitions include game, aquaculture, wildlife, hunt, and take. (See also Chapter 37. Game and Parks. Article 4. Permits and Licenses. (B) Special Permits and Licenses).	Neb. Rev. St. § 37-201 to 248
Sterilization	Dogs and cats must be sterilized before adoption, or adopters must enter into a sterilization agreement.	Neb. Rev. St. § 54-638).
Vaccination	(Regulations for cat importation and rabies, see Neb. Admin. R. & Regs. Tit. 23, Ch. 2, § 009)	
Tethering	NONE	
Parked Vehicles	NONE	
Leash	The owner of any dog running at large for ten days without a collar as required shall be fined an amount not to exceed $25.	Neb. Rev. St. § 54-607
	In counties having a population of eighty thousand or more inhabitants and cities of the first class contained in such counties, it shall be unlawful for any person, firm, partnership, limited liability company, or	Neb. Rev. St. § 54-608

Law	Requirements	Reference
	corporation to have any dog which is owned, kept, harbored, or allowed to be habitually in or upon premises occupied by him, her, or it or under his, her, or its control to be at large.	
	A municipality may regulate, license, or prohibit the running at large of dogs.	Neb. Rev. St. § 17-526
Leash—wildlife management region	NONE	
Chasing Wildlife	Any person who brings or permits to run at large his or her pets on any area where the game commission has not permitted them to run at large shall be guilty of a Class V misdemeanor.	Neb. Rev. St. § 37-307
Strict Liability	The owner of any dog that causes any damage to person, firm or corporation. Presumably any place where person has legal right to be. Exception: Trespasser included.	Neb. Rev. St. § 54-601
Dog Bites	Any dog. Damage to person, firm or corporation. Presumably any place where person has legal right to be. Exception: Trespasser included.	Neb. Rev. St. § 54-601
Dangerous Dog	Must securely confine a dangerous dog while the dog is unattended on the owner's property. Must post warning signs on the property. Must sterilize the dog. Must implant a microchip on the dog. Must securely restrain the dog by a chain or leash when off the owner's property. Must not transport such dog or permit such dog to be transported to another county, city, or village in this state, unless for a reasonable veterinary purpose. If moving, must obtain written permission prior to such relocation from the animal control authority of the county, city, or village in which the owner resides and from the county, city, or village in which the owner will reside.	Neb. Rev. St. §§ 54-618, 619

Law	Requirements	Reference
Breed specific	Many cities ban and/or restrict pit bulls and other breeds. See city website for more information.	
Cruelty	Cruelty to animals (Cruelly Mistreat) is defined as: "knowingly and intentionally kill, maim, disfigure, torture, beat, mutilate, burn, scald, or otherwise inflict harm upon any animal." Cruelly neglect is defined as: "fail to provide any animal in one's care, whether as owner or custodian, with food, water, or other care as is reasonably necessary for the animal's health." Abandonment or cruel neglect is a Class I Misdemeanor with a fine up to $1000 and/or imprisonment up to 1 year. Cruelty to animals is a Class I Misdemeanor with a fine up to $1000 and/or imprisonment up to 1 year. A second or subsequent offense is a Class IV Felony with a fine up to $10,000 and/or imprisonment up to 5 years.	Neb. Rev. St. § 28-1008
Minimum age sale of puppies	Must be at least 8 weeks old.	Neb. Rev. St. § 28-1018

NEVADA

Law	Requirements	Reference
Exotic Pets	Under this Nevada statute, unless otherwise provided by statute no person may possess any live wildlife unless he is licensed by the division to do so, capture live wildlife in this state to stock a commercial or noncommercial wildlife facility, or possess or release from confinement any mammal for the purposes of hunting. However, the provisions of this section do not apply to alternative livestock and products made therefrom.	Nev. Rev. Stat. §504.295
	"Wildlife" means any wild mammal, wild bird, fish, reptile, amphibian, mollusk or crustacean found naturally in a wild state, whether indigenous to Nevada or not and whether raised in captivity or not.	Nev. Rev. Stat. §501.097
Sterilization	Dogs and cats must be sterilized before adoption, or adopters must enter into a sterilization agreement.	Nev. Rev. Stat. Ann. §574.640).
Vaccination	An owner of a cat shall maintain the dog, cat or ferret currently vaccinated against rabies in accordance with the provisions of this section and the recommendations set forth in the Compendium of Animal Rabies Prevention and Control, 2008 edition, published by the National Association of State Public Health Veterinarians, Inc.	Nev. Admin. code §441A.435
Tethering	A person shall not restrain a dog using a tether, chain, tie, trolley, or pulley system that: is less than 12 ft. in length, fails to allow the dog to move at least 12 ft., allows the dog to reach a fence or other object in which it could become entangled, uses a prong, pinch, or choke collar, for more than 14 hrs. in a 24-hr. period.	Nev. Rev. Stat. §574.100
Parked Vehicles	Unattended in a parked or standing motor vehicle during a period of extreme heat or cold or in any other manner that endangers the health or safety of the cat or dog.	Nev. Rev. Stat. §574.195
Leash	NONE	

Law	Requirements	Reference
Leash– wildlife management region	It is unlawful for the owner of any dog to permit such dog to run at large if such dog is actively tracking, pursuing, harassing, attacking or killing any wildlife in a state-owned wildlife management area.	Nev. Rev. Stat. §503.636
Chasing Wildlife	It is unlawful for the owner of any dog to permit such dog to run at large if such dog is actively tracking, pursuing, harassing, attacking or killing any wildlife in a state-owned wildlife management area. A peace officer may kill the dog without any liability.	Nev. Rev. Stat. §503.636
Strict Liability	NONE	
Dog Bites	NONE	
Dangerous Dog	NONE	
Breed specific	NONE	
Cruelty	Cruelty to animals is defined as: "Overdrive, overload, torture, cruelly beat or unjustifiably injure, maim, mutilate or kill an animal, whether belonging to himself or to another; deprive an animal of necessary sustenance, food or drink, or neglect or refuse to furnish it such sustenance or drink; or abandon an animal" or cause, instigate or encourage such acts. The first offense is a Misdemeanor with a $200 to $1000 fine, imprisonment from 2 days to 6 months, and community service of 48 to 120 hours. The second offense within 7 years is a Misdemeanor with a fine of $500 to $1000, imprisonment of 10 days to 6 months, and community service for 100 to 200 hours. A third or subsequent offense within 7 years is a Class C Felony with a fine up to $10,000 and/or imprisonment for 1 to 5 years. Exemptions are made for rodeos, livestock show, normal practices of ranching, hunting, dangerous animals, research, and veterinary care.	Nev. Rev. Stat. §574.050
Minimum age sale of puppies	Shall not separate a dog or cat from its mother until it is eight weeks of age or accustomed to taking food or Nourishment other than by nursing, whichever is later.	Nev. Rev. Stat. §574.500

New Hampshire

Law	Requirements	Reference
Exotic Pets	This section of laws comprises New Hampshire's wolf-dog hybrid act. Under the law, no person shall sell or resell, offer for sale or resale, or release or cause to be released a wolf hybrid in the state of New Hampshire. A person may temporarily import a wolf hybrid provided that he or she shows proof of spaying or neutering and has accurate vaccination records. Each wolf hybrid shall be under the physical control of the owner or confined in an enclosure or structure sufficient to prohibit escape. Any person in violation of this chapter or any rule adopted under this chapter shall be guilty of a class A misdemeanor. (See also link to 207:14 Import, Possession, or Release of Wildlife).	N.H. Rev. Stat. § 466-A:1 to 466-A:6
	This New Hampshire section states that no person shall import, possess, sell, exhibit, or release any live marine species or wildlife, or the eggs or progeny thereof, without first obtaining a permit from the executive director except as otherwise permitted. The executive director has the authority to determine the time period and any other conditions governing the issuance of such permit. The executive director may refuse to issue a permit if he determines that such issuance may pose significant disease, genetic, ecological, environmental, health, safety, or welfare risks to persons, marine species or wildlife. Any wildlife release or imported contrary to these provisions are subject to seizure. (See also Chapter 466-A. Wolf Hybrids).	N.H. Rev. Stat. § 207:14 - 207:15-a
Sterilization	NONE	
Vaccination	Cats: Three month of age and older.	N.H. Rev. Stat. § 436:100
Tethering	NONE	

Law	Requirements	Reference
Parked Vehicles	It shall be cruelty to confine an animal in a motor vehicle or other enclosed space in which the temperature is either so high or so low as to cause serious harm to the animal.	N.H. Rev. Stat. § 644:8-aa
Leash	A dog is considered to be a nuisance, a menace, or vicious to persons or to property if a dog is "at large," which means it is off the premises of the owner or keeper and not under the control of any person by means of personal presence and attention as will reasonably control the conduct of such dog, unless accompanied by the owner or custodian (excluding hunting, supervised competition, exhibition, or training dogs with restrictions; also a dog which is guarding, working, or herding livestock, with restrictions).	N.H. Rev. Stat. § 466:31
	The city councils shall have power to regulate the keeping of dogs and their running at large, require them to be licensed, and authorize the destruction of those kept or running at large contrary to the ordinance.	N.H. Rev. Stat. § 47:17
Leash– wildlife management region	It is unlawful for the owner or custodian of any dog to permit such dog to run at large in territory inhabited by game birds or quadrupeds, or on lands where livestock is pastured, at any time of the year (with exceptions for hunting and farm dogs).	N.H. Rev. Stat. § 466:33
Chasing Wildlife	If any dog, at any time, shall maim, injure or destroy any wild animal protected by law, the owner thereof shall be fined the same amount which the statutes impose upon persons for killing the same animal contrary to law.	N.H. Rev. Stat. § 466:35
Strict Liability	The owner of any dog that causes any damage to person or property, presumably any place where the person injured has a legal right to be, except in cases where person injured was committing a trespass or other tort.	N.H. Rev. Stat. § 466:19

Law	Requirements	Reference
Dog Bites	Any dog. Damage to person or property. Presumably any place where person injured had a legal right to be. Exception: Person injured was committing a trespass or other tort.	N.H. Rev. Stat. § 466:19
Dangerous Dog	NONE	
Breed specific	NONE	
Cruelty	Cruelty to animals is defined as: "deprived any animal in his possession or custody necessary care, sustenance or shelter; Negligently beats, cruelly whips, tortures, mutilates or in any other manner mistreats or causes to be mistreated any animal; overdrives, overworks, drives when overloaded, or otherwise abuses or misuses any animal intended for or used for labor; transports any animal in his possession or custody in a manner injurious to the health, safety or physical well-being of such animal; abandons any animal previously in his possession or custody by causing such animal to be left without supervision or adequate provision for its care, sustenance or shelter; or otherwise negligently permits or causes any animal in his possession or custody to be subjected to cruelty, inhumane treatment or unnecessary suffering of any kind." Cruelty to animals is a Misdemeanor with a fine up to $2000 and/or imprisonment up to 1 year. A second or subsequent offense, or "purposely beats, cruelly whips, tortures, or mutilates" or causes the same is a Class B Felony, with a fine up to $4000 and/or imprisonment up to 7 years. In addition, an animal may be confiscated, and decided whether or not the person should be allowed to maintain custody of the animal. The court may decide to bar them from owning animals for a period of time. Exemptions are made for licensed veterinarians.	N.H. Rev. Stat. Ann. § 644:8 (Criminal Code)
Minimum age sale of puppies	NONE	

New Jersey

Law	Requirements	Reference
Exotic Pets	NONE	
Sterilization	Dogs and cats must be sterilized before adoption, or adopters must submit a deposit and certification that the animal has been sterilized within 180 days of adoption.	N.J. Stat. Ann. § 4:19-15.30, 15.31).
Vaccination	NONE	
Tethering	NONE	
Parked Vehicles	Unattended in a vehicle under inhumane conditions adverse to the health or welfare of the living animal or creature.	N.J. Stat. Ann. § 4:22-26
Leash	The governing body of every municipality may make, amend, repeal and enforce ordinances To prohibit or regulate the running at large of dogs.	N.J. Stat. Ann. § 40:48-1
Leash— wildlife management region	NONE	
Chasing Wildlife	If any dog, at any time, shall maim, injure or destroy any wild animal protected by law, the owner thereof shall be fined the same amount which the statutes impose upon persons for killing the same animal contrary to law.	N.J. Stat. Ann. § 466:35
Strict Liability	The owner of any dog that cause a bite to a person, in any public or private place where person has the legal right to be, including dog owner's property, except in case of trespassing and person injured was not lawfully on property.	N.J. Stat. Ann. § 4:19-16
Dog Bites	Any dog. Bite to person. Public place, or private place where person has legal right to be, including dog owner's property. Exceptions: Trespass – person inured was not lawfully on property.	N.J. Stat. Ann. § 4:19-16

Law	Requirements	Reference
Dangerous Dog	Notify animal control when the dog is at large, has an attacked a human being or animal, dies, sold or donated. Prior to selling or donating the dog, inform the prospective owner that the dog has been declared potentially dangerous. Upon the sale or donation of the dog to a person residing in a different municipality, notify the department and the licensing authority, police department or force, and animal control officer of that municipality of the transfer of ownership. May have to pay a potentially dangerous dog fee. Register the dog and obtain a number and red identification tag. Tattoo the registration number on the dog. Erect and maintain an enclosure to keep the dog. If taken out of the enclosure, dog must be securely muzzled and restrained with a tether. May require the owner to maintain liability insurance in an amount determined by the municipal court. Display a warning sign.	N.J. Stat. Ann. §§4:19-24, 28
Breed specific	Some cities declare or presume pit bulls dangerous, vicious or potentially dangerous. See city website for more information.	
Cruelty	Cruelty to animals is defined as: "Overdrive, overload, drive when overloaded, overwork, deprive of necessary sustenance, abuse, or needlessly kill a living animal or creature; or inflict unnecessary cruelty upon a living animal or creature, or unnecessarily fail to provide a living animal or creature of which the person has charge either as an owner or otherwise with proper food, drink, shelter or protection from the weather, or leave it unattended in a vehicle under inhumane conditions adverse to the health or welfare of the living animal or creature." Cruelty to animals is a Disorderly Persons Offense with a fine from $250 to $1000 and/or imprisonment up to 6 months.	N.J. Stat. Ann. § 4:22-17
Minimum age sale of puppies	NONE	

New Mexico

Law	Requirements	Reference
Exotic Pets	NONE	
Sterilization	Adopters must enter into a sterilization agreement and pay a sterilization deposit.	N.M. Stat. Ann. § 77-1-20
Vaccination	Cats: Over the age of three months.	N.M. Stat. Ann. § 77-1-3 (1978)
Tethering	NONE	
Parked Vehicles	NONE	
Leash	Each municipality and each county shall make provision by ordinance for the seizure and disposition of dogs and cats running at large.	N.M. Stat. Ann. § 7-1-12 (1978)
Leash— wildlife management region	NONE	
Chasing Wildlife	NONE	
Strict Liability	NONE	
Dog Bites	NONE	
Dangerous Dog	Animal control will issue a certificate of registration if the owner: pays an annual fee if applicable; has written permission of the property owner or homeowner's association where the dangerous dog will be kept, if applicable; will maintain the dangerous dog exclusively on the owner's property except for medical treatment or examination; cages or muzzles and restrains the dog with a lead no longer than four feet if the dog is taken off the owner's property will	N.M. Stat. Ann. §§ 77-1A-5, 77-1A-6

Law	Requirements	Reference
	not allow the dog to be transported in a vehicle that might allow the dog to escape or gain access to any person or animal outside the vehicle posts a warning sign notify animal control about changes in the dog's circumstances.	
Breed specific	A couple of cities determine certain breeds to be potentially dangerous and ban pit bulls. See city website for more information.	
Cruelty	Cruelty to animals is defined as: "negligently mistreating, injuring, killing without lawful justification or tormenting an animal; or abandoning or failing to provide necessary sustenance to an animal under that person's custody or control." Extreme cruelty to animals is defined as: "intentionally or maliciously torturing, mutilating, injuring or poisoning an animal; or maliciously killing an animal. maliciously killing an animal." Cruelty to animals is a Misdemeanor with a fine up to $1000 and/or imprisonment up to 1 year. On a fourth or subsequent conviction of cruelty to animals, or extreme cruelty to animals, it is a 4th Degree Felony with a fine up to $5000 and/or imprisonment up to 18 months. The court may also order participation, at the convicted's expense, in an animal cruelty prevention program or an animal cruelty education program, and/or undergo psychological treatment. Children must be assessed and treated psychologically. Exemptions are made for humanely destroying a sick or injured animal, protecting a person or animal from injury or death, fishing, hunting, falconry, taking and trapping, the practice of veterinary medicine, rodent or pest control, accepted agricultural animal husbandry practices, rodeo practices and research facilities.	N.M. Stat. Ann. § 30-18-1
Minimum age sale of puppies	NONE	

NEW YORK

Law	Requirements	Reference
Exotic Pets	New York state law requires anyone in possession of dangerous dogs and dangerous wild animals (which include non-human primates, non-domesticated dogs and cats, bears, venomous, constrictors and python snakes, and certain crocodiles) to report the presence of that animal to the clerk of the city, town, or village in which the animal resides. The report must be filed by April 1st every year and must list all of the physical locations where the animal may be kept. The clerk must then notify all local police, fire, and emergency medical service departments of the presence of that animal. Any person who fails to report the presence may be fined up to $250 dollars for the first offense and $1,000 dollars for each subsequent offense. Zoos and other U.S. Department of Agriculture-licensed exhibitors are exempt from the reporting requirement.	N.Y. Agric. & Gen. Mun. Law § 209-cc
	This New York laws begin by stating that wild game and other wildlife may only be possessed if lawfully taken in compliance with the Fish and Wildlife Law and the accompanying regulations. Skunk, bobcat, mink, raccoon and muskrat may be bought and sold alive during their respective open seasons. No live wolf, coyote, coy dog, fox, skunk, venomous reptile or raccoon shall be possessed or transported, except under a license or permit issued by the department. Every such license or permit shall contain a prominent notice warning the licensee or permittee of his or her duty to exercise due care in safeguarding the public from attack; failure to do so is a crime under section three hundred seventy of the agriculture and markets law.	N.Y. Envtl. Conserv. Law § 11-0917

Law	Requirements	Reference
	This set of New York statutes provides some of the state's fish and wildlife laws. Among the provisions include a prohibition against interference with wildlife, restriction on the possession and importation of certain wildlife such as wolves, wolfdogs, coyotes, coy dogs, foxes, skunks, and venomous reptiles, and laws that allows individuals to take destructive wildlife. No person shall knowingly possess, harbor, sell, barter, transfer, exchange or import any wild animal for use as a pet in New York state, except that any person who possessed a wild animal for use as a pet at the time that this section went effect may retain possession of such animal for the remainder of its life.	N.Y. Envtl. Conserv. Law § 11-0501 to 11-0539
	This New York law provides that any person who owns or possesses a wild animal or reptile capable of inflicting bodily harm upon a human being, who fails to exercise due care in safeguarding the public from attack by such wild animal or reptile, is guilty of a misdemeanor. The punishment for violation is imprisonment for not more than one year, or by a fine of not more than five hundred dollars, or by both. The second part of the law imposes strict liability upon owners of dangerous wild animals.	N.Y. Agric. & Mkts. Law § 370
	This New York statute provides that no person who owns, operates or manages a facility that harbors non-native big game mammals shall knowingly permit the taking on such premises by any person who pays a fee to take a live non-native big game mammal by any of the following means: the shooting or spearing of a non-native big game mammal that is tied or hobbled; the shooting or spearing of a non-native big game mammal that is staked or attached to any object; the shooting or spearing of a non-native big game mammal that is confined in a box, pen, cage or similar container of ten or less contiguous acres from which there is no means for such mammal to escape, among other things.	N.Y. Envtl. Conserv. Law § 11-1904

Law	Requirements	Reference
	This section provides that no person shall knowingly possess, harbor, sell, barter, transfer, exchange or import any wild animal for use as a pet in New York state, except that any person who possessed a wild animal for use as a pet at the time that this section went effect may retain possession of such animal for the remainder of its life. Certain other entities are also excepted from this ban.	N.Y. Envtl. Conserv. Law § 11-0512
	This set of statutes represents the definitional portion of New York's Fish and Wildlife Law. Among the provisions include definitions for game and non-game, a definition for "wild animal," which includes big cats, non-domesticated dogs, bears, and venomous reptiles, and the state's hunter harassment law. The section also provides that the State of New York owns all fish, game, wildlife, shellfish, crustacea and protected insects in the state, except those legally acquired and held in private ownership.	N.Y. Envtl. Conserv. Law § 11-0101 to 11-0113
Sterilization	Dogs and cats must be "spayed or neutered" before adoption, or adopters must enter into a sterilization agreement.	N.Y. Agric. & Mkts. Law § 377-a).
Vaccination	Cats: No later than 4 months of age.	N.Y. Pub. Health Law § 2141
Tethering	NONE	
Parked Vehicles	Confined in motor vehicle in extreme heat or cold without proper ventilation or other protection where confinement places companion. Any person who knowingly violates this section is guilty of a violation: 1st offense - fine of not less than $50 not more than $100 2nd offense – fine of not less than $100 not more than $250. Police, peace officer, or peace officer acting as agent of humane society may take necessary steps to remove animal from vehicle. Will not be civilly or criminally liable if actions taken in reasonably good faith.	N.Y. Agric. & Mkts. Law § 353-d

Law	Requirements	Reference
Leash	Any municipality may enact a local law or ordinance upon the keeping or running at large of dogs and the seizure thereof, provided no municipality shall vary, modify, enlarge or restrict the provisions of this article relating to rabies vaccination and euthanization.	N.Y. Agric. & Mkts. Law § 122
	The governing body of any municipality may at any time by order require that all dogs in such municipality shall be securely confined between sunset and one hour after sunrise during the period of time designated in the order, or, if no time is so designated, until the order is revoked.	N.Y. Agric. & Mkts. Law § 121
Leash— wildlife management region	No owner or trainer of a dog shall allow it to run at large in fields or woods inhabited by deer outside the limits of any city or village, except on lands actually farmed or cultivated by the owner or trainer of the dog or a tenant of such owner or trainer.	N.Y. Envtl. Conserv. Law § 11-0923
Chasing Wildlife	Cats: Any person over the age of twenty-one years possessing a hunting license may, and environmental conservation officers and peace officers, acting pursuant to their special duties, or police officers shall humanely destroy cats at large found hunting or killing any protected wild bird or with a dead bird of any protected species in its possession. Dogs: Any person may kill a dog pursuing or killing game in protected areas (no action may be taken against the person).	N.Y. Envtl. Conserv. Law § 11-0529
Strict Liability	The owner of dangerous dogs only causes an injury to a person, companion, farm or domestic animal in any place, except in cases where dog was coming to the aid or defense of a person during a murder, robbery, burglary, arson, rape, criminal sexual act, or kidnapping within the dwelling or upon the property of the dog's owner.	N.Y. Agric. & Mkts. Law § 123

ﻝﻝ

Law	Requirements	Reference
Dog Bites	Dangerous dogs only (dog previously declared "dangerous"). Injury caused to a person, companion, farm or domestic animal. Exception: Dog was coming to the aid or defense of a person during a murder, robbery, burglary, arson, rape, criminal sexual act, or kidnapping within the dwelling orupon the property of the dog's owner.	N.Y. Agric. & Mkts. Law § 123
Dangerous Dog	Sterilize the dog. Microchip the dog and one or more of the following as deemed appropriate under the circumstances and as deemed necessary for the protection of the public: Evaluation of the dog. Secure, humane confinement of the dog. Restraint of the dog on a leash by an adult of at least 21 years of age. Muzzling the dog. Maintenance of a liability insurance policy in an amount determined by the court, not to exceed $100,000.	N.Y. Agric. & Mkts. Law § 123
Breed specific	Some cities ban or declare pit bulls and Rottweilers dangerous. See city website for more information.	
Cruelty	Cruelty to animals is defined as: "overdrives, overloads, tortures or cruelly beats or unjustifiably injures, maims, mutilates or kills any animal, whether wild or tame, and whether belonging to himself or to another, or deprives any animal of necessary sustenance, food or drink, or neglects or refuses to furnish it such sustenance or drink, or causes, procures or permits" such acts. This is a Misdemeanor, punishable with a fine of up to $1000 and/or imprisonment up to 1 year.	N.Y. Agric. & Mkts. Law § 353
Minimum age sale of puppies	Not younger than eight weeks old.	N.Y. Agric. & Mkts. Law § 402

North Carolina

Law	Requirements	Reference
Exotic Pets	These two North Carolina statutes provide that a city or county may by ordinance regulate, restrict, or prohibit the possession or harboring of animals which are dangerous to persons or property.	N.C. Gen. Stat. Ann. § § 153A-131, 160A-187
Sterilization	NONE	
Vaccination	Cats: Over four months of age.	N.C. Gen. Stat. Ann. § 130A-185
Tethering	A person who maliciously restrains a dog using a chain or wire grossly in excess of the size necessary to restrain the dog safely violates this law. For purposes of this section, "maliciously" means the person imposed the restraint intentionally and with malice or bad motive.	N.C. Gen. Stat. Ann. § 362.3
Parked Vehicles	An animal that is confined in a motor vehicle under conditions that are likely to cause suffering, injury, or death to the animal due to heat, cold, lack of adequate ventilation, or under other endangering conditions.	N.C. Gen. Stat. Ann. § 14- 363.3
Leash	No person shall allow his dog over six months old to run at large in the Nighttime unaccompanied by the owner or by some member of the owner's family, or some other person by the owner's permission. Any person intentionally, knowingly, and willfully violating this section shall be guilty of a Class 3 misdemeanor, and shall also be liable in damages to any person injured or suffering loss to his property or chattels.	N.C. Gen. Stat. Ann. § 67-12
Leash— wildlife management region	NONE	

Law	Requirements	Reference
Chasing Wildlife	The owner of a dangerous dog shall be strictly liable in civil damages for any injuries or property damage the dog inflicts upon a person, his property, or another animal. On game lands, wildlife refuges, and public hunting grounds the Wildlife Resources Commission may regulate the possession and use of dogs and may impound dogs found running at large without supervision or, if unsupervised, without means of identification.	N.C. Gen. Stat. Ann. §§ 67- 4., 113-291.5
Strict Liability	The owner of a dangerous dog causes injury or property damage inflicted upon a person, place, or animal, presumably in any place.	N.C. Gen. Stat. Ann. § 67-4.4
Dog Bites	Dangerous dogs only (dog previously declared "dangerous"). Injuries or property damage inflicted upon a person, property, or animal. Presumably any place.	N.C. Gen. Stat. Ann. § 67-4.4
Dangerous Dog	Dog must be confined indoors, in a securely enclosed and locked pen, or in another structure designed to restrain the dog; Dog must be leashed and muzzled or otherwise restrained beyond the owner's real property. Provide written notice to the authority that made the determination and the person taking ownership of the dog when ownership is transferred.	N.C. Gen. Stat. Ann. § 67-4.2
Breed specific	Some cities declare certain breeds to be potentially vicious. See city website for more information.	
Cruelty	Cruelty to animals is defined as: "intentionally over-drive, overload, wound, injure, torment, kill, or deprive of necessary sustenance, or cause or procure to be overdriven, overloaded, wounded, injured, tormented, killed, or deprived of necessary sustenance," which is a Class 1 Misdemeanor with fines and imprisonment at the discretion of the court.	N.C. Gen. Stat. Ann. § 14-360
Minimum age sale of puppies	NONE	

North Dakota

Law	Requirements	Reference
Exotic Pets	This Chapter of North Dakota laws deals with the state board of animal health, state veterinarian, and special provisions for keeping certain non-traditional livestock. Section 36-01-08.2 states that any person who keeps a mountain lion, wolf, or wolf hybrid in captivity must obtain an identification number from the state board. Section 36-01-08.4 also provides that a person may not keep a skunk or raccoon in captivity, and that the state board must adopt rules concerning the keeping of a primate, wolf, or wolf-hybrid in captivity. The remainder of the chapter deals primary with infectious disease control in livestock, although section 36-01-31 contains a ban on the keeping of a live venomous reptile.	N.D. Cent. Code §36-01-00.1-35
Sterilization	Dogs and cats must be sterilized before adoption, or adopters must enter into a sterilization agreement.	N.D. Cent. Code §40-05-19
Vaccination	NONE	
Tethering	NONE	
Parked Vehicles	Unattended in a stationary or parked motor vehicle in a manner that endangers the animal's health or safety.	N.D. Cent. Code §36-21.2-12
Leash	NONE	
Leash— wildlife management region	NONE	
Chasing Wildlife	Any district game warden may kill any unattended dog harassing or killing big game. No action for damages may be maintained against the person for the killing.	N.D. Cent. Code §20.1-05-02.1
Strict Liability	NONE	

Law	Requirements	Reference
Dog Bites	NONE	
Dangerous Dog	NONE	
Breed specific	Many cities ban pit bulls and other large breeds. See city website for more information.	
Cruelty	Cruelty to animals is defined as: "overdrive, overload, torture, cruelly beat, neglect, or unjustifiably; injure, maim, mutilate, or kill any animal, or cruelly work any animal when unfit for labor; deprive any animal over which the person has charge or control of necessary food, water, or shelter; keep any animal in any enclosure without exercise and wholesome change of air; abandon any animal; allow any maimed, sick, infirm, or disabled animal of which the person is the owner, or of which the person has custody, to lie in any street, road, or other public place for more than three hours after notice." Also included are statutes for Cruelty in Transportation, Unattended Dog or Cat in a Motor Vehicle, Poisoning Animals, Exposure of Animals (neglect), Cockfights, Dogfights, Artificially Colored Animals, Use of Certain Birds as Advertising Devices - Use of Live Beef or Dairy Cattle as Raffle Prizes - Gifts of Animals. Cruelty to animals is a Class A Misdemeanor with up to $2000 in fines and up to 1 year imprisonment.	N.D. Cent. Code §36-21-1-01
Minimum age sale of puppies	NONE	

OHIO

Law	Requirements	Reference
Exotic Pets	Formerly, this Ohio law provides than an owner or keeper of any non-indigenous or exotic animal that presents a risk of serious physical harm to persons or property must report the animal's escape within one hour after discovering its escape. Failure to do so is a first degree misdemeanor. However, this law was repealed in 2012.	Ohio Rev. Code Ann. § 2927.21
	On June 5, 2012, Ohio governor Kasich signed the "Dangerous Wild Animal Act" into law. Under this new section, no person shall possess a dangerous wild animal on or after January 1, 2014 unless he or she is authorized under an unexpired wildlife shelter/propagation permit or other exception. Dangerous wild animals include big cats, some smaller exotic cats, bears, elephants, hyenas, gray wolves, alligators, crocodiles and nonhuman primates other than lemurs. Except as provided, no person shall acquire, buy, sell, trade, or transfer possession or ownership of a dangerous wild animal on or after the effective date of this section.	Ohio Rev. Code Ann. § 935.01 - .99
Sterilization	NONE	
Vaccination	NONE	
Tethering	NONE	
Parked Vehicles	NONE	
Leash	Ordinances or resolutions to control dogs include the restraint of dogs, except that such ordinances or resolutions shall not prohibit the use of any dog which is lawfully engaged in hunting or training for the purpose of hunting while accompanied by a licensed hunter.	Ohio Rev. Code Ann. § 955.221

Law	Requirements	Reference
Leash—wildlife management region	NONE	
Chasing Wildlife	No person shall disturb, injure, or destroy a tree, plant, lawn, embankment, decoration, or other property or kill, injure, or disturb a waterfowl, water animal, bird, or game or fur-bearing animal, kept as a semidomestic pet upon an island or within the boundary lines of Buckeye Lake, Indian Lake, The Portage Lakes, Lake St. Marys, Guilford Lake, and Lake Loramie, or any other territory over which the state has jurisdiction or an embankment or state land adjacent thereto. No person shall take or disturb fish in any lagoon or any other portion of any of the waters over which the state has jurisdiction and which have been set aside by the chief for the propagation of fish.	Ohio Rev. Code Ann. § 1531.07
Strict Liability	The owner of any dog that causes any injury, death, or loss to a person, presumably in any place where the person has the legal right to be, except in cases of provocation where person injured was teasing, tormenting, or abusing the dog on the owner's property. Other exceptions include; person injured was committing criminal trespass or another criminal offense (other than a minor misdemeanor) on the property of the owner, or a criminal offense other than a minor misdemeanor against any person.	Ohio Rev. Code Ann. § 955.28
Dog Bites	Any dog. Any injury, death, or loss to person or property. Presumably any place where person had a legal right to be. Provocation exception: Person injured was teasing, tormenting, or abusing the dog on the owner's property. Other exceptions: Person injured was committing criminal trespass or another criminal offense (other than a minor misdemeanor) on the property of the owner, or a criminal offense other than a minor misdemeanor against any person.	Ohio Rev. Code Ann. § 955.28

Law	Requirements	Reference
Dangerous Dog	When transferring ownership, seller must inform buyer about dog's behavior and must inform the proper authorities of the transfer. Must have the dog on a leash and possibly a muzzle when off the owner's property. Must obtain liability insurance. Must register the dog to someone 18 years or older. Must notify the proper authority if the dog is loose, bites a person, attacks another animal, the owner and dog relocate, or the dog is sold, transferred, or dies. Must not debark or surgically silence the dog. Must not possess a dog known or reasonably believed to be dangerous. Must keep dog current in rabies vaccinations. Must sterilize the dog. Must post warning signs. Must implant dog with microchip.	Ohio Rev. Code Ann. § §955.11, 955.22
Breed specific	Many cities have different laws. Some restrict certain breeds and other ban certain breeds. See city website for more detailed information.	
Cruelty	Cruelty to animals is defined as: "Torture an animal, deprive one of necessary sustenance, unnecessarily or cruelly beat, needlessly mutilate or kill, or impound or confine an animal without supplying it during such confinement with a sufficient quantity of good wholesome food and water; affording it access to shelter; carry or convey an animal in a cruel or inhuman[e] manner." (Note, there are other provisions which govern the conditions in which production animals are cared for and transported.) Cruelty to animals is a 2nd degree Misdemeanor with a fine up to $750 and/or imprisonment up to 90 days.	Ohio Rev. Code Ann. § 959.01
Minimum age sale of puppies	Must be at least eight weeks of age.	Ohio Rev. Code Ann. § 955.50

OKLAHOMA

Law	Requirements	Reference
Exotic Pets	No exotic wildlife may be released into the wilds of Oklahoma without first obtaining written permission of the Director. Violation is a misdemeanor punishable of a fine of $100 to $2000, and/or imprisonment up to 30 days.	Okla. Stat. Ann. tit. 29, § 7-801
	This Oklahoma statute states that no person may breed, possess or raise native wildlife, except fish, amphibians, aquatic reptiles, aquatic invertebrates or exotic livestock, for commercial purposes without first obtaining a commercial wildlife breeder's license from the Director. Further, no person licensed with a commercial wildlife breeder's license may sell native cats or bears to any person who does not possess a commercial wildlife breeder's license. The initial and annual fee for such a license is $48 for a resident. Violation of any provision of this section results in a fine of not less than $500.00 and, if applicable, revocation of the wildlife license. Circuses are exempted from this provision.	Okla. Stat. Ann. tit. 29, §§ 4-107, 4-107.1
Sterilization	Dogs and cats must be sterilized before adoption, or adopters must enter into a sterilization agreement.	Okla. Stat. Ann. tit. 4, § 499.2
Vaccination	Cats: Four months of age.	Okla. Admin. Code §310: 599-3-9.1
Tethering	NONE	
Parked Vehicles	NONE	
Leash	The board of county commissioners of any county with a population of 200,000 or more may regulate or prohibit the running at large of dogs within said county, and cause such dogs as may be running at large to be impounded and disposed of.	Okla. Stat. Ann. tit. 4, § 43

Law	Requirements	Reference
Leash– wildlife management region	Notwithstanding any other provision of law, no person may enter a state park with a dog, unless the dog is on a leash, or permit any dog to enter a state park or recreation area under the jurisdiction of the Commission.	Okla. Stat. Ann. tit. 74, § 2217
Chasing Wildlife	Except as otherwise provided by law, no person may enter upon any state or federal wildlife refuge or Wildlife Management Area with dog, gun or bow.	Okla. Stat. Ann. tit. 29, § 7-304
Strict Liability	The owner of any dog that causes any damages, any place where the victim has the legal right to be, except in cases of provocation.	Okla. Stat. Ann. tit. 4, § 42.1
Dog Bites	Any dog. Any damages. Any place where the victim has the legal right to be. Provocation exception.	Okla. Stat. Ann. tit. 4, § 42.1
Dangerous Dog	Must register the dog (city or county may charge a registration fee). Must confine the dog in a proper enclosure. Must post a warning sign. Must obtain liability insurance. Must be muzzled and restrained when off the property.	Okla. Stat. Ann. tit. 4, §§ 45, 46
Breed specific	NONE	
Cruelty	Cruelty to animals is defined as: "overdrive, overload, torture, destroy or kill, or cruelly beat or injure, maim or mutilate, any animal in subjugation or captivity, whether wild or tame, and whether belonging to himself or to another, or deprive any such animal of necessary food, drink or shelter, or who shall cause, procure or permit, or who shall willfully set on foot, instigate, engage in, or in any way further any act of cruelty to any animal." This is a Felony with a fine up to $5,000, or imprisonment in a county jail for up to one year, or imprisonment in a state penitentiary for up to 5 years. Abandoning an animal or cruelty in transit is a Misdemeanor with a fine of $100 to $500, and/or imprisonment up to 1 year. In addition, the person may be required to pay for cost of care and boarding of the victimized animal, there are no exemptions.	Okla. Stat. Ann. tit. 21, § 1685
Minimum age sale of puppies	Cat or dog must be at least eight weeks of age.	Okla. Admin. Code §35:55-5-2

OREGON

Law	Requirements	Reference
Exotic Pets	These Oregon laws concern the regulation of exotic pets in the state. An "exotic animal" for purposes of the section means a member of the family Felidae not indigenous to Oregon (except the domestic cat), any nonhuman primate, any nonwolf member of the family Canidae not indigenous to Oregon (except the domestic dog), any bear except the black bear, and any member of the order Crocodylia. A person may not keep an exotic animal in this state unless the person possesses a valid State Department of Agriculture permit for that animal issued prior to the effective date of this 2009 Act.	Or. Rev. Stat § 609.205 - 335
Sterilization	NONE	
Vaccination	NONE	
Tethering	In 2013, the state enacted a new law called "Unlaw- ful Tethering." A person commits the offense of unlawful tethering if the person tethers a domestic animal in the person's custody or control: (a) With a tether that is not a reasonable length given the size of the domestic animal and available space and that allows the domestic animal to become entangled in a manner that risks the health or safety of the domestic animal; (b) With a collar that pinches or chokes the domestic animal when pulled; (c) For more than 10 hours in a 24-hour period; or (d) For more than 15 hours in a 24-hour period if the tether is attached to a running line, pulley or trolley system. Note that if the tethering causes physical injury or death, a person can be charged with animal neglect in the first or second degree.	Or. Rev. Stat §§167.343, 167.325, 167.330
Parked Vehicles	NONE	

Law	Requirements	Reference
Leash	If the governing body of a county by ordinance, or a measure approved by the electors in an election prohibits dogs from running at large, the county shall give notice, by publication in a newspaper having a general circulation in the county. After 60 days from the date of the notice, every person keeping a dog shall prevent the dog from running at large in any county or city where prohibited. A person who is the keeper of a dog commits a Class B violation if the dog runs at large where prohibited.	Or. Rev. Stat § 609.060
Leash— wildlife management region	NONE	
Chasing Wildlife	No person shall hunt or trap on a wildlife refuge. A dog found unlawfully hunting or tracking any game mammal or bird (subject to specific enumerated hunting provisions) may be killed if not licensed and wearing a collar or if while wearing a collar, the owner is notified and the dog continues to hunt or track the game animal.	Or. Rev. Stat §§ 501.015, 498.102
Strict Liability	NONE	
Dog Bites	NONE	
Dangerous Dog	NONE	
Breed specific	A couple of cities ban or restrict certain breeds. See city website for more information.	
Cruelty	Animal abuse in the second degree is defined as: "intentionally, knowingly or recklessly causes physical injury to an animal." This is a Class B Misdemeanor with a fine up to $2000 and/or imprisonment up to 6 months. Exemptions are made for good animal husbandry.	Or. Rev. Stat § 167.310

Law	Requirements	Reference
	Animal abuse in the first degree is defined as: "intentionally, knowingly or recklessly: causes serious physical injury to an animal; or cruelly causes the death of an animal." This is a Class A Misdemeanor with a fine up to $5000 and/or imprisonment up to 1 year. However, animal abuse in the first degree is a Class C Felony with a fine up to $100,000 and/or imprisonment up to 5 years IF the person has been convicted of two or more of the following: Assault in the first, second, third or fourth degree if the case involved domestic violence or was committed against a minor child; if the animal abuse was knowingly committed in the presence (was seen or directly perceived) of a minor child or has previous convictions of animal abuse in the first degree or aggravated animal abuse in the first degree.	
Minimum age sale of puppies	NONE	

PENNSYLVANIA

Law	Requirements	Reference
Exotic Pets	These Pennsylvania statutes represent the state's exotic pet laws. "Exotic wildlife" includes all bears, coyotes, lions, tigers, leopards, jaguars, cheetahs, cougars, wolves and any crossbreed of these animals. The commission may issue a permit to a person to act as an exotic wildlife dealer. No permit shall be granted by the commission until it is satisfied that the provisions for housing and caring for the exotic wildlife and protection for the public are proper and adequate and in accordance with the standards which may be established by regulations. It is unlawful to release any exotic wildlife into the wild, fail to exercise due care in safeguarding the public, or recklessly engage in conduct that places another person in danger of attack from exotic wildlife.	34 Pa. Cons. Stat. Ann. § 2961 - 2965; 58 Pa. Code § 147.261 – 262
	This chapter of Pennsylvania laws allows the commission to issue permits to take wildlife. Among the permit categories include endangered or threatened species permits, wildlife menagerie, wildlife (exotic) dealer, and wildlife (exotic) possession permits. It is unlawful to exercise any of the privileges granted by a permit issued under this title without first securing the required permit.	34 Pa. Cons. Stat. Ann. § 2901 - 2908
Sterilization	Dogs and cats must be sterilized before adoption, or adopters must enter into a sterilization agreement.	3 Pa. Cons. Stat. § 459-902-A
Vaccination	Cats: Attains at 12 weeks of age.	3 Pa. Cons. Stat. § 455.8
Tethering	NONE	
Parked Vehicles	NONE	

Law	Requirements	Reference
Leash	Confinement and control. It shall be unlawful for the owner or keeper of any dog to fail to keep at all times the dog in any of the following manners: (1) confined within the premises of the owner; (2) firmly secured by means of a collar and chain or other device so that it cannot stray beyond the premises on which it is secured; or (3) under the reasonable control of some person, or when engaged in lawful hunting, exhibition, performance events or field training.	3 Pa. Cons. Stat. § 459-305
Leash— wildlife management region	NONE	
Chasing Wildlife	It is unlawful for any person controlling or harboring a dog to permit the dog to chase, pursue, follow upon the track of, injure or kill any game or wildlife at any time.	34 Pa. Cons. Stat. Ann. § 2381
Strict Liability	The owner of any dog is liable for any cost of medical treatment, in any place.	3 Pa. Cons. Stat. § 459-502
Dog Bites	Any dog. Any cost for medical treatment. Any place.	3 Pa. Cons. Stat. § 459-502
Dangerous Dog	Must keep the dog properly confined. Must leash and muzzle the dog if outside of proper enclosure. Must register the dog and pay a registration fee. Must post a warning sign. Must pay court-ordered restitution to a victim of a dangerous dog. Must implant dog with a microchip. Must obtain liability insurance. Must sterilize the dog. Must obtain a surety bond of liability insurance. Must notify the proper authorities if the dangerous dog is on the loose, is unconfined, has attacked another animal, has attacked a human being, has died or has been sold or donated. New owner or keeper of the dangerous dog shall be required to comply with all of the provisions of this act and regulations pertaining to a dangerous dog.	3 Pa. Cons. Stat. §§ 459-503-A, 459-504-A
Breed specific	A few cities restrict or declare pit bulls as dangerous or vicious. See city website for more information.	

Law	Requirements	Reference
Cruelty	Cruelty to animals is defined as: "wantonly or cruelly ill-treats, overloads, beats, otherwise abuses any animal, or neglects any animal as to which he has a duty of care, whether belonging to himself or otherwise, or abandons any animal, or deprives any animal of necessary sustenance, drink, shelter or veterinary care, or access to clean and sanitary shelter which will protect the animal against inclement weather and preserve the animal's body heat and keep it dry." This is a summary offense with a fine of $50-750 and/or imprisonment up to 90 days. It is a Misdemeanor in the second degree if a person: "Kills, maims or disfigures any domestic animal of another person or any domestic fowl of another person; administers poison to or exposes any poisonous substance with the intent to administer such poison to any domestic animal of another person or domestic fowl of another person; harasses, annoys, injures, attempts to injure, molests or interferes with a dog guide, hearing dog or service dog." This is punishable with a fine of not less than $500. It is a Felony in the third degree if a person: "Kills, maims or disfigures any zoo animal in captivity; or administers poison to or exposes any poisonous substance with the intent to administer such poison to any zoo animal in captivity." This is punishable by a fine up to $15,000 and/or up to 7 years in prison. It is a Misdemeanor in the first degree if a person: "Kills, maims, mutilates, tortures or disfigures any dog or cat, whether belonging to himself or otherwise; or administers poison to or exposes any poisonous substance with the intent to administer such poison to any dog or cat, whether belonging to himself or otherwise" This is punishable by a fine of not less than $1,000 and/or imprisonment for up to 2 years. A subsequent conviction is a Felony in the 3rd Degree, punishable by a fine up to $15,000 and/or imprisonment up to 7 years. Exemptions to these clauses are veterinary care, protecting other domestic animals or fowl, game laws, pest control, and farming.	18 Pa. Cons. Stat. § 5511
Minimum age sale of puppies	Eight weeks old.	3 Pa. Cons. Stat. § 459-603

Rhode Island

Law	Requirements	Reference
Exotic Pets	This chapter of Rhode Island laws proclaims that its intent is to provide safeguards for the protection of persons in the state from disease hazards associated with imported wild animals. Under the chapter, no person shall import into, receive, or possess in this state without first obtaining a permit from the department, animals of the following orders, families, and genera: primates, carnivores, amphibia, reptilia, canidae, and insecta. Personal pets under a special permit are exempted from the importation permit requirement. A permit may be granted by the department to import a wild animal as a personal pet, if a written affidavit or declaration under penalty of perjury is completed at the time of entry at the site of first arrival. This chapter also requires that certain species undergo quarantine for specified periods of time. Any person who violates any provisions of this chapter shall be fined not less than one hundred dollars ($100), and the loss of any specimen referred to in this chapter.	R.I. Gen. Laws § 4-18-1 to 15 (1956)
Sterilization	Dogs and cats must be "spayed or neutered" before adoption, or adopters must enter into a sterilization agreement.	R.I. Gen. Laws § 4-19-16
Vaccination	Except as otherwise amended by board regulation, the owner or keeper of a dog, cat, or ferret shall have the animal vaccinated not earlier than three (3) months of age nor later than four (4) months of age.	R.I. Gen. Laws § 4-13-31 (1956)
Tethering	It is a violation for an owner or keeper to: Keep any dog on a permanent tether that restricts movement of the tethered dog to an area less than one hundred thirteen square feet (113 sq. ft.), or less than a six-foot (6') radius at ground level. Tether a dog with a choke-type collar or prong-type collar. Keep any dog tethered for more than ten (10) hours during a twenty-four (24) hour period or keep	R.I. Gen. Laws § 4-13-42 (1956)

Law	Requirements	Reference
	any dog confined in a pen, cage or other shelter for more than fourteen (14) hours during any twenty-four (24) hour period.	
Parked Vehicles	No owner or person shall confine any animal in a motor vehicle which is done in a manner that places the animal in a life threatening or extreme health threatening situation by exposing it to a prolonged period of extreme heat or cold, without proper ventilation or other protection from such heat or cold.	R.I. Gen. Laws § 4-1-3.2 (1956)
Leash	City or town councils may make any ordinances concerning dogs in their cities or towns as the councils deem expedient, pertaining to the conduct of dogs, which ordinances shall include regulations relating to unrestricted dogs, leash laws, confinement, and destruction of vicious dogs.	R.I. Gen. Laws § 4-13-15.1 (1956)
Leash—wildlife management region	NONE	
Chasing Wildlife	A person may not in any manner molest or destroy any wild animal in a state protected wildlife management area.	R.I. Gen. Laws § 20-18-2
Strict Liability	The owner of any dog that cause an assault, bite, or other injury to any person, while traveling the highway or outside of the enclosure of the dog's owner or keeper, except in cases of provocation where the dog was in enclosure on owner's property or was not traveling the public highway. Another exception is, the dog was in enclosure on owner's property or was not traveling the public highway.	R.I. Gen. Laws § 4-13-16
Dog Bites	Any dog. Assault, bite, or other injury to any person. While traveling the highway or outside of the enclosure of the dog's owner or Keeper. Provocation: Dog was in enclosure on owner's property or was not traveling the public highway. Other exceptions: Dog was in enclosure on owner's property or was not traveling the public highway.	R.I. Gen. Laws § 4-13-16

Law	Requirements	Reference
Dangerous Dog	Vicious Dog Ownership Conditions: May require liability insurance. Must tattoo license number on the dog. Must display a sign. Must keep dog in a proper enclosure. Must notify the proper authorities if a vicious dog is on the loose, is unconfined, has attacked another animal or has attacked a human being, or has died. When the dog is off the owner's property, it shall be leashed and/or muzzled. When the dog is outdoors on the owner's property, it must be leashed and/or muzzled, or tie-out, or in an enclosed area which prevents its escape. Must sterilize the dog. If an owner or keeper moves, he or she shall notify the dog officer of the city or town in which he/she resides and the dog officer of the city or town in which he or she is to reside. Must leave dog under the care of someone who is over 16 years of age. Must not sell or give away the dog.	R.I. Gen. Laws § 4-13.1-3 (1956)
Breed specific	One city bans pit bulls. See city website for more information.	
Cruelty	Unnecessary Cruelty is defined as: "Overdrives, overloads, drives when overloaded, overworks, tortures, torments, deprives of necessary sustenance, cruelly beats, mutilates or cruelly kills, or causes or procures to be so overdriven, overloaded, driven when overloaded, overworked, tortured, tormented, deprived of necessary sustenance, cruelly beaten, mutilated or cruelly killed, any animal, and whoever, having the charge or custody of any animal, either as owner or otherwise, inflicts cruelty upon that animal, or willfully fails to provide that animal with proper food, drink, shelter or protection from the weather." This is punishable with a fine from $50 to $500 and/or imprisonment up to 11 months for each offense. Malicious Injury to or Killing of Animals is defined as: "cuts out the tongue or otherwise dismembers any animal, maliciously, or maliciously kills or wounds any animal, or maliciously administers poison to or exposes any poisonous substance with	R.I. Gen. Laws § 4-1-1

Law	Requirements	Reference
	intent that the poison shall be taken or swallowed by any animal, or who maliciously exposes poisoned meat with intent that the poison meat is taken or swallowed by any wild animal." This is punishable with a fine up to $1,000 and/or imprisonment up to 2 years, shall be liable to the owner of the animal for triple damages in civil court, and serve 10 hours of community service which is not deferrable. Exemptions are made for licensed hunters during hunting season and businesses licensed to kill animals for human consumption.	
Minimum age sale of puppies	NONE	

SOUTH CAROLINA

Law	Requirements	Reference
Exotic Pets	This South Carolina law states that it is unlawful for a person to import, possess, or transport for the purpose of release or to introduce or bring into this State the following live wildlife: a furbearer which includes but is not limited to, red and gray fox, raccoon, opossum, muskrat, mink, skunk, otter, bobcat, weasel, and beaver; a member of the family Cervidae, a nondomestic member of the families Suidae (pigs), Tayassuidae (peccaries), Bovidae (bison, mountain goat, mountain sheep), coyote, bear, or turkey (genus Meleagris); or a non-native species of fish, crustacean, mollusk, or invertebrate. A permit may be granted only after the investigations and inspections of the wildlife have been made as the department considers necessary and the department approves the possession, transportation, or importation into the State. § 50-11-1765 provides that it is unlawful to sell live wolves or to ship, import, or possess live wolves into this State without a permit.	S.C. Code Ann. §§ 50-11-1700 – 1950 (1976); 50-16-10 – 70 (1976)
	This South Carolina law provides that no carnivores, which normally are not domesticated, may be sold as pets in this State. A carnivore kept by an individual must not be allowed to run at large and then returned to confinement. A normally wild animal indigenous to this State, if held captive for a period of time, may be released to the wild. This section does not apply to domesticated ferrets. Each business that sells ferrets must also display a notice about the potential danger of unprovoked attacks against humans.	S.C. Code Ann. §§ 47-5-20, 47-5-50

Law	Requirements	Reference
	This set of South Carolina laws relates to the possession of live wildlife. A permit is required for the following: the family Cervidae, a nondomestic member of the families Suidae (pigs), Tayassuidae (peccaries), Bovidae (bison, mountain goat, mountain sheep), coyote, bear, or turkey (genus Meleagris), and a "furbearer," which includes, but is not limited to, red and gray fox, raccoon, opossum, muskrat, mink, skunk, otter, bobcat, weasel, and beaver. However, wildlife imported for exhibition purposes only by state wildlife departments, municipal zoos or parks, public museums, public zoological parks, and public scientific or educational institutions operated not for profit, and transient circuses are not required to procure a permit. Under another section, release of a member of the family Suidae (pig) into the wild is prohibited except as provided by law. Further, it is unlawful for a person to possess, transport, or otherwise bring into the state or release or introduce into the state any diseased wildlife or other animal that reasonably might be expected to pose a public health or safety hazard. Violating any permitting requirement under the chapter results in a misdemeanor with a mandatory fine of not more than $1,000 or up to 6 months' imprisonment, or both.	S. C. Code Ann. §§ 50-16-10 to 70; 50-11-1765 (1976)
Sterilization	Dogs and cats must be sterilized before adoption, or adopters must enter into a sterilization agreement.	S.C. Code Ann. § 47-3-480
Vaccination	NONE	
Tethering	NONE	
Parked Vehicles	NONE	
Leash	It is unlawful in any county or municipality adopting penalty provisions pursuant to the provisions of this article for any dog or cat owner or other keeper of a dog or cat to allow his dog to run at large off of property owned, rented, or controlled by him.	S. C. Code Ann. § 47-3-50 (1976)

Law	Requirements	Reference
Leash– wildlife management region	It shall be unlawful for any person at any park or facility under the jurisdiction of the Department of Parks, Recreation and Tourism to bring a dog or any other animal into the park or facility unless it is crated, caged, or upon a leash not longer than six feet or otherwise under physically restrictive control at all times.	S. C. Code Ann. §51-3-145 (1976)
Chasing Wildlife	There are a number of designated wildlife refuges, each with their own set of regulations. Generally speaking, pets are no allowed. Pets are not allowed at "wildlife management areas" - owners who bring pets to one of these areas may be convicted of a misdemeanor.	S. C. Code Ann. §50-11-2200
Strict Liability	The owner of any dog that causes a bite or attack, in a public place or private place where the person has the legal right to be, except in cases of provocation. Another exception is trespassing, victim not in a place where s/he has the legal right to be.	S. C. Code Ann. § 47-3-110
Dog Bites	Any dog. Bite or other attack. Public place, or private place where person has legal right to be, including dog owner's property. Provocation exception. Other exception: Trespass - victim not in a place where s/he has a legal right to be.	S. C. Code Ann. § 47-3-110
Dangerous Dog	Must not go unconfined on the premises.	S. C. Code Ann. § 47-3-720 (1976)
	Must clearly mark the pen or run area contains a dangerous animal. Must be safely restrained when permitted off the premises.	S. C. Code Ann. § 47-3-730 (1976)
	No person may possess with intent to sell, offer for sale, breed, or buy or attempt to buy a known dangerous animal.	S. C. Code Ann. § 47-3-740 (1976)
	Must register dangerous animal with local law enforcement.	S. C. Code Ann. § 47-3-760 (1976)
Breed specific	A few cities declare some breeds as dangerous or vicious. See city website for more information.	

Law	Requirements	Reference
Cruelty	Ill treatment of animals, generally, is defined as: "knowingly or intentionally overloads, overdrives, overworks, ill-treats any animal, deprives any animal of necessary sustenance or shelter, inflicts unnecessary pain or suffering upon any animal, or by omission or commission knowingly or intentionally causes these things to be done." Each offense is a misdemeanor and is punishable by imprisonment for up to 60 days and/or a fine of $100 to $500 for the first offense; imprisonment not exceeding 90 days and/or a fine up to $800 for a second offense; and imprisonment up to 2 years and/or a fine up to $2000 for a third or subsequent offense. A second provision to Ill Treatment of Animals is: "Whoever tortures, torments, needlessly mutilates, cruelly kills, or inflicts excessive or repeated unnecessary pain or suffering upon any animal or by omission or commission causes the acts to be done." This is a felony punishable by imprisonment of not less than 180 days and not to exceed 5 years AND a fine of $5000. Exemptions are made for fowl, accepted animal husbandry practices of farm operations and the training of animals, the practice of veterinary medicine, agricultural practices, forestry and silvacultural practices, wildlife management practices. Abandonment or neglect of providing "the necessities of life", defined as adequate water, food and shelter is a misdemeanor and is punishable by a fine of $200 to $500 OR imprisonment up to 30 days. If a non-profit animal humane organization is involved in prosecuting the individual, 1/2 of the fine imposed shall be given to that organization.	S.C. Code Ann. §47-1-10
Minimum age sale of puppies	NONE	

үү

SOUTH DAKOTA

Law	Requirements	Reference
Exotic Pets	These South Dakota statutes establish the Animal Industry Board, which promulgate rules to allow nondomestic mammals that are safe to the public and to the free-roaming animals of the state to be imported or possessed. The Board regulates the breeding, raising, marketing, and transportation of any captive nondomestic mammals. The Board may also develop and implement programs to identify animals and premises involved to further animal health and food safety.	S.D. Codified Laws § 40-3-23 - 29
Sterilization	NONE	
Vaccination	NONE	
Tethering	NONE	
Parked Vehicles	Unattended in a standing or parked vehicle in a manner that endangers the health or safety of such animal.	S.D. Codified Laws § 40-1-36
Leash	The board of county commissioners of each of the counties of the State of South Dakota shall have the power to regulate, restrain, or prohibit the running at large of dogs.	S.D. Codified Laws § 40-34-5
	The board of county commissioners of each of the counties of the State of South Dakota may provide that if any person owning or keeping more than five dogs shall fail to keep such dogs within the confines of his own property, such failure shall amount to a public nuisance.	S.D. Codified Laws §40-34-4
Leash— wildlife management region	Any person who permits a dog to run at large in a state park is guilty of a Class 2 misdemeanor.	S.D. Codified Laws § 41-17-18.1

Law	Requirements	Reference
Chasing Wildlife	Dogs may not be used to hunt big game and may be charged with a misdemeanor (1st offense) or a felony (2nd offense) for doing so. The Department of Game, Fish, and Parks can seize and dispose of all dogs unlawfully used to take, pursue, or kill protected game.	S.D. Codified Laws §§ 41-8-15, 41-15-14
Strict Liability	NONE	
Dog Bites	NONE	
Dangerous Dog	NONE	
Breed specific	One city restricts certain breeds. See city website for more information.	
Cruelty	Cruelty to animals is defined as: "mistreatment, torture, or cruelty of an animal is any act or omission whereby unnecessary, unjustifiable, or unreasonable physical pain or suffering is caused, permitted, or allowed to continue including acts of mutilation." Inhumane treatment is defined as: "any act of mistreatment, torture, cruelty, neglect, abandonment, mutilation, or inhumane slaughter." Poisoning, intentionally killing and inhumane treatment of an animal are all Class 1 Misdemeanors, with a fine up to $1000 and/or imprisonment up to 1 year. Exceptions are made for generally accepted practices of training, use of animal, animal husbandry, farming, hunting, protection of life, limb or property, research and veterinary care.	S.D. Codified Laws §40-1-1
Minimum age sale of puppies	NONE	

Ψψ

TENNESSEE

Law	Requirements	Reference
Exotic Pets	This Tennessee law makes it an offense for a person to display, exhibit, handle, or use a poisonous or dangerous snake or reptile in a manner that endangers the life or health of any person. Violation is a Class C misdemeanor.	Tenn. Code Ann. § 39-17-101
	This Tennessee chapter relates to the private possession of wildlife. It is unlawful for any person to possess, transport, import, export, buy, sell, barter, propagate or transfer any wildlife, whether indigenous to this state or not, except as provided by this part and rules and regulations promulgated by the Tennessee wildlife resources commission pursuant to this part. Additionally, no person shall possess Class I (all species inherently dangerous to humans such as wolves, bears, lions and poisonous snakes) or Class II (native species that are not listed in other classes) wildlife without having documentary evidence showing the name and address of the supplier of such wildlife and date of acquisition. In order to obtain a permit to possess Class I wildlife, a person must be 21, have at least 2 years of experience handling such animals (or take an approved written exam), have a full-time resident caretaker, and must have a plan for the quick and safe recapture of the wildlife, among other provisions. The annual permits and fees for personal possession of Class I wildlife are $150/animal or $1,000/facility.	Tenn. Code Ann. § 70-4-401 - 418
Sterilization	Dogs and cats must be "spayed or neutered" before adoption, or adopters must enter into a sterilization agreement.	Tenn. Code Ann. § 44-17-502
Vaccination	Cat: Six months of age or older.	Tenn. Code Ann. §§ 68-8-103, 68-8-101

234 · APPENDIX A

Law	Requirements	Reference
Tethering	Offense to knowingly tie, tether, or restrain a dog in a manner that results in the dog suffering bodily injury.	Tenn. Code Ann. § 39-14-202
Parked Vehicles	Any animal.	Tenn. Code Ann. § 29-34-209
Leash	The owner of a dog has a duty to keep that dog under reasonable control at all times, and to keep that dog from running at large.	Tenn. Code Ann. § 44-8-413
Leash— wildlife management region	NONE	
Chasing Wildlife	A person may not use a dog to hunt or trail deer. A person may not take, injure, or kill protected wildlife. Unlawfully killing or injuring protected wildlife is a misdemeanor.	Tenn. Code Ann. §§ 70-4-118, 70-5-101
Strict Liability	The owner of any dog running at large and not under reasonable control that cause any damages, in any public or private place where the person has a legal right to be, except in cases of provocation where the injured person was enticing, disturbing, alarming, harassing, or otherwise provoking the dog. Other exceptions: Military or police dog. Trespass upon the private, nonresidential property of the dog's owner. Dog protecting the owner or innocent person. Dog was securely confined (i.e., kennel, crate, etc.). If dog causes damage while on its owner's property, then claimant must show owner knew of vicious propensities.	Tenn. Code Ann. § 44-8-413

Law	Requirements	Reference
Dog Bites	Dogs running at large/not under reasonable control. Any damages. Public or private place where person has the legal right to be. Provocation exception: Injured person was enticing, disturbing, alarming, harassing, or otherwise provoking the dog. Other exception: Military or police dog. Trespass upon the private, nonresidential property of the dog's owner. Dog protecting the owner or innocent person. Dog was securely confined (i.e., kennel, crate, etc.). If dog causes damage while on its owner's property, then claimant must show owner knew of vicious propensities.	Tenn. Code Ann. § 44-8-413
Dangerous Dog	NONE	
Breed specific	Many cities ban, restrict or declare certain breed vicious or dangerous. See city website for more information.	
Cruelty	Cruelty to animals is defined as: "Tortures, maims or grossly overworks an animal; Fails unreasonably to provide necessary food, water, care or shelter for an animal in the person's custody; Abandons unreasonably an animal in the person's custody; Transports or confines an animal in a cruel manner; or inflicts burns, cuts, lacerations, or other injuries or pain, by any method, including blistering compounds, to the legs or hooves of horses in order to make them sore." This is a Class A Misdemeanor punishable with a fine up to $2500 and/or 11 months, 29 days to 30 years' imprisonment.	Tenn. Code Ann. §39-14-202;
Minimum age sale of puppies	NONE	

TEXAS

Law	Requirements	Reference
Exotic Pets	Under these Texas statutes, no person may take, sell, purchase, or possess an alligator, an alligator egg, or any part of an alligator without a permit. An offense is a misdemeanor.	Tex. Parks & Wild. Code Ann. § 65.001 – 104
	Chapter 822, Subchapter E regulates the keeping of dangerous wild animals. It imposes a registration requirement upon the owner of a dangerous wild animal and also sets forth insurance requirements. One thing to note is that Texas animal cruelty laws do not apply to these wild animals.	Tex. Health & Safety Code Ann. § 822.101 – 116
	In this subchapter, "wild animal" is defined as a nondomestic animal that the commissioners court of a county determines is dangerous and is in need of control in that county. The commissioners court of a county by order may prohibit or regulate the keeping of a wild animal in the county. A person commits a Class C misdemeanor if the person violates an order adopted under this subchapter and the order defines the violation as an offense.	Tex. Loc. Gov't Code § 240.001 – 004
	This Texas statute provides that no person may kill or attempt to injure a dangerous wild animal that is in captivity in this state or released from captivity in this state for the purpose of being killed.	Tex. Parks & Wild. Code Ann § 62.101 – 107
	This Texas law provides that no person on a public road or on the right-of-way of a public road may hunt an exotic animal. In addition, no person may hunt on the land of another for an exotic animal without the express consent of the owner of the land to hunt for exotic animals. A person who violates this section commits an offense that is a Class A Parks and Wildlife Code misdemeanor.	Tex. Parks & Wild. Code Ann § 62.015

Law	Requirements	Reference
Sterilization	Dogs and cats must be sterilized before adoption, or adopters must enter into a sterilization agreement.	Tex. Health & Safety Code § 828.002
Vaccination	Cats: By the time the animal is four (4) months of age.	Tex. Health & Safety Code Ann. § 826.021
Tethering	Owner may not leave a dog outside and unattended by use of a restraint that unreasonably limits the dog's movement during certain times of day or during extreme weather. A restraint unreasonably limits a dog's movement if the restraint is a length shorter than the greater of 5x the length of the dog or 10 feet. Also if it's in an unsafe condition or causes injury to the dog. Law does not apply to running line, pulley, or trolley system if the collar meets requirements.	Tex. Health & Safety Code Ann. § 821.076 - 081
Parked Vehicles	NONE	
Leash	The owner of a dog has a duty to keep that dog under reasonable control at all times, and to keep that dog from running at large.

The owner or person having control of a dog at least six months of age in a county adopting this subchapter may not allow the dog to run at large unless the dog the dog is registers and is wearing an identification tag. | Tex. Health & Safety Code Ann. § 822.012 Tex. Health & Safety Code Ann. § 822.031 |
| Leash— wildlife management region | NONE | |

Law	Requirements	Reference
Chasing Wildlife	A person may not use a dog to hunt or trail deer. A person may not take, injure, or kill protected wildlife. Anyone unlawfully kills or injures protected wildlife is liable to the state for the value of the animal and may also be criminally prosecuted.	Tex. Parks & Wild. Code Ann §§ 62.0065, 61.021, 12.301, 12.306 and 68.015
Strict Liability	NONE	
Dog Bites	NONE	
Dangerous Dog	Must register the dog and pay a registration fee. Must restrain the dog at all times or keep dog in a proper enclosure. Must obtain liability insurance. Must comply with applicable municipal ordinances. Must keep current on rabies vaccinations. Must notify animal control if the owner relocates with the dog. Must notify the proper authority if the dangerous dog attacks someone.	Tex. Health & Safety Code Ann. §§ 22.042, 822.043
Breed specific	A couple of cities ban or restrict pit bulls. See city website for more information.	
Cruelty	Cruelty to animals is defined as: " (1) tortures an animal; (2) fails unreasonably to provide necessary food, care, or shelter for an animal in the person's custody; (3) abandons unreasonably an animal in the person's custody; (4) transports or confines an animal in a cruel manner; (5) kills, seriously injures, or administers poison to an animal, other than cattle, horses, sheep, swine, or goats, belonging to another without legal authority or the owner's effective consent; (6) causes one animal to fight with another; (7) uses a live animal as a lure in dog race training or in dog coursing on a racetrack; (8) trips a horse; (9) injures an animal, other than cattle, horses, sheep, swine, or goats, belonging to another without legal authority or the owner's effective consent; or (10) seriously overworks an animal."	Tex. Penal Code, Ann. §42.09

Law	Requirements	Reference
	Sections (2),(3),(4),(9), or (10) (provide necessary food, care, shelter; abandons; transports in a cruel manner; injures, or seriously overworks) are a Class A Misdemeanor with a fine up to $4000 and/or imprisonment up to 1 year. The third conviction of the above is a State Jail Felony, with a fine up to $10,000 and/or imprisonment from 180 days to 2 years. Sections (1),(5),(6),(7), or (8) (tortures; kills, seriously injures or poisons; animal fighting; uses as a lure; trips a horse) is a State Jail Felony with a fine up to $10,000 and/or imprisonment from 180 days to 2 years. A third conviction of the above is a Felony of the Third Degree with a fine up to $10,000 and/or imprisonment from 2 to 10 years. Exemptions are made for bona fide scientific research, protection of property or persons, fishing, hunting or trapping, wildlife control, and animal husbandry.	
Minimum age sale of puppies	A dog or cat at least eight weeks of age.	16 Tex. Admin. Code § 91.113

UTAH

Law	Requirements	Reference
Exotic Pets	NONE	
Sterilization	Dogs and cats must be sterilized before adoption, or adopters must enter into a sterilization agreement.	Utah Code Ann. § 11-46-203
Vaccination	NONE	
Tethering	NONE	
Parked Vehicles	NONE	
Leash	NONE	
Leash— wildlife management region	NONE	
Chasing Wildlife	It is a misdemeanor to allow a dog to take any protected wildlife or any nest or egg of protected wildlife. There is a schedule of fines describing the minimum restitution value of each protected animal.	Utah Code Ann. §§ 23-20-3, 23-20-4.5
Strict Liability	The owner of any dog that causes any injury, presumably any place, except in cases of state, county, city, town, and peace officers not liable for injury committed by a dog when: Dog has been trained to assist in law enforcement, and injury occurs while the dog is reasonably and carefully being used in the apprehension, arrest, or location of a suspected offender, or injury occurs in maintaining or controlling the public order.	Utah Code Ann. § 18-1-1
Dog Bites	Any dog. Any injury. Presumably any place. Exception: State, county, city, town, and peace officers not liable for injury committed by a dog when: Dog has been trained to assist in law enforcement, and injury occurs while the dog is reasonably and carefully being used in the apprehension, arrest, or location of a suspected offender, or injury occurs in maintaining or controlling the public order.	Utah Code Ann. § 18-1-1

Law	Requirements	Reference
Dangerous Dog	NONE	
Breed specific	One city restricts certain breeds. See city website for more information.	
Cruelty	Cruelty to animals is defined as: "intentionally, knowingly, recklessly, or with criminal negligence: fails to provide necessary food, care, or shelter for an animal in his custody; abandons an animal in the person's custody; transports or confines an animal in a cruel manner; injures an animal; causes any animal, not including a dog, to fight with another animal of like kind for amusement or gain; or causes any animal, including a dog, to fight with a different kind of animal or creature for amusement or gain." If these acts are committed "intentionally or knowingly", it is a Class B Misdemeanor with a fine up to $1000 and/or imprisonment up to 6 months. If these acts are committed "recklessly or with criminal negligence" it is a Class C Misdemeanor with a fine up to $750 and/or imprisonment up to 90 days.	Utah Code Ann. 76-9-301
Minimum age sale of puppies	No puppies or kittens less than 8 weeks of age.	Utah Admin. Code r. 58-1-13(3)

VERMONT

Law	Requirements	Reference
Exotic Pets	These Vermont statutes comprise the state's dog laws. Among the provisions include licensing and control laws for both domestic dogs and wolf-hybrids, laws concerning the sale of dogs, and various wildlife/hunting laws that implicate dogs.	Vt. Stat. Ann. tit. 20 § 3511 - 3513; 3541 - 3817, 3901 - 3915, 4301 - 4304; Vt. Stat. Ann. tit. 10 §§ 5001 - 5007, 4748
	This Vermont law provides that a person may not bring into the state or possess any live wild bird or animal of any kind, unless the person obtains from the commissioner a permit to do so. Applicants shall pay a permit fee of $100.00.	Vt. Stat. Ann. tit. 10 § 4709
Sterilization	NONE	
Vaccination	NONE	
Tethering	A person commits the crime of cruelty to animals if he or she ties, tethers, or restrains an animal, either a pet or livestock, in a manner that is inhumane or is detrimental to its welfare.	Vt. Stat. Ann. tit. 13 § 352
Parked Vehicles	Unattended in a standing or parked motor vehicle in a manner that would endanger the health or safety of the animal.	Vt. Stat. Ann. tit. 13 § 386
Leash	NONE	
Leash— wildlife management region	NONE	

Law	Requirements	Reference
Chasing Wildlife	Vermont has a point system for hunting licenses similar to that used for driver's licenses. Certain enumerated violations, including taking bear or deer with dogs, earn points which can result in the suspension or revocation of a hunting license. A game warden may shoot a dog who is pursuing a deer or moose close enough to endanger its life, or a fine may be issued.	Vt. Stat. Ann. tit. 10 § § 4502, 4748
Strict Liability	NONE	
Dog Bites	NONE	
Dangerous Dog	NONE	
Breed specific	One city bans pit bulls. See city website for more information.	
Cruelty	Cruelty to animals is defined as: "intentionally kills or attempts to kill any animal belonging to another person without first obtaining legal authority or consent of the owner; overworks, overloads, tortures, torments, abandons, administers poison to, cruelly beats or mutilates an animal, exposes a poison with intent that it be taken by an animal; ties, tethers, or restrains an animal, either a pet or livestock, in a manner that is inhumane or is detrimental to its welfare; deprives an animal of adequate food, water, shelter, rest or sanitation, or necessary medical attention, or transports an animal in overcrowded vehicles; owns, possesses, keeps or trains an animal engaged in an exhibition of fighting; acts as judge or spectator at events of animal fighting or bets or wagers on the outcome of such fight; as pound keeper, officer, agent of a humane society or as an owner or employee of an establishment for treatment, board or care of an animal, knowingly receives, sells, transfers or otherwise conveys an animal in his or her care for the purpose of research or vivisection;	Vt. Stat. Ann. tit. 13 § 351

Law	Requirements	Reference
	intentionally torments or harasses an animal owned or engaged by a police department or public agency of the state or its political subdivisions, or interferes with the lawful performance of a police animal; knowingly sells, offers for sale, barters or displays living baby chicks, ducklings or other fowl which have been dyed, colored or otherwise treated so as to impart to them an artificial color, or fails to provide poultry with proper brooder facilities; uses a live animal as bait or lure in a race, game or contest." The classification of the crimes is not defined in the statutes. Cruelty to animals is punishable with a fine up to $2000 and/or imprisonment for up to 1 year. A second or subsequent is punishable with a fine up to $5000 and/or imprisonment up to 2 years. Animal fighting (either statute) is punishable with a fine of up to $5000 and/or imprisonment up to 5 years.	
Minimum age sale of puppies	NONE	

VIRGINIA

Law	Requirements	Reference
Exotic Pets	This Virginia section provides three definitions related to hybrid dogs (wolf or coyote crossbreeds), including, adequate confinement, hybrid canine, responsible ownership. The section also allows any locality may, by ordinance, establish a permit system to ensure the adequate confinement and responsible ownership of hybrid canines. Violation of an ordinance enacted pursuant to this section is a Class 3 misdemeanor for the first violation and a Class 1 misdemeanor for any subsequent violation.	Va. Code Ann. § 3.2-6581 – 6584
	This section provides Virginia's hybrid canine laws (registered or described to a veterinarian, animal control, or other listed authority as a wolf or coyote-dog cross). Under the section, any locality may, by ordinance, establish a permit system to ensure the adequate confinement and responsible ownership of hybrid canines. Violation of an ordinance enacted pursuant to this section is a Class 3 misdemeanor for the first violation and a Class 1 misdemeanor for any subsequent violation. Further, it is the duty of any animal control officer or other officer who may find a hybrid canine in the act of killing or injuring livestock or poultry to kill such hybrid canine forthwith, whether such hybrid canine bears a tag or not.	Va. Code Ann. § 3.2-6581 - 6584
Sterilization	Dogs and cats must be sterilized before adoption, or adopters must enter into a sterilization agreement.	Va. Code Ann. § 3.2-6574
Vaccination	Four (4) months of age and older.	Va. Code Ann. § 3.2-6521

Law	Requirements	Reference
Tethering	Each owner shall provide for companion animals adequate space. "Adequate space" means a tether that: is appropriate to the age and size of the animal, is attached to the animal by a properly applied collar, halter, or harness, configured so as to protect the animal from injury and prevent the animal or tether from becoming entangled with other objects or animals, is at least three times the length of the animal.	Va. Code Ann. § 3.2-6500
Parked Vehicles	Companion animal.	Va. Code Ann. § 3.2-6504.1
Leash	The governing body of any locality may adopt ordinances requiring that dogs within any such locality be kept on a leash or otherwise restrained and may, by resolution directed to the circuit court, request the court to order a referendum as to whether any such ordinance so adopted shall become effective. The results of the referendum shall not be binding upon the governing body of the locality but may be used in ascertaining the sense of the voters.	Va. Code Ann. § 3.2-6539
Leash– wildlife management region	NONE	
Chasing Wildlife	It is a misdemeanor to allow a dog to enter a game refuge.	Va. Code Ann. § 29.1-554
Strict Liability	NONE	
Dog Bites	NONE	
Dangerous Dog	Register dog for $150, other fees may apply. Dog given a tag that declares it dangerous--annually renewed for $85. Post proof of registration on Virginia Dangerous Dog registry. Owner must be 18 years or older. Dog must be current on rabies. Dog must be sterilized. Dog must be confined in a proper enclosure when on owner's property.	Va. Code Ann. § 3.2-6540

Law	Requirements	Reference
	Dog must be muzzled and confined until a proper enclosure is constructed. Must be leashed and muzzled when off owner's property. Must post signs. The owner must notify the local animal control in certain instances. Must microchip the dog. Must obtain liability insurance or surety bond.	
Breed specific	NONE	
Cruelty	Cruelty to animals is defined as: "overrides, overdrives, overloads, tortures, ill-treats, abandons, willfully inflicts inhumane injury or pain, or cruelly or unnecessarily beats, maims, mutilates, or kills any animal, whether belonging to himself or another; deprives any animal of necessary food, drink, shelter or emergency veterinary treatment; sores any equine for any purpose or administers drugs or medications to alter or mask such soring for the purpose of sale, show, or exhibition of any kind, unless such administration of drugs or medications is within the context of a veterinary client-patient relationship and solely for therapeutic purposes; willfully sets on foot, instigates, engages in, or in any way furthers any act of cruelty to any animal; carries or causes to be carried in or upon any vehicle, vessel or otherwise any animal in a cruel, brutal, or inhumane manner; or causes or permits any of the above things," or killing a dog or cat for its hide, fur or pelt. This is a Class 1 Misdemeanor with a fine up to $2500 and/or imprisonment up to 1 year.	Va. Code Ann. § 3.1-796.122
Minimum age sale of puppies	Under seven weeks old without its dam or queen.	Va. Code Ann. § 3.2-6510

WASHINGTON

Law	Requirements	Reference
Exotic Pets	This Washington chapter passed in 2007 regulates the keeping of dangerous wild animals. By definition, a potentially dangerous wild animal includes, among others, lions, tigers, captive-bred cougars, jaguars, cheetahs, leopards, wolves, (but excluding wolf-hybrids), bears, hyenas, non-human primates, elephants, rhinoceroses, certain reptiles, and venomous snakes. A person shall not own, possess, keep, harbor, bring into the state, or have custody or control of a potentially dangerous wild animal. A person in legal possession of a potentially dangerous wild animal prior to July 22, 2007, and who is the legal possessor of the animal may keep possession of the animal for the remainder of the animal's life.	Wash. Rev. Code Ann. §16.30.005 - 900
	These laws set forth the laws for importation and health requirements of certain imported animals. It also allows the director to establish inspection procedures for the transportation of animals. A section provides that it is unlawful for a person to bring an animal into Washington state without first securing a certificate of veterinary inspection, reviewed by the state veterinarian of the state of origin, verifying that the animal meets the Washington state animal health.	Wash. Rev. Code Ann. §16.36.005 - 160
Sterilization	NONE	
Vaccination	NONE	
Tethering	NONE	
Parked Vehicles	Leave or confine any animal unattended in a motor vehicle or enclosed space if the animal could be harmed or killed by exposure to excessive heat, cold, lack of ventilation, or lack of necessary water.	Wash. Rev. Code Ann. §16.52.340

Law	Requirements	Reference
Leash	The council of said town shall have power to prohibit dogs running at large, and to provide for the killing of all dogs found at large and not duly licensed.	Wash. Rev. Code Ann. §35.27.370
	It shall be the duty of the sheriff or any deputy sheriff to kill any dog found running at large (after the first day of August of any year and before the first day of March in the following year) without a metal identification tag.	Wash. Rev. Code Ann. §16.08.030
Leash— wildlife management region	NONE	
Chasing Wildlife	The unlawful use of a dog, preventing the dog from chasing or hunting deer, elk, or any endangered animal, is a misdemeanor and could result in the dog being declared a public nuisance, which allows fish and wildlife officers to destroy the dog without warrant or process. Negligently allowing a dog on a game reserve is a misdemeanor.	Wash. Rev. Code Ann. §§ 77.15.240, 77.12.315, and 77.15.440
Strict Liability	The owner of any dog that bites, in any public or private place where a person has the legal right to be, except in cases of provocation and trespassing.	Wash. Rev. Code Ann. §§ 16.08.040, 16.08.060
Dog Bites	Any dog bite. Public or private place where person has the legal right to be. Provocation exception. Other exception: Trespass.	Wash. Rev. Code Ann. §§ 16.08.040, 16.08.060
Dangerous Dog	Dog must be registered; an annual fee may be charged. Dog must be kept in a proper enclosure. Owner must post signs. Owner must obtain a surety bond or liability insurance. If outside the proper enclosure, the dog is muzzled and restrained by a substantial chain or leash and under physical restraint of a responsible person.	Wash. Rev. Code Ann. §§ 16.08.080, 16.08.090

Law	Requirements	Reference
Breed specific	Many cities ban, restrict or declare certain breeds to be potentially dangerous or dangerous. See city website for more information.	
Cruelty	Animal Cruelty in the First Degree is defined as: "intentionally inflicts substantial pain on, causes physical injury to, or kills an animal by a means causing undue suffering, or forces a minor to inflict unnecessary pain, injury, or death on an animal." This is a Class C Felony, with a fine up to $10,000 and/or imprisonment up to 5 years. Animal Cruelty in the Second Degree is defined as: "under circumstances not amounting to first degree animal cruelty, the person knowingly, recklessly, or with criminal negligence inflicts unnecessary suffering or pain upon an animal, fails to provide the animal with necessary food, water, shelter, rest, sanitation, ventilation, space, or medical attention and the animal suffers unnecessary or unjustifiable physical pain as a result of the failure; or abandons the animal." This is a Misdemeanor with a fine up to $1000 and/or imprisonment up to 90 days. However, "In any prosecution of animal cruelty in the second degree, it shall be an affirmative defense, if established by the defendant by a preponderance of the evidence, that the defendant's failure was due to economic distress beyond the defendant's control." In addition to the above sentencing provisions, the following are also included: If convicted of a misdemeanor or gross misdemeanor, the court may decide to defer the above sentencing provisions in lieu of 2 years' probation; in cases of multiple misdemeanor convictions, the sentences shall be consecutive, but the probation period shall remain 2 years; forfeiture of all animals held if any one of the animals dies as a result of the actions by the convicted or if there is a prior conviction under these provisions, if animals are forfeited the convicted shall not be permitted to own or care for similar animals for 2 years; cost of care,	Wash. Rev. Code Ann. §§ 16.52.011, 16.52.200, 16.52.205, 16.52.207

Law	Requirements	Reference
	euthanasia or adoption; civil penalty of $1000 that will go to the SPCA; animal cruelty or prevention educational program. Exceptions are made for "game laws", killing of venomous reptiles, protection of life, limb or property, killing animals for food, scientific research, animal husbandry, and rodeo.	
Minimum age sale of puppies	NONE	

WEST VIRGINIA

Law	Requirements	Reference
Exotic Pets	This West Virginia statute provides that the state fish and game director may issue a permit to a person to keep and maintain in captivity as a pet, a wild animal acquired from a commercial dealer or during the legal open season. The fee is charged is two dollars.	W. Va. Code, §§ 20-2-51, 20-2-52
	The State of West Virginia found the possession of dangerous wild animals to present a serious public health and safety concern. Because of this, the state prohibits a person from possessing a dangerous wild animal unless the animal was owned prior to June 1, 2015 and the owner obtained a permit. Under this statute, a "Dangerous wild animal" means a mammal, bird, reptile, amphibian or aquatic animal, including a hybrid that is dangerous to humans, other animals or the environment due to its inherent nature and capability to do significant harm.	W. Va. Code § 19-34-1 to 9
Sterilization	Dogs and cats must be "spayed or neutered" before adoption, or adopters must enter into a sterilization agreement.	W. Va. Code § 19-20B-2
Vaccination	Cats: Before the age of three months old.	W. Va. Code § 19-20A-3
Tethering	It is unlawful for any person to intentionally, knowingly or recklessly cruelly chain or tether an animal.	W. Va. Code § 61-18-19
Parked Vehicles	Unattended and confined in a motor vehicle when physical injury to or death of the animal is likely to result.	W. Va. Code § 61-8-19
Leash	NONE	

Law	Requirements	Reference
Leash— wildlife management region	Dogs or cats vaccinated in compliance with the provisions of this article may run at large in any area or locality: Provided, That the commissioner of agri-culture may, pursuant to article nine of this chapter, exercise his discretion to establish a quarantined area or locality and to require all dogs and cats within the limits of any quarantined area or locality to be confined as provided in article nine.	W. Va. Code § 19-20A-8
	It shall be unlawful, during the continuance of such quarantine, after notice as aforesaid, for the owner of any dog to permit such dog to run at large in any such quarantined locality.	W. Va. Code § 19-9-18
Chasing Wildlife	Dogs may not hunt or chase deer. The dog might be held by a conservation officer for ten days until the owner picks him up or he might be put to death. There are also a few hunting regulations prohibiting dogs from hunting wild game between May and mid-August.	W. Va. Code § 20-2-16
Strict Liability	The owner of any dog running at large causing any damage to person or property, presumably any place except the owner's property and if the dog is on owner's property.	W. Va. Code § 19-20-13
Dog Bites	Dog running at large. Any damage to person or property. Presumably any place but owner's property. Exception: Dog on owner's property.	W. Va. Code § 19-20-13
Dangerous Dog	NONE	
Breed specific	Some cities ban, restrict or declare certain breeds to be vicious. See city website for more information.	

Law	Requirements	Reference
Cruelty	Cruelty to animals is defined as: "cruelly mistreats, abandons or withholds proper sustenance, including food, water, shelter or medical treatment necessary to sustain normal health and fitness or to end suffering or abandons any animal to die, or uses, trains or possesses any domesticated animal for the purpose of seizing, detaining or maltreating any other domesticated animal." This is a Misdemeanor with a fine of $300 to $1000 and/or imprisonment up to 6 months. A second conviction is a Misdemeanor with a fine of $500 to $1000 and/or imprisonment of 90 days to 1 year. Imprisonment is mandatory. With a second or subsequent conviction, the convicted cannot be granted probation until they have undergone a complete psychiatric or psychological evaluation that is reviewed by the court. There is a Felony provision for "intentionally tortures or maliciously kills an animal, or causes, procures or authorizes any other person to torture or maliciously kill an animal...For the purposes of this subsection, "torture" means an action taken for the primary purpose of inflicting pain." This Felony conviction carries a fine of $1000 to $5000 and imprisonment of 1 to 3 years. Additional sentencing provisions include forfeiture of the animals, cost of care, prohibition of possession or ownership of animals for 5 years if convicted of a Misdemeanor, 15 years if convicted of a Felony. Exemptions are made for veterinary care, hunting, fishing, trapping, animal training, farming, game farms, and scientific research.	W. Va. Code § 61-8-19
Minimum age sale of puppies	NONE	

WISCONSIN

Law	Requirements	Reference
Exotic Pets	The Wisconsin wildlife laws require a license to take a wild animal from the wild or to import one into the state. A license is also required to exhibit, breed, reha-bilitate, hunt, and/or purchase wild animals. Violations can result in fines, forfeiture, and/or imprisonment.	Wis. Stat. Ann §169.01 – 46
	This Wisconsin statute prohibits the killing or aiding in killing or wounding by use of deadly weapon of any animal that is tied, staked out, caged or otherwise intentionally confined in a man-made enclosure, regardless of size. However, nothing in this section prohibits the shooting of any wild game in its wild state.	Wis. Stat. Ann §951.09
	Under this Wisconsin statute, the importation or movement of animals may be prohibited or regulated if it is necessary to prevent the introduction or spread of a disease that threatens the health of animals or of humans.	Wis. Stat. Ann § 95.20
Sterilization	NONE	
Vaccination	NONE	
Tethering	NONE	
Parked Vehicles	NONE	
Leash	A dog is considered to be running at large if it is off the premises of its owner and not under the control of the owner or some other person. A dog that is actively engaged in a legal hunting activity, including training, is not considered to be running at large if the dog is monitored or supervised by a person and the dog is on land that is open to hunt-ing or on land on which the person has obtained permission to hunt or to train a dog. Dog running at large or untagged dog subject to impoundment. An officer shall attempt to capture and restrain any dog running at large and any untagged dog.	Wis. Stat. Ann §174.042

Law	Requirements	Reference
Leash— wildlife management region	NONE	
Chasing Wildlife	A game warden may kill a dog found running, injuring, or killing any deer, elk, or game bird (eggs and nests) if immediate action is necessary to protect the animal.	Wis. Stat. Ann §29.921
Strict Liability	The owner of any dog that causes an injury to a person, domestic animal or property, presumably any place, except in cases of provocation and when dog used in law enforcement.	
Dog Bites	Any dog. Any injury to a person, domestic animal or property. Presumably any place. Provocation exception; comparative negligence. Other exception: dog used in law enforcement.	Wis. Stat. Ann §174.02
Dangerous Dog	NONE	
Breed specific	Some cities ban, restrict or declare certain breeds to be vicious or dangerous. See city website for more information.	
Cruelty	Cruelty to animals is defined as: "No person may treat any animal, whether belonging to the person or another, in a cruel manner." Intentional or negligent violation is a Class A Misdemeanor punishable with a fine up to $10,000 and/or imprisonment up to 6 months. Intentional violation that results in the mutilation, disfigurement or death of an animal is a Class E Felony punishable with a fine up to $10,000 and/or imprisonment up to 2 years. Additional sentencing provisions include forfeiture of animals, cost of care, and forbidding the convicted from owning, possessing or training any animal of the type or species of the abused for not more than 5 years. Exceptions are made for laws regarding wild animals, scientific research and veterinary care.	Wis. Stat. Ann §951.02
Minimum age sale of puppies	NONE	

WYOMING

Law	Requirements	Reference
Exotic Pets	This section of Wyoming statutes states that all wildlife in the state is considered the property of the state. It further provides that there is no private ownership of live animals classified in this act as big or trophy game animals. "Exotic species" means any wild animals, including amphibians, reptiles, mollusks, crustaceans or birds not found in a wild, free or unconfined status in Wyoming. This section also contains the management laws for delisted gray wolves that were repealed in 2012.	Wyo. Stat. Ann. § 23-1-101 to 109 (1977)
Sterilization	NONE	
Vaccination	Cats: Three (3) months of age or older.	Wyo. Stat. Ann. § 11-31-213
Tethering	NONE	
Parked Vehicles	NONE	
Leash	A board of county commissioners may declare the running at large of any specified animals in unincorporated areas within the county limits a public nuisance.	Wyo. Stat. Ann. § 11-31-301 (1977)
Leash— wildlife management region	NONE	
Chasing Wildlife	Hunting, running, or harassing any of the named classes of animals may result in the dog being put to death or the owner being charged with a misdemeanor. There is an exception if the dog is protecting livestock.	Wyo. Stat. Ann. § 23-3-109
Strict Liability	NONE	
Dog Bites	NONE	

Law	Requirements	Reference
Dangerous Dog	NONE	
Breed specific	A couple of cities ban pit bulls and other breeds. See city website for more information.	
Cruelty	Cruelty to animals is defined as: "knowingly and with intent to cause death, injury or undue suffering: overrides an animal or drives an animal when over-loaded; or unnecessarily or cruelly beats, tortures, torments, injures, mutilates or attempts to kill an animal; or carries an animal in a manner that poses undue risk of injury or death; or unnecessarily fails to provide it with the proper food, drink or protection from the weather, or cruelly abandons the animal, or in the case of immediate, obvious, serious illness or injury, fails to provide the animal with appropriate care." Cruelty to animals is a Misdemeanor with a fine up to $750 and/or imprisonment up to 6 months.	Wyo. Stat. Ann. § 6-3-203
Minimum age sale of puppies	NONE	

CONTRACT TEMPLATES

The templates provided here are for educational purposes only and should not be considered legal advice. Please contact a licensed legal professional to customize contracts and other documents for the specific needs of you and your organization.

CONTENTS

TEMPLATE 1 ANIMAL SURRENDER

SURRENDER AGREEMENT

This is a legally binding document for the irrevocable surrender of your animal(s) to [NAME OF ORGANIZATION].

I/We, _____state that I/we am/are at least eighteen (18) years of age and by voluntarily signing this Agreement irrevocably give, donate, surrender and release to [NAME OF ORGANIZATION], hereinafter referred to as [ACRONYM], the following animal(s), referred to collectively in this Agreement as "Animal(s)".

Animals(s) name(s): _____

Male _____ Female _____ (If multiples, list numbers)

Color(s): _____

Age(s): _____

I/We confirm the fact that I/We am/are the legal owner of the Animal(s), and I/We have full power and authority to surrender the Animal(s) to [ACONYM]. No other person or organization (including by way of example a breeder or rescue organization] has any legal or ownership interest in the Animal(s).

I/We agree to provide all medical records and disclose information known to me/us pertaining to the Animal(s), including its medical and behavioral history, at the same time as I/We surrender the Animal(s). [ACRONYM] has my/our permission to contact my/our veterinarian for any necessary information pertaining to the Animal(s), and I/We agree by signing this Agreement that my/our veterinarian and any other current or prior caretakers of the Animal(s) may release any and all information known by them to [ACRONYM].

Veterinarian's Name: _____

Phone Number: _____

Address: _____

List medical history, behavioral history, and any other information [ACRO-NYM] should know about the Animal(s) – good and not so good:

I/We understand that by surrendering the Animal(s) to [ACRONYM], I/We am/are giving up all ownership or other interest in the Animal(s). I/We will not seek further information about the Animal(s) from [ACRONYM] and understand that [ACRONYM] is under no obligation to provide any follow up information about the Animal(s) to me/us.

By signing this surrender agreement, I/We release [ACRONYM] from any and all rights, claims, obligations, liabilities, and causes of action whatsoever arising out of or relating to my/our ownership, possession, or disposition of the Animal(s), and I/we agree to indemnify and hold harmless [ACRONYM] from and against any and all such rights, claims, obligations, liabilities, and causes of action which may be asserted by third parties.

I/We have fully read and understand this Surrender Agreement. I accept and agree to abide by its terms.

If the Animal(s) are jointly owned by more than one owner (husband, wife, adult-aged child, all owners must sign this Agreement. Separate copies of the Agreement may be signed if all the owners are unable to sign the same copy, with the combined copies of the document making up one original, signed Agreement.

DATE: _____

OWNER'S SIGNATURE: _____

OWNER'S NAME: _____

OWNER'S ADDRESS: _____

_____

NUMBER STREET   CITY   STATE   ZIP

OWNER'S PHONE NUMBERS:

(Home) _____

(Work) _____

OWNER'S E-MAIL: _____

DONATION AMOUNT: $_____

Additional owner(s) names and signatures:

_____   _____

NAME   SIGNATURE

....

APPROVED ON BEHALF OF THE ORGANIZATION

_____   _____

NAME, TITLE   DATE

TEMPLATE 2 FOSTER CARE AGREEMENT

FOSTER CARE AGREEMENT

I, _____ [ENTER NAME], volun-
tarily enter into this Agreement to provide temporary care and custody to: _
_____ [ENTER NAME & OTHER IDENTIFYING
INFORMATION AS APPROPRIATE REGARDING THE ANIMAL] (referred to as
the "Foster Animal" in this Foster Care Agreement).

I agree that the opportunity given to me to help rehabilitate the Foster
Animal, as well as the chance of a potential future adoption, is of significant
benefit to me, and serves as proper legal consideration in exchange for my
agreements stated in this contract.

On behalf _____[NAME OF RESCUE],
(referred to as "Rescue" in this Agreement), I agree to perform all the following services to take care of the Foster Animal:

1. provide the Rescue and its designated individuals(s) access to all parts
   of my home and property for a home inspection before my application
   to foster is approved;

2. provide foster care to the Foster Animal for any period as determined
   in the sole discretion of the Rescue, understanding that I may have the
   Foster Animal for a short and temporary period or an extended and
   indefinite period, and understanding that the Rescue provides no guar-
   antee as to the health of the Foster Animal, and that the Foster Animal
   may have significant medical needs, socialization problems, and not be
   housebroken;

3. provide, including being fully financially responsible for the cost, of food
   and shelter for the Foster Animal;

4. provide for the Foster Animal, including being fully financially responsible for the cost of proper and routine veterinary care including a yearly wellness exam, current required and recommended vaccinations and medications (including regular heartworm and flea & tick preventative medication if recommended by veterinarians in my area, in addition to any other medications as prescribed by my veterinarian), and urgent and emergency care as needed; I understand and agree, however, that unless I have the express written permission of an authorized representative of the Rescue, I may not arrange or pay or otherwise cause:

    a. any elective veterinary procedure to be performed on the Foster Animal; or,

    b. the sterilization (spay or neuter) of the Foster Animal.

5. take all necessary precautions to prevent the foster animal from either impregnating another animal or becoming impregnated; in the event that such happens despite my precautions I will alert the Rescue immediately;

6. provide all foster care to the Foster Animal to the Rescue's satisfaction;

7. provide the Rescue with quarterly reports on the health status of the Foster Animal;

8. contact the Rescue with any and all questions or concerns about the Foster Animal or the fostering program, as well as with updated contact information;

9. keep possession of the Foster Animal always and not transfer possession or custody of the Foster Animal to any other person at any time, except for temporary, short-term possession for vet care, grooming, etc.

10. notify the Rescue if I plan to move at any time during the period of this Agreement, providing the address of where I plan to move and agreeing

to return the Foster Animal to the Rescue if the Rescue asks for the Foster Animal to be returned due to the planned move;

11. notify the Rescue immediately if at any point I can no longer, or do not want to continue to, provide care, food, shelter or veterinary care for my foster animal, and arrange for surrender and return of the Foster Animal back to Rescue;

12. return the Foster Animal to the Rescue at any time and for any reason or no reason at all upon the request of the Rescue, agreeing that the decision to require my surrender of the Foster Animal back to the Rescue shall be made in the sole determination of the Rescue; I further understand and agree that if the Rescue is forced to undertake any action to enforce this provision of the Agreement that I agree to pay for all court costs, attorneys' fees and any other costs directly connected to and incurred by the Rescue to enforce this provision and obtain the return of the Foster Animal; I also hereby specifically provide consent to provide Rescue with access to my premises if necessary to facilitate the return of the Foster Animal.

I UNDERSTAND THAT THE RESCUE RETAINS ALL OWNERSHIP AND LEGAL RIGHTS TO THE FOSTER ANIMAL. I FURTHER UNDERSTAND THAT FOSTERING THE FOSTER ANIMAL DOES NOT PROVIDE ME WITH ANY LEGAL RIGHTS TO THE FOSTER ANIMAL AND THAT ALWAYS THE RESCUE'S RIGHTS IN AND TO THE FOSTER ANIMAL ARE SUPERIOR TO MINE.

I understand, however, that I will be given the first right of adoption of the Foster Animal when the Rescue decides to offer the Foster Animal for adoption. I understand and agree that the Foster Animal must be spayed / neutered immediately upon its adoption.

I understand that the provisions of this Agreement are legally binding and that any violation of this Agreement may result in legal liabilities for myself. I state that I am over 21 years of age, have read this Agreement in its

entirety, understand and agree to abide by all its terms and voluntarily sign
and enter into this Agreement as of the date signed by me below.

_____   _____

PRINTED NAME   SIGNATURE

_____

DATE

....

APPROVED ON BEHALF OF THE RESCUE

_____   _____

NAME, TITLE   DATE

TEMPLATE 3 SHELTER/RESCUE COOPERATIVE AGREEMENT

[Ownership Transferred]

COOPERATIVE AGREEMENT BETWEEN
[ANIMAL SHELTER] AND [ANIMAL RESCUE]

This Cooperative Agreement is made this _____ day of _____ [MONTH], 20 ___ [YEAR] by and between:

Name of animal shelter: _____

Address of animal shelter: _____

Contact person: _____

Phone: _____

Email: _____

Known as the "Animal Shelter" in this Cooperative Agreement; and,

Name of animal rescue: _____

Address of animal rescue: _____

Contact person: _____

Phone: _____

Email: _____

Known as the "Rescue" in this Cooperative Agreement.

WHEREAS, the Animal Shelter desires to engage one or more Rescues to help care for the animal population that it serves; and

WHEREAS, the Rescue has the capacity to provide the services needed to provide the help needed by the Animal Shelter;

NOW THEREFORE, the Animal Shelter and Rescue agree to the following terms and conditions:

1. The Rescue agrees with respect to the animals transferred into Rescue's care to:

   a. provide appropriate food, water, temperature-controlled and ventilated shelter, health and medical care, proper animal separation, pest control, sanitation and waste disposal for all animals transferred into Rescue's care;

   b. comply with all applicable federal, state and local laws with respect to the care, transport and welfare of the animals;

   c. hold ownership of the animals as the property of the Rescue, including during any period in which the animal(s) are placed in a foster home or care, until an outgoing animal adoption/placement is completed and ownership is transferred;

   d. allow the Animal Shelter to periodically inspect the Rescue's facilities, procedures and care of animals transferred to it.

2. The Animal Shelter agrees to:

   a. transfer ownership and full legal responsibility of animals to the Rescue at the time of their physical transfer to Rescue, including full liability for all future costs associated with the care, health, behavior and/or recuperation from damage or injury associated with the animal(s);

   b. inspect the Rescue's facilities and procedures from time to time to ensure compliance with all requirements of this Cooperative Agreement and applicable animal welfare laws.

3. This Cooperative Agreement shall become effective on the date written above and remain in effect for a period of _____ months from the effective date.

4. This Cooperative Agreement may be terminated by the Animal Shelter or the Rescue at any time upon written notice to the other party to this Agreement.

The undersigned, by signing this Cooperative Agreement, state that they understand its terms and are authorized to sign the Agreement on behalf of their organization.

For Rescue: For Animal Shelter:

_____   _____

_____   _____
PRINTED NAME/TITLE   PRINTED NAME/TITLE

TEMPLATE 4 VOLUNTEER AGREEMENT

[NAME OF ORGANIZATION]
VOLUNTEER AGREEMENT

The person signing below states that he/she is voluntarily signing this Agreement to serve as a volunteer with _____
_____[ORGANIZATION NAME] known as "Shelter" in this Agreement, and agrees to all the following terms and conditions in consideration for the opportunity to volunteer:

1. I accurately and truthfully completed this volunteer agreement.

2. I understand that working with animals is unpredictable and necessarily involves risk of bodily harm and injury. Specifically I understand by way of example but not limitation that I may be bitten, scratched, attacked or otherwise injured or frightened while volunteering with the Shelter and working with the Shelter's animals. By applying to become a volunteer and signing this Volunteer Agreement, I agree to assume all risk of injury, bodily harm or any and all other damage to myself or my personal property. I agree that in no event will the Shelter be liable to me, and I agree to hold the Shelter harmless from any injuries, damages, liabilities, costs, expenses or claims of whatsoever nature which I might suffer or sustain about the performance of my volunteer activities for Shelter, except for any claims that may arise due to the gross negligence of the Shelter and its employees.

3. I agree to abide by the mission, rules, regulations, policies, and programs of Shelter as now existing, changed, modified or later developed.

4. If I volunteer to provide shelter, foster care or boarding of animals in my home, or transport any of Shelter's animals in my car (transport only), I consent to a visit by a Shelter representative periodically to observe the animals and their living conditions.

5. I understand that minors under the age of 18 must be accompanied at all times by a Shelter approved volunteer over the age of 18; I further agree that, at no time, will a minor accompanying me on my volunteer duties be left alone with or in charge of a Shelter animal.

6. I understand and agree that the Shelter may refuse my volunteer application for any reason, and that the Shelter may terminate its relationship with me at any time for any reason or no reason at all.

7. When my volunteer relationship is terminated, or otherwise upon the request of the Shelter, I agree to immediately return all supplies, equipment, records, moneys, and other items that are the property of the Shelter.

8. I agree that any changes to this Agreement must be in writing and signed by both myself and an authorized Shelter representative.

9. I agree and understand that this Agreement is binding upon the Shelter and myself and our respective heirs, successors, assigns, executors, and personal representatives.

By signing below I state that I have read and understand all the terms of this Volunteer Agreement and voluntarily agree to abide by all the terms.

_____   _____

PRINTED NAME   SIGNATURE

_____

DATE

TEMPLATE 5 ADOPTION AGREEMENT

[RESCUE NAME]
ANIMAL ADOPTION AGREEMENT

This Animal Adoption Agreement ("Agreement") is made by and between [RESCUE NAME], located at _____
_____ [ADDRESS], and known as "Rescue" in this Agreement, and:

Adopter's name: _____
Address:

_____

NUMBER STREET   CITY   STATE   ZIP

Phone: _____
Email: _____

Known as "Adopter" in this Agreement, with respect to the adoption of the following animal:

Animal description (known as "Animal" in this Agreement)

DOG/CAT _____ BREED _____
SEX _____FIXED _____NAME _____
DOB _____ COLOR _____
Distinguishing mark: _____

_____

The Adopter agrees to the following terms and responsibilities:

1. **Adoption donation**. The Adopter understands that the average cost to the Rescue to house, feed, provide medical care and other services to animals prior to adoption is $ _____ [INSERT DESIRED DONATION AMOUNT]. Adopter agrees to make a voluntary donation to the Rescue of $ _____ to help the Rescue continue its services caring for

animals and finding animals forever homes. I understand that donation is not a payment for the adoption of this Animal but rather is a non-refundable contribution to the Rescue's general funds. This donation may be tax-deductible.

2. **Animal care**. The Adopter states that he/she is adopting the Animal solely as a companion animal for his/herself and/or his/her immediate family with the intent to provide the Animal a warm and loving forever home. The Adopter agrees to provide the following care for the Animal:

   a. To keep the Animal primarily indoors and when outdoors protect the Animal from long term exposure to adverse weather;

   b. Provide the Animal with proper food, clean water, exercise and appropriate preventative vaccines, wellness and emergency medical care;

   c. Not subject the Animal to cosmetic appearance changing procedures, including but not limited to tail docking, ear cropping, declawing, or any type of alterations that are not necessary and are done only for cosmetic reasons;

   d. Ensure that the Animal wear a collar with an identification tag at all times;

   e. Attach a leash to the Animal's harness or collar EVERY TIME this animal is out of doors and not in a safely enclosed area;

3. **Inhumane activities**. That Adopter agrees that the Animal will never be subject to cruel or inhumane treatment by him/herself or anyone with whom he/she interacts, and further that the Animal will never be used as an aggressive guard dog or for dog fighting or any other activity in which one animal is pitted against another.

4. **Adopter responsible for Animal behavior**. The Adopter understands and agrees that the Rescue takes in animals with unknown backgrounds, including possible neglect or abuse by previous owners and/or health, behavioral or other issues unknown to the Rescue at the time the animal is adopted by you. **The Rescue makes no guarantees or express**

or implied warranties of any kind regarding the animal including without limitation as to the Animal's age, breed, physical or mental characteristics, prior experiences, current or future health, behavior or temperament. The Adopter understands and agrees that he/she is responsible for any behavioral problems you may have with the Animal, including injuries to yourself, your family or others by biting, scratching or other physical attack, and/or damage to property caused by the Animal. By adopting this Animal and entering in to this Agreement the Adopter agrees to indemnify and hold harmless the Rescue and its officers, directors, employees and volunteers, against liability from any such injuries or damage caused by the Animal.

5. **Adopter responsible for compliance with laws**. The Adopter understands and agrees that he/she is responsible for complying with all applicable city, county, state and federal laws governing ownership, control and custody of animals, including if the Animal is adopted as a puppy, compliance with spay/neuter requirements as described in the attached agreement.

6. **Adopter responsible for providing a forever home**. The Adopter agrees that he/she will not sell, give away or otherwise dispose of the Animal to any person(s), dealer, retailer, auction, institute or any other entity for any reason. The Adopter agrees that if at a later date he/she is unable or unwilling to keep the Animal, the Adopter shall notify the Rescue and provide the Rescue with the first opportunity to reclaim the Animal at no charge.

7. **Failure to abide by Agreement**. The Adopter understands and agrees that should he/she violate any term(s) of this Agreement the Rescue may revoke the Agreement and retrieve the Animal.

By signing this Agreement below, I confirm that I have read and understand the terms of this Agreement and agree to be bound by all of the terms stated above. I understand that the terms above are the entire agreement between the Rescue and myself as the Adopter and that these terms may not be changed or modified unless agreed to in writing by both parties. I also agree that in the event that any part of this Agreement is determined to be invalid, the rest of the Agreement shall remain in full force and effect.

Adopter: Rescue:

_____   _____

SIGNATURE   SIGNATURE

_____   _____

PRINTED NAME   PRINTED NAME

_____   _____

DATE   DATE

TEMPLATE 6 SPAY/NEUTER AGREEMENT

Permanent ownership of this dog is contingent upon your compliance with this Spay/Neuter Agreement. Proof of the spay/neuter must be received by the (ADOPTER'S NAME) within fourteen (14) days after the surgery. If the dog's health does not allow the procedure to be performed immediately after adoption of the dog, you agree to provide [NAME OF RESCUE] with a statement from your veterinarian that this dog is not yet in physical or emotional condition for surgery, including the earliest date that the procedure may be performed. Once the delayed procedure is performed, you agree to provide proof of the spay/neuter to [NAME of RESCUE] within fourteen (14) days after the surgery.

It is the responsibility of the person(s) adopting the dog, and not your veterinarian, that our rescue timely receives notice that the procedure has been performed. Failure to comply with this Agreement by the date below, unless otherwise agreed to in writing, is a breach of the adoption agreement requiring you to return the dog to our rescue. You are not entitled to a refund of any donation or adoption fee when returning the animal due to breach of this agreement and the spay/neuter requirement.

Your signature below indicates that you have read and understand this Spay/Neuter Agreement and will abide by its requirement to spay/neuter the animal that you are adopting by the date indicated below or return the animal to our rescue.

Adopter's signature

Signature: _____

Date: _____, 20 _____

Printed name: _____

Date by which animal must be spayed/neutered: _____

ϒϒ

SPAYING OR NEUTERING YOUR DOG IS HEALTHIER FOR THEM

Neutering a male eliminates the possibility of testicular tumors and reduces the chance of prostate problems. Neutering decreases the chance of perianal tumors and hernias. In addition, neutered males are less likely to escape a yard and find a female in heat, reducing the risk of your dog getting hit by a car, getting lost or otherwise getting injured.

Spayed females are less likely to get mammary tumors, ovarian cancer and uterine infection.

Spaying and neutering also benefits your dog's temperament. Males neutered early in life tend to be less aggressive and are less likely to mark in the house. Spayed females do not have hormonal mood swings. Females who do not give birth tend to be less aggressive. Breeding also brings significant risk to your dog.

There are so many unwanted animals filling shelters. Please abide by spay/neuter requirements.

APPENDIX C

FORMATION DOCUMENTS

CONTENTS

C-1 ARTICLES OF INCORPORATION—SAMPLE

SAMPLE ARTICLES OF INCORPORATION

Most states provide an online fill-in form to incorporate a nonprofit corporation. However, many state forms do not include the required IRS language. You must add the IRS language to the state form or as an addendum prior to incorporating to qualify for IRS 501(c)(3) status. The IRS language is highlighted in the following sample Articles of Incorporation.

TO STATE CORPORATION COMMISSION:

The undersigned natural person of the age of twenty-one years or more, acting as incorporator, adopts the following Articles of Incorporation pursuant to Chapter 10 of Title 13.1 of the Code of Virginia as follows:

FIRST: The name of the corporation is [INSERT YOUR ORGANIZATION, INC.].

SECOND: The period of duration is perpetual.

THIRD: The corporation is organized and will be operated exclusively for charitable and educational purposes within the meaning of 501(c)(3) of the Internal Revenue Code. (All references to sections in these Articles refer to the Internal Revenue Code of 1986 as amended or to comparable sections of subsequent internal revenue laws.) Specifically, the corporation is organized to [INSERT BROAD MISSION STATEMENT].

In pursuance of these purposes it shall have the powers to carry on any business or other activity which may be lawfully conducted by a corporation organized under the Virginia Non-stock Corporations Act, whether or not related to the foregoing purposes, and to do all things necessary, proper and consistent with maintaining tax exempt status under section 501(c)(3).

Commentary: The above bolded language is one section of the required IRS to qualify for 501(c)(3) tax-exempt status. In addition to the IRS language, insert a brief mission statement, such as "operate an animal welfare organization".

FOURTH: The corporation shall not have members.

Commentary: Most animal welfare organizations do not have members. However, if your organization has members you might state, "The corporation may have one or more classes of members, the qualifications and rights, including voting rights, of which shall be designated in the bylaws.

FIFTH: The registered agent is [INSERT NAME], who is a resident of the state of Virginia and a director of the corporation, and the address of its initial registered office is [INSERT STREET ADDRESS, CITY, STATE, ZIP CODE], which is physically located in the County of [INSERT COUNTY NAME].

Commentary: The registered agent is the person who receives correspondence from the state, including any annual corporate report that must be filed to maintain your organization's corporate status. States vary on who may serve as the registered agent. Generally, if a person serves in this role he/she must be a resident of the state with a street address in the state. Many states require the person to be a member of the corporation's board of directors or an officer. Another option is to use a commercial registered agent service. You may find a commercial registered agent service by searching online "registered agent". The state must be notified, and a fee often must be paid, to change the registered agent.

SIXTH: The number of directors constituting the initial Board of Directors is [INSERT NUMBER OF DIRECTORS], and the name(s) and address(es), including street number, of the persons who are to serve as the initial directors until the first annual meeting, or until their successors are elected and qualified, are:

[INSERT NAMES AND ADDRESSES OF INITIAL BOARD MEMBERS]

The members of the Board of Directors shall be those individuals elected, from time to time, in accordance with the Bylaws. Directors shall elect their successors.

Commentary: States vary on the minimum number of board members required. Some states allow as few as one; other states require at least three. A board of 3-5 members often works well for new nonprofit organizations.

SEVENTH: The internal affairs of the corporation shall be regulated by its Board of Directors as described in the Bylaws. **Upon dissolution of the corporation, its assets shall be disposed of exclusively for the purposes of the corporation or distributed to such organizations organized and operated exclusively for charitable purposes which shall, at the time, qualify as exempt organizations under section 501(c)(3).**

Commentary: The bolded dissolution language above is part of the required IRS language to qualify under section 501(c)(3) of the Internal Revenue Code.

EIGHTH: **No part of the net earnings of the corporation shall inure to the benefit of or be distributed to any director, employee or other individual, partnership, estate, trust or corporation having a personal or private interest in the corporation. Compensation for services rendered and reimbursement for expenses incurred in attending to the affairs of this corporation shall be limited to reasonable amounts. No substantial amount of the activities of the corporation shall be the carrying on of propaganda, or otherwise attempting to influence legislation and this corporation shall not intervene in (including the publishing or distributing of statements) any political campaign on behalf of or in opposition to any**

candidate for public office. Notwithstanding any other provision of these Articles or of any Bylaws adopted thereunder, this corporation shall not take any action not permitted by the laws which then apply to this corporation.

Commentary: The bolded language above is part of the required IRS language to qualify under section 501(c)(3) of the Internal Revenue Code.

NINTH: The name and address, including street and number, of the incorporator is:

[INSERT STREET ADDRESS, CITY, STATE, ZIP CODE]

Commentary: The incorporator(s) serves as the person stating that he/ she wants to form and incorporate this organization. Their duties end when the initial board meeting of the corporation is held. Most states require only one incorporator.

IN WITNESS THEREOF, I have hereunto set my hand and seal this [INSERT DAY] day of [INSERT MONTH], [INSERT YEAR].

_____

PRINTED NAME (Signature above)

Commentary: The incorporator must sign the articles. Some states also required the registered agent to sign the articles accepting their role as the registered agent. Most states have a filing fee ranging from as little as $25 to as much as several hundred dollars. Many states provide for filing articles of incorporation online at their corporate services website. A few states require that pen and ink signed originals be mailed into the state. You should carefully read all the instructions provided by your state prior to filing articles of incorporation.

C-2 BYLAWS—SAMPLE

BYLAWS of
[YOUR RESCUE NAME HERE]

ARTICLE I

Name and Purposes

Section 1.01. Name. The name of the organization is [INSERT RESCUE NAME]

Section 1.02. Purpose. The Corporation is organized to [INSERT BRIEF, BROAD PURPOSE STATEMENT].

SAMPLE PURPOSE STATEMENT: The ABC rescue provides temporary housing for the pets of women undergoing breast cancer treatment.

ARTICLE II
AUTHORITY AND DUTIES OF DIRECTORS

Section 2.01. Authority of Directors. The Board of Directors is the policy-making body and may exercise all the powers and authority granted to the Corporation by law.

Section 2.02. Number, Selection, and Tenure. The Board shall consist of a minimum of three (3) directors. Directors shall serve a three-year term and may be re-elected for any number of additional terms in office, consecutive or otherwise. Directors shall elect their successors.

Commentary: IRS rules require that public charitable 501(c)(3) organizations have an independent board of directors. A minimum of three directors, who are not related to each other (e.g. husband, wife, children) is recommended.

Section 2.03. Resignation. Resignations are effective upon receipt by the Secretary of the Corporation of written notification.

Section 2.04. Regular Meetings. The Board of Directors shall hold at least one (1) regular meeting per calendar year.

Commentary: Most state nonprofit laws require board to meet at least once a year to adopt a budget and set the year's program. Best practice is for nonprofit boards to meet at these 3 times per year.

Section 2.05. Special Meetings. Meetings shall be at such dates, times and places as the Board shall determine.

Section 2.06. Notice. Meetings may be called by the President or at the request of any two directors by notice mailed, telephoned, or sent electronically (e.g. emailed, texted, or instant messaging) to each member of the Board not less than forty-eight (48) hours before such meeting.

Section 2.07. Quorum. A quorum shall consist of a majority of the Board attending in person or through teleconferencing. All decisions will be by majority vote of those present at a meeting at which a quorum is present. If less than a majority of the directors is present at said meeting, a majority of the directors present may adjourn the meeting on occasion without further notice.

Section 2.08. Action Without a Meeting. Any action required or permitted to be taken at a meeting of the Board of Directors (including amendment of these Bylaws) or of any committee may be taken without a meeting if all the members of the Board or committee consent in writing (including by email ballot) to taking the action without a meeting and to approving the specific action. Such consents shall have the same force and effect as a unanimous vote of the Board or of the committee as the case may be.

Commentary: Most state laws require that if a board action is taken by written ballot (including by way of example an email vote) without an in-person or other type of meeting during which all board members may discuss the issue, the vote must be unanimous of all board members currently in office.

Section 2.09. Participation in Meeting by Conference Telephone. Members of the Board may participate in a meeting through use of conference telephone or similar communications equipment, so long as members participating in such meeting can hear one another.

Commentary: Most state statutes allow boards to meet by conference telephone. A vote by conference call is considered the same, and follows the same rules, as a vote at an in-person meeting.

Section 2.10. Reimbursement. Directors shall serve without compensation with the exception that expenses incurred in the furtherance of the Corporation's business are allowed to be reimbursed with documentation and prior approval. In addition, Directors serving the organization in any other capacity are allowed to receive compensation therefore.

Commentary: While it is not illegal to pay nonprofit corporation board members, it is very uncommon and strongly discouraged.

ARTICLE III
AUTHORITY AND DUTIES OF OFFICERS

Section 3.01. Officers. The officers of the Corporation shall be a President and such other officer(s) as the Board may determine from time to time in its discretion.

Section 3.02. Appointment of Officers; Terms of Office. The officers of the Corporation shall be elected by the Directors immediately following the election of the Directors at the annual meeting. Officers shall serve any number of one-year terms, consecutive or otherwise.

Section 3.03. Resignation. Resignations are effective upon receipt by the Secretary of the Board of a written notification.

Section 3.04. Removal. An officer may be removed by the Board of Directors at a meeting, or by action in writing pursuant to Section 2.08, whenever in the Board's judgment the best interests of the Corporation will be served thereby. Any such removal shall be without prejudice to the contract rights, if any, of the person so removed.

Section 3.05. President. The President shall be a director of the Corporation and will preside at all meetings of the Board of Directors. The President shall perform all duties attendant to that office, subject, however, to the control of the Board of Directors, and shall perform such other duties as on occasion shall be assigned by the Board of Directors.

Section 3.08. Paid Staff. The Board of Directors may hire such paid staff as they deem proper and necessary for the operations of the Corporation. The powers and duties of the paid staff shall be as assigned or as delegated to be assigned by the Board. The procedures recommended by the Internal Revenue Service (see Part V, 4 of IRS Form 1023 Rev. 10-2004) shall be followed in determining appropriate compensation.

ARTICLE IV
INDEMNIFICATION

Every member of the Board of Directors, officer or employee of the Corporation may be indemnified by the corporation against all expenses and liabilities, including counsel fees, reasonably incurred or imposed upon such members of the Board, officer or employee in connection with any threatened, pending, or completed action, suit or proceeding to which she/he may become involved by reason of her/his being or having been a member of the Board, officer, or employee of the corporation, or any settlement thereof, unless adjudged therein to be liable for negligence or misconduct in the performance of her/his duties. Provided, however, that in the event of a settlement the indemnification herein shall apply only when the Board approves such settlement and reimbursement as being in the best interest of the corporation. The foregoing right of indemnification shall be in addition and not exclusive of all other rights which such member of the Board, officer or employee is entitled.

Commentary: State laws regarding indemnification vary. review your state's nonprofit laws with respect to board indemnification and the specific language allowed.

ARTICLE V
FINANCIAL ADMINISTRATION

Section 5.01. Fiscal Year. The fiscal year of the Corporation shall be January 1 – December 31 but may be changed by resolution of the Board of Directors.

Commentary: A fiscal year is your tax year. It may start on the first of any month and run through the last day of the 12th month following your start date. You may change your fiscal year from time to time with the IRS if your financial and tax situation calls for a change in your fiscal year.

Section 5.02. Checks, Drafts, Etc. All checks, orders for the payment of money, bills of lading, warehouse receipts, obligations, bills of exchange, and insurance certificates shall be signed or endorsed by the President of the Corporation and in such manner as shall from time to time be determined by resolution of the Board of Directors or of any committee to which such authority has been delegated by the Board.

Section 5.03. Deposits and Accounts. All funds of the Corporation, not otherwise employed, shall be deposited from time to time in general or special accounts in such banks, trust companies, or other depositories as the Board of Directors or any committee to which such authority has been delegated by the Board may select, or as may be selected by the President or by any other officer or officers or agent or agents of the Corporation, to whom such power may from time to time be delegated by the Board. For the purpose of deposit and for the purpose of collection for that account of the Corporation, checks, drafts, and other orders of the Corporation may be endorsed, assigned, and delivered on behalf of the Corporation by any officer or agent of the Corporation.

Section 5.04. Investments. The funds of the Corporation may be retained in whole or in part in cash or be invested and reinvested on occasion in such property, real, personal, or otherwise, or stock, bonds, or other securities, as the Board of Directors in its sole discretion may deem desirable, without regard to the limitations, if any, now imposed or which may hereafter be imposed by law regarding such investments, and which are permitted to organizations exempt from Federal income taxation under Section 501(c)(3) of the Internal Revenue Code.

Section 5.05. Contracts. The President is authorized to enter into any contract or execute and deliver any instrument in the name of and on behalf of the Corporation, provided that the Board of Directors has authorized the contract.

Section 5.06. Financial Controls. The Corporation is committed to maintaining best practices in its financial controls, reporting and record keeping. To that end, proper separation of financial controls shall be maintained including requiring transactions to be authorized by a person(s) other than the person(s) signing or executing the transaction with a third person(s) reviewing financial transactions, including bank statements. The Board shall ensure that an internal or external audit, as appropriate in conformance with best practices for nonprofit organizations of the same or similar budget size, be performed each year.

Commentary: It is critically important the financial duties be separate to protect the assets of the organization.

Section 5.07. Accountability. The financial records of the Corporation shall be subject to review and audit as determined by the Board of Directors. The organization shall adopt, and financial records shall be maintained, in accordance with an approved record retention policy.

ARTICLE VI
BOOKS AND RECORDS

Correct books of account of the activities and transactions of the Corporation shall be kept at the office of the Corporation. These shall include a minute book, which shall contain a copy of the Certificate of Incorporation, a copy of these Bylaws, and all minutes of meetings of the Board of Directors.

ARTICLE VII
CONFLICTS OF INTEREST

Commentary: The IRS expects all nonprofit organizations to have in place, and abide by, specific rules for when conflicts of interest arise.

Section 7.01. Existence of Conflict, Disclosure. Directors, officers, employees and contractors of Corporation should refrain from any actions or activities that impair, or appear to impair, their objectivity in the performance of their duties on behalf of the Corporation. A conflict of interest may exist when the direct, personal, financial or other interest(s) of any director, officer, staff member or contractor competes or appears to compete with the interests of the Corporation. If any such conflict of interest arises the interested person shall call it to the attention of the Board of Directors for resolution. If the conflict relates to a matter requiring board action, such person shall not vote on the matter. When there is a doubt as to whether any conflict of interest exists, the matter shall be resolved by a vote of the Board of Directors, excluding the person who is the subject of the possible conflict.

Section 7.02. Nonparticipation in Vote. The person having a conflict shall not participate in the final deliberation or decision regarding the matter under consideration and shall retire from the room in which the Board is meeting. However, the person may be permitted to provide the Board with any and all relevant information.

Section 7.03. Minutes of Meeting. The minutes of the meeting of the Board shall reflect that the conflict was disclosed and the interested person was not present during the final discussion or vote and did not vote on the matter.

Section 7.04. Annual Review. A copy of this conflict of interest statement shall be furnished to each director or officer, employee and/or contractor who is presently serving the corporation, or who hereafter becomes associated with the corporation. This policy shall be reviewed annually for information and guidance of directors and officers, staff members and contractors, and new officers and directors, staff members and contractors shall be advised of the policy upon undertaking the duties of their offices.

ARTICLE VIII
NON-DISCRIMINATION/HARASSMENT

Section 8.01. Equal opportunity. Consultants and volunteers will be recruited without unlawful discrimination due to race, color, age, religion, national origin, sexual orientation, sex disability, veteran status, marital status or any other classification protected by applicable discrimination laws.

Section 8.02. Discrimination against any consultant or volunteer based on race, color, sex, religion, national origin, disability, veteran status, sexual orientation or any other illegal basis is not tolerated.

Section 8.03. Harassment includes verbal or physical conduct that demeans or shows hostility toward an individual because of his/her race, color, sex, religion, age, disability or other illegal basis, conduct that creates a hostile or offensive work environment. See section below for reporting.

ARTICLE IX
WHISTLEBLOWER PROTECTION

Section 9.01. No retaliation. Consultants and volunteers are encouraged to report any conduct or activities that they believe are inappropriate or illegal. The Corporation does not retaliate or punish in any way, including without limitation by firing, demotion, suspension, harassment or failure to consider for promotion, anyone who reports truthful information.

Section 9.02. Reporting procedures. Consultants or volunteers who are subject to, or aware of, inappropriate conduct or activity should immediately report it to his/her supervisor or the Corporation President. Consultants or volunteers should not report the conduct to anyone who they believe is involved in the conduct. Information reported remains confidential to the extent possible. Failure to report an incident of harassment or discrimination may indicate that the consultant or volunteer does not consider the conduct unwelcome or problematic.

Section 9.03. Investigation. The Corporation investigates all reports and takes appropriate action to correct the situation and /or to discipline involved parties, including termination. If, after investigation, substantial facts cannot be established, the situation will be monitored for a period of time.

ARTICLE X
PARLIAMENTARY AUTHORITY

Meetings shall be conducted pursuant to general rules of parliamentary procedure, provided such rules of conduct are not inconsistent with these bylaws.

ARTICLE XI
AMENDMENT OF BYLAWS

These Bylaws may be amended by a majority vote of the Board of Directors, provided prior notice is given of the proposed amendment in the notice of the meeting at which such action is taken, or provided all members of the Board waive such notice, or by unanimous consent in writing without a meeting pursuant to Section 2.08.

C-3 IRS FORM 1023EZ

IRS Form 1023EZ is fillable online at www.pay.gov. Only organizations that anticipate gross income of $50,000 or less during each of their first three years may file for 501(c)(3) status with this form. Organizations also must meet all eligibility requirements on the IRS 1023EZ checklist (below).

Recommendations for completing form 1023EZ:

1. Addresses—Form 1023EZ is a public document. As a result, we recommend using the business address for your organization as the address for each of your board members. You do not need to include the officer and director personal home addresses.

2. NTEE Code—Part III, Item 1 asks for the appropriate 3-character NTEE Code that best describes your activities. Code: "D20" is applicable to animal welfare organizations, including rescues.

The IRS eligibility requirements do not permit certain types of organizations to file Form 1023EZ, regardless of their annual income. Among the types of organizations that may not apply with Form 1023EZ are:

• Organizations set-up under the laws of a foreign country, or that have a primary mailing address in a foreign country;
• Organizations set up as LLCs;
• A successor to a for-profit entity; and,
• An organization that is seeking status as a private operating foundation

C-4 IRS FORM 1023

The IRS provides several versions of the IRS Form 1023, all of which are accessible at https://www.irs.gov/pub/irs-pdf/f1023i.pdf. Form 1023 requires the submission of a narrative description of your organizations activities as well as financial information showing your anticipated income and expense.

You must complete Form 1023 by providing accurate responses that best represent how you will operate and manage your rescue. Following are the responses that are common for many rescues. However, you should seek professional help if you are unsure how to complete Form 1023 for your organization.

Part I

Box 1. Name—the legal name of your organization should include "Inc." or "Company" or a similar designation so that the public is on notice that this is an incorporated entity.

Box 4. EIN—you must apply and obtain an EIN to include on the application. Instructions for obtaining an EIN online are included in this appendix.

Box 7. Authorized representative. Check "no" unless you have hired an attorney or other professional to help complete this form.

Box 8. Paid advisor. Check "no" unless you are using a paid advisor of some type to help with this application and to set-up and manage your activities.

Box 10. Most organizations are now required to file an IRS Form 990 return (990N, 990EZ or the full 990); in most cases the answer here is "no".

Part II

Line 1. Most rescues are set up as nonprofit corporations, making the answer here "yes".

Lines 2, 3, 4. If you are a nonprofit corporation, the answer to lines 2-4 is "no".

Line 5. Bylaws. You should adopt and attach a copy of your bylaws to this form and answer "yes".

Part III

This section asks that you indicate exactly the location in your articles of incorporation that certain required IRS language is located. The required language is included in the sample articles of incorporation included at the beginning of this appendix (C-1).

Part IV

You are required to include a description of your intended activities with the application. The description is normally a few paragraphs and may include a bulleted list of your planned activities. Following is an example of a narrative description we used in an animal rescue organization's Form 1023:

Activities

[NAME] is organized to provide medical and surgical care for animals in underdeveloped countries, emphasizing sterilization to prevent unwanted pet animals and unnecessary suffering where veterinary care is unattainable for most domestic animals. Specifically, the organization plans to:

1. *Send volunteers to [COUNTRY] to perform spays and neuters;*

2. *Train volunteers on techniques to improve efficiency in high volume spay/neuter clinics; and,*

3. *Plan, coordinate and send volunteers to operate spay/neuter clinics in [COUNTRIES].*

[NAME] will operate on contributions from the public, including donations made by clients who receive care for their animals by the founding veterinarian.

Analysis of Activities

Section 1.501(c)(3)-1(d)(1)(i)(g) of the Income Tax Regulations defines "charitable" as including organizations operated to prevent cruelty to children or animals. For example, an organization that prevented the birth of unwanted animals and the eventual suffering of others by providing funds for pet owners who cannot afford the spaying or neutering operation was ruled tax-exempt under this provision. Rev. Rul. 74-194, 1974-1 C.B. 129.

[NAME] activities of planning and conducting animal care clinics in underdeveloped countries qualifies as a charitable activity to prevent cruelty to animals and is similar to the organization described in Rev. Rul. 74-194 discussed above.

Part V

Items 1(a) and 1(b). The IRS requires nonprofit charitable organizations to have an independent board of directors. Best practice is for nonprofit directors to serve voluntarily without pay. Founders of rescue often serve both on the board, and as a paid Executive Director to manage the organization. In this case, I list the founder as an unpaid director in section 1a, and list their staff title and compensation in section 1b. This shows the IRS that you are serving in two roles: (1) as an unpaid member of the board of directors, and (2) as a paid staff person.

Item 2—you are required to disclose any family and/or business relationships among your board members.

Item 3—include in the attachments a brief description of the duties of your highest paid staff person, such as,

Sally Smith, Executive Director. Sally has served as a foster home for rescue animals for the past five years and is the founder of this rescue. Sally will manage the day-to-day operations of the rescue, including fundraising, caring for the animals, and recruiting, training and supervising volunteers. Sally expects to work full-time managing the rescue.

Item 4 – to ensure that compensation provided to your staff meets IRS guidelines for "reasonable compensation", you should check "yes" and follow all the guidelines provided in this section.

Item 5 – the IRS expects your organization to adopt and follow a conflict of interest policy. A sample policy is found in Article VII of the sample bylaws included earlier in this appendix.

Item 6 – most smaller rescues do not provide non-fixed payments and answer "no to these questions.

Item 7 – the IRS wants to ensure that organizations do not operate in any way to provide financial or other benefit to their founders or others who control the organization. As a result, you must disclose if the rescue will have any business arrangements with the founder. Some rescues, for example, operate from their homes and may want to add a barn or other facility for the rescue to their personal property. You must be very careful with any activity or transaction like this to make sure that you don't violate IRS rules.

Items 8(a) and 9(a) – similar to item 7 above, you must disclose any type of arrangement that may provide the officers and directors with personal benefit.

Part VI

This section asks questions regarding any goods, services or benefits that you provide to individuals. Most rescues operate to benefit animals and not people and therefore may answer "no" to these questions. Providing an animal to foster, or adopting animals, does not constitute providing a good or service. You may always, however, answer "yes" and then provide a description of your activities. If you are unsure if your activities qualify as a tax-exempt animal welfare organization, seek professional advice.

Part VII

Does not normally apply to new animal welfare organizations. If you are a successor organization, seek professional advice for any questions that you may have.

Part VIII

Item 1 – political campaign activity. 501(c)(3) tax-exempt organizations are prohibited from engaging in any political campaign activity in support of, or opposition to, any candidate for public office.

Item 2 – 501(c)(3) organizations may engage in a very limited amount of lobbying activity, meaning any activity in which you seek to have a legislator vote a particular way on a legislation, or to introduce specific legislation. We recommend that you seek professional advice if you plan to engage in any lobbying activities.

Item 3 – bingo or gaming. Your organization may engage in bingo or gaming activities to raise money provided you follow the applicable federal, state and local laws. Many state governments have specific rules and registration requirements relating to bingo and gaming.

Item 4 – fundraising activities. Check all the boxes for the types of activities you may engage in. Answer the questions as appropriate for your organization. Note that many state governments require that you file a "charity registration" with the attorney general's office prior to engaging in fundraising in the state. If you plan to seek contributions from residents in multiple states, you may need to register to fundraise in each state prior to beginning your fundraising.

Item 5 – answer appropriately.

Item 6—generally not applicable to animal rescues therefore making the answer "no".

Item 7—most start-up rescues manage their own activities making this answer "no".

Item 8—most start-up rescues do not engage in joint ventures or partnerships making this answer "no".

Item 9—generally answered "no".

Item 10—generally answered "no". However, if you develop any intellectual property, the IRS expects that your nonprofit holds the ownership rights to what you develop.

Item 11—generally answered "no" but you may include in the attachments that your organization, "has no current plans to accept contributions of real property but reserves the right to do so in the future in accordance with IRS rules and regulations."

Item 12—nonprofit organizations may operate in foreign countries. The U.S. government restricts organizations from engaging in activities with certain countries listed on the OFAC (Office of Foreign Assets Control) sanctions list.

Item 13—nonprofit organizations may make grants to other organizations provided that the grants are used to further your organization's tax-exempt mission. Your answer to this question must show the IRS that you understand this rule.

Item 14—nonprofit 501(c)(3) groups may make grants to foreign organizations; however, you must show that by doing so you further your tax-exempt mission and that you oversee how the grants are used. You also must make sure that you do not work with any groups in a country on the OFAC sanctions list.

Items 15-21—generally do not apply to animal welfare organizations.

Item 16 – scholarships. If you plan to provide any type of scholarship or grant to an individual you must complete Schedule H.

Part IX

A. Budgets. You must include financial information showing the IRS you expected sources of income and amounts and expected expenses. We often write "see attached" on this form and include, instead, a simple spreadsheet.

B. Balance sheet. For start-ups that have only a bank account, you can complete this form by including your bank balance on a specific date on line 1- Cash; if you don't have any liabilities or debts, this same amount of cash on hand then goes on line 17 – Total Fund Balances.

Part X

1a – generally "no" for animal welfare groups that will receive donations from a variety of sources. Organizations that are funded entirely, or almost entirely by the founder or a limited number of sources may be qualified as private foundations and answer "yes" here.

Item 5 – animal welfare groups that receive most of their funding from donations or government or other grants check box "g". Animal welfare groups that expect to receive at least one-third of their funding from fees – such as adoption fees – should check box "h".

Item 6 – skip this. The IRS no longer provides advance rulings.

Part XI

You are probably completing the full IRS Form 1023 because you expect your gross income to exceed $50,000/year. If so, on line 1 check box "no" and then check the box on line 3 indicating that you understand the filing fee for this form is $850.

Sign, print your name and date.

C-5   HOW TO APPLY ONLINE FOR AN IRS EIN

(federal tax identification number)

1. Go to the IRS EIN online filing page at
   https://www.irs.gov/Businesses/Small-Businesses-&-Self-Employed/
   Apply-for-an-Employer-Identification-Number-(EIN)-Online

2. Select **"Apply Online Now "** blue button

3. Selec**t ok**, IRS.gov message

4. Select **"Begin Application"**

5. Select last Radio button **"View Additional Types, Including Tax Exempt Governmental Organizations"** then **Continue**

6. Select radio button **"Other Non-Profit/Tax-Exempt Organizations"** then **Continue**

7. **Continue** again to next screen

8. Why are you requesting an EIN: select "**started new business**"

9. Who is the responsible party? Select **"individual"**

10. Selected individual. Complete your first and last name and your social security number. Then select **"I am a responsible and duly authorized officer or member of this organization"** and **Continue** to next screen.

11. Where is the organization located? Complete the address and phone number boxes. Answer the questions regarding "care of" and a different address as applicable, and then **continue** to the next screen. If the "verify your address" screen comes up, verify (usually by accepting the "database version").

12. On the next screen fill in

- Legal name of your rescue—this should be listed exactly as listed on the articles of incorporation copy (note however that the IRS form will not accept punctuation including commas and periods)
- Trade Name /DBA—leave blank unless you are using a DBA
- Start date is normally the current month and year
- **Continue** to next screen

13. This screen contains YES/NO questions about your organization. Answer as appropriate, then **Continue.**

14. What does your business organization do?

- Select "other" at the end, then **Continue**
- Next screen select "organization" then **Continue**
- Next screen select "other" then specify "animal welfare"

15. How would you like to receive your EIN confirmation letter? Select "**receive letter online**" then **Continue** and

- Save the application by selecting Print, then saving it as a PDF
- Next verify info entered correctly
- Then click **"Submit"**

16. The next screen should show you the EIN # assigned. We recommend taking a screen print of the number, then "**Click Here for your EIN"** and a .pdf copy of your EIN Confirmation letter should appear.

17. **Save the EIN letter** (called a "CP575" letter). The IRS does not issue new ones.

APPENDIX D

ADDITIONAL RESOURCES

CONTENTS

D-1 AGENDA FOR YOUR FIRST ("ORGANIZATIONAL") BOARD MEETING

The first or organizing meeting of your board of directors is essential to getting your animal welfare group off the ground. At this meeting you should:

- Adopt the bylaws
- Elect additional members to the board of directors (the number of directors, how they are elected or appointed, and the length of their terms should be listed in your bylaws)
- Elect officers (the number of officers, their titles, terms how they are elected should be listed in your bylaws)
- Adopt a program plan for the first year
- Adopt a budget
- Appoint an executive director.
- Delegate authority to appropriate officers and/or staff to open a bank account, complete and file the IRS tax-exemption application and required state registrations.
- Determine how often the board will meet and the date of the next meeting.

....

How often should the board meet?

State law generally requires very few meetings. However, best practice calls for at least three evenly spaced meetings per year. See Better Business Bureau nonprofit guidelines at www.give.org.

....

ΨΨ

D-2 TIPS AND STRATEGIES TO RUN GREAT MEETINGS

It's not easy to lead a meeting and successfully encourage participation and different points of view. Establishing an agenda that includes standard financial and other reports made at each meeting is the first step to a well-run meeting. While using basic parliamentary procedure is a good idea, I recommend that you steer clear of trying to enforce Roberts Rules of Order. The few people who understand Robert's Rules may use the complicated procedures to control a meeting, rather than to encourage participation by all. Here are a few tips to help you lead effective meetings:

Prepare a detailed agenda in advance

• Give each agenda item a specific amount of time, to help ensure that the meeting runs accordingto plan and no one person or topic overruns the entire meeting.
• Place topics that may require more discussion at the beginning of the agenda.
• Use action verbs on each agenda item (i.e., decide, share, review, select, discuss, finish, adjust,etc.) to ensure a clear outcome..

Start on time / end on time

• Schedule time to socialize 15 minutes before meeting begins, or encourage socializing after themeeting ends.
• Start on time. End on time. It shows that you respect everyone's time.
• Set a timer or stopwatch to go off at the time the meeting is to begin, as a signal for all to bequiet.
• Designate a timekeeper to watch the clock during the meeting, and give feedback to meetingparticipants to let them know when the time for discussion on an agenda item is almost up, tokeep the meeting on track.

Stay on topic

- Have the meeting Chair stop the "runaway" discussions and return to the agenda item being discussed.
- Create a "Parking Lot" on a piece of paper, where important issues not related to currentdiscussion can be listed, to be discussed at a later date.
- Use the "Parking Lot" when creating the next month's agenda.

D-3 PARLI-PRO BASICS FOR CONDUCTING A MEETING

Simplified parliamentary rules are a good choice when it comes to running effective school support organization meetings. Having no rules for meetings leads to unorganized, often chaotic meetings, while using a strict Roberts Rules of Order method may lead to imbalanced meetings, dominated by those few who understand Roberts Rules. Following these simple rules ensures that all voices are heard and hopefully better decisions are made.

1. Chair calls the meeting to order.
2. Meeting participants review agenda. Amendments, if any, are proposed to the agenda. Participants approve agenda.
3. Once the agenda has been approved, including the time period to begin and end discussion of each item, the agenda may not be changed or amended without a motion to amend the agenda, a second, and approval by a 2/3 majority affirmative vote.
4. The Chair conducts the meeting, allowing the indicated time period for discussion and/or presentation of each item.

Six Steps to Every Motion

1. A member is recognized and makes a motion.
2. Another member seconds the motion.
3. Without rewording, the presiding officer restates the motion to the assembly.
4. The members debate the motion. No member may speak for a second time until all members who wish to speak are heard once.
5. The presiding officer asks for affirmative votes & then negative votes.
6. The presiding officer announces the results of the vote.

D-4 WHAT TO INCLUDE (AND LEAVE OUT) OF MEETING MINUTES

Minutes serve as the official record of the actions that occurred at a meeting. While there is often a desire to make minutes as complete as possible so that they serve as a historical record, including too much detail may be unwise from a legal perspective.

Minutes should include four basic types of information:

1. time, date and place of the meeting;
2. the fact that proper, prior notice was given or that such notice was waived by those attending the meeting;
3. the names of those in attendance and whether a quorum was present; and
4. the official actions taken by the meeting participants (motions made and approved or defeated).

Not required to be included in minutes are:

1. names of those who move and second motions;
2. the vote (number voting for and against) for each motion;
3. detail of the debate that occurred regarding each motion.

Minutes may be looked at if your group is ever investigated or sued. Therefore, it is important to keep an accurate record of your meetings but not include unnecessary information that could prove harmful in the future. Including the names of those who move and second motions can help potential plaintiffs find "friends" and "foes." Providing vote counts in the minutes makes public how divided the assembly was, and are unnecessary. Only the fact that a motion passed or failed is needed. Unless a meeting participant specifically requests that their negative (but not prevailing) vote be recorded, you can leave it out of the minutes. Because debates infrequently reflect a balanced view or consensus of the members (either the minority or majority view may be more strongly argued) inclusion of debates in the minutes may create a skewed historical record. In addition, including debate detail may create a public appearance of divisiveness when a united public front may be more desirable.

The minutes should include the date, time and place of the meeting, along with a list of who attended, whether a quorum was present, and that proper notice of the meeting was given (or waived). To make the minutes easier to draft and use, it is a good idea to have the minutes follow the agenda. For each item on the agenda, there should be a corresponding item in the minutes. In this way, the supporting reports and documents may be attached to, and kept as part of, the agenda. Someone reviewing the minutes may then easily reference the agenda and attachments.

Keeping minutes simple by recording only the actions approved, but not the detailed debate, balances the need for a complete record against the risks of including too much information.

D-5 SAMPLE MEETING MINUTES

NOTE: Report on actions taken. It is not recommended to report on discussions and the actual vote count, unless unanimous. Minutes are a public record.

[BOOSTER CLUB NAME]
[DATE]
[LOCATION]

Proper written notification of this meeting was provided to board members XX days in advance of the meeting. The following board members were present: [NAME, NAME, NAME].

1. **Call to Order**
   The meeting was called to order at [TIME] by [NAME].

2. **Approval of Minutes**
   [NAME] moved to approve the minutes of the last board meeting held on [DATE]. Motion was seconded and the minutes were approved.

3. **Financial Policies**
   Financial policies for the organization were discussed. The following policies were approved:

   The President and Treasurer shall have check signing authority. To ensure proper financial controls, the Vice President (who does not have check signing authority) shall review monthly bank statements.

4. **Programs**
   The next event of [DESCRIPTION] was discussed. [NAME] reported that donations have been secured to cover all costs of the event.

5. **Other Business**
   No other business was discussed.

6. Next Meeting

The next board meeting shall be held on [DATE], [TIME] at [LOCATION].

7. Adjourn

The meeting was adjourned at [TIME].

D-6 RECRUITING, TRAINING, AND RETAINING VOLUNTEERS

Volunteers can be invaluable in assisting with fundraising and providing extra helping hands for animal rescue staff. Here's a few tips on how to obtain, train, and retain volunteers.

Recruiting Volunteers

1. Recruit widely. Don't limit your request for volunteers to your usual circle of friends, but reach broadly into the school and community. For example, my church provides volunteers to the nearby school, and my elementary school PTO received help from the local Coast Guard facility for our labor-intensive fall festival. Some community members simply want to help make their community a better place.

2. Recruit more volunteers than you think you'll need. Remember, many hands make light work, and no-shows and dropouts are inevitable.

3. Seek out volunteers at the beginning of the year, providing a form with many options. Also include how much time each volunteer opportunity takes. You will get more volunteers if they understand the time commitment and don't feel like they are jumping into a black hole of unending obligations.

4. Provide as much detail as you can about the volunteer roles and what you hope to accomplish. Descriptions, photos, and outcomes from prior years will help engage your prospective volunteers. Testimonials from prior volunteers who enjoyed working with your group also may help.

5. Don't stop at one appeal. Many times prospective volunteers are busy when first asked but may be more receptive if you ask again at another time. This also shows that you are not a closed group, but encourage wider participation.

6. Ask people personally for their help. Don't rely entirely on an email notice or written appeal. Go beyond passive messaging by reaching out personally to potential volunteers and ask your other officers and volunteers to do the same. Some people respond better if they are asked personally.

7. Make an appeal for volunteers prior to each new event. This lets people who have a connection or interest in the type of event to get involved.

8. Sometimes local businesses will provide staff to nonprofits as volunteers. It doesn't hurt to ask!

9. Sometimes people like to contribute what they know how to do best, their special or unique skills. A painter may contribute a painting. A baker might donate a cake. However, other people prefer a break from their day jobs. Keep an open mind, and encourage people to volunteer where they feel best.

10. Check with your school and, if required, make sure volunteers complete all required school information forms and background checks.

Training Volunteers

1. Provide volunteers with any training and/or tools needed to do their jobs properly. Don't assume a volunteer understands what to do and how to do it. However, also encourage volunteers to offer suggestions for improving how things are done.

2. Group training can be a time saver; however, make sure you consider the normal work schedules of your volunteers. You may need to do both a work-hour, and an evening, training.

3. Make sure your trainers are good with volunteers. Working with a volunteer work force requires more collaboration than an employer/employee relationship.

4. Develop and keep written records of your programs, processes, and procedures. Having a guidebook for your key fundraising events or monthly

adoption events that lists the number of volunteers needed, the steps to take to organize, set-up and run the event, is a good idea.

5. Holding a "launch" meeting for a new project or fundraiser helps get everyone on the same page regarding expectations and responsibilities, and helps everyone get excited about the new challenge.

6. If a volunteer is struggling with an assignment, consider sending in reinforcements and finding the volunteer an assignment that is a better match.

7. Competitions and inexpensive incentives help recruit and retain volunteers and keep them excited about the work along the way.

Retaining Volunteers

1. To keep people happily working without pay, you need to understand what motivates them, and keeps them fulfilled.

2. Flexibility with respect to volunteer tasks, hours, and the way things get done is helpful.

3. Balance difficult tasks with fun ones.

4. Some volunteers stay motivated if they feel like they have special privileges or perks. These are perks that cost the group nothing (i.e. a special parking place for the volunteer of the month), but go a long way to say thank you.

5. Give praise and kudos to volunteers in your newsletter and other communications.

6. But remember, while some folks like awards, praise and thanks, others may prefer to be anonymous. Make sure you ask!

7. Make sure your volunteers have something to do. When I went to help at the church food pantry, and there were so many volunteers I had nothing to do, I was less motivated to go back. I felt like they didn't need me.

APPENDIX E

FINANCIAL PROCEDURE GUIDELINES & TEMPLATES

CONTENTS

E-1 FINANCIAL POLICY WORKSHEET

1. **Approve an annual budget**
   a. Include expected sources of income & amounts
   b. Include expected types of expenses & amounts
   c. Review periodically budget versus actual income/expenses

2. **Implement financial controls**
   a. Check signor(s) only signs checks
   b. Consider requiring 2 signors on every check
   c. Have all expenditures approved by someone other than check signor
   d. Have bank statements reviewed/reconciled by someone other than check signor
   e. Always use 2 people (other than check signor) to count cash on site at each fundraiser/event; record receipts on cash tally sheet; deposit funds immediately to bank

3. **Keep good records**
   a. Receipts for all expenditures
   b. Deposit slips
   c. Cash tally sheets
   d. Bank statements
   e. Federal (IRS Form 990) and state tax returns/fundraising reports

4. **Use bookkeeping software**

5. **Conduct an annual financial review**
   a. Use a committee of at least 2 people who were not routinely responsible for money handling
   b. Follow guidelines for what to look at and for
   c. Consider allowing the school business or other officer to review the booster club's books

E-2 SAMPLE BUDGET WORKSHEET

	Budget	Actual
INCOME		
Adoption fees		
Individual donations		
Business donations		
Total Income		
EXPENSES		
Animal food		
Vet expenses		
Supplies		
Salaries		
Other		
Total Expenses		
Net (carry-over to next year)		

E-3 SAMPLE FINANCIAL POLICES

Financial Controls for the [NAME OF RESCUE]

Annual Budget. An annual budget should be developed each year and approved by the Board of Directors. The budget should show all the expected sources of income and amounts for each, and the expected expenses and amounts for each. The annual budget may be amended from time to time by the board as needed.

Purchase Approval. All purchases on behalf of the organization must be pre-approved, either by detailed line item in the annual budget or vote of the board. The officer(s) authorized to sign contracts on behalf of the organization shall be designated in the bylaws, or by vote of the Board of Directors.

Bank Account(s)

1. **Bank accounts.** All bank accounts of the organization shall be opened in an FDIC insured institution, approved by the Board of Directors, in the legal name of the organization using the organization's own EIN (employer identification number).

2. **Investments.** All investments and investment accounts shall approved by the Board of Directors. Investment accounts shall generally be limited to Certificates of Deposit in FDIC insured institutions.

3. **Bill payment.** All bills of the organization shall be paid by check from the organization's bank account. Online or e-checks are permissible, however all procedures for paper checks be followed, regardless of the banks procedures (prior approval of processing the online payment should be obtained by way, for example, of email approval by the required number of signatories before processing the payment).

   a. All checks shall be numbered and shall be held in the custody of an officer authorized by the Board, such as the Treasurer.

b. All payments by check shall correlate to an invoice or receipt, on which the check number and date paid shall be written. If a receipt or invoice is not available, an officer shall write and sign a description of what was purchased.

c. Pre-signing blank checks is prohibited.

d. All expenses must be pre-authorized by (i) approval in the annual budget, or (ii) subsequent amendment to the budget, or (iii) vote of the Board if authorized by the bylaws.

e. Bank statements shall be reviewed by treasurer and one or more other officers without signature authority to ensure separation of financial controls.

4. **Bank cards.** If debit/credit cards are established in the name of the organization, a policy approved by the Board shall be established that includes a list of the authorized users, daily/monthly/annual spending limits, and limits use to charges for the organization. No personal charging on the card by the authorized users shall be allowed.

Cash

1. All cash must be kept in a secure location, such as in a lock box. A cash box ledger shall be kept and monthly cash box reports, including starting balance, expenditures, additions, and ending balance shall be provided to the Board.

2. The Board shall establish a maximum amount of cash kept on hand, such as $250.

3. A receipt shall be provided whenever cash is turned over or collected.

a. Receipts shall be numbered and kept in a bound book, with one copy provided to the person turning in the cash, and one copy kept in the receipt book as a record. Alternatively, a receipt ledger on which the date, amount, and signature of both the giver and recipient of the funds may be used.

b. Cash should always be counted by two (2) individuals, on the day the funds are collected, and at the site where the funds are collected. A cash tally sheet showing the date and amount collected, and signed by the counters, should be maintained. If the Treasurer is not one of the counters, the Treasurer should re-count the funds, and counter-sign the tally sheet,

c. Cash should be deposited immediately into the organization's bank account. A copy of the deposit slip shall be immediately forwarded and kept by the Treasurer. The deposit slip should be cross-referenced against the cash tally sheet, and saved for the bank reconciliation.

Financial Reports. The Treasurer should provide a financial report to the board monthly that includes:

1. Statement of receipts and disbursements (also known as a Statement of Activities);
2. Balance sheet (includes cash on hand, other assets, liabilities and equities);
3. A copy of the bank statement, bank reconciliation, monthly cash reports and imaged checks;
4. A copy of the cash tally sheets; and,
5. Any outstanding receipts/expenses/purchase orders/contractual obligations.

The monthly treasurer's reports shall be compiled and kept in the organization's records for three (3) years. Bank statements, canceled checks, check registers, invoices, receipts, cash tally sheets, investment statements, and related documents should be kept for seven (7) years. The year-end treasurer's report, annual financial review report, and IRS Form 990 shall be kept permanently.

E-4 SAMPLE CASH TALLY SHEET

Cash Box Tally Sheet

Beginning Cash Box	Event Proceeds
Date: _____	Date: _____
Function: _____	Function: _____
Cash Box: _____	Cash Box: _____

Coin:	**Coin:**
_____ X $0.01 = $_____	_____ X $0.01 = $_____
_____ X $0.05 = $_____	_____ X $0.05 = $_____
_____ X $0.10 = $_____	_____ X $0.10 = $_____
_____ X $0.25 = $_____	_____ X $0.25 = $_____
_____ X $0.50 = $_____	_____ X $0.50 = $_____

Total Coins _____	**Total Coins** _____

Currency:	**Currency:**
_____ X $1 = $_____	_____ X $1 = $_____
_____ X $5 = $_____	_____ X $5 = $_____
_____ X $10 = $_____	_____ X $10 = $_____
_____ X $20 = $_____	_____ X $20 = $_____
_____ X $50 = $_____	_____ X $50 = $_____
_____ X $100 = $_____	_____ X $100 = $_____

Total Currency _____

Beg. Cash Box Total _____

Signatures
Rec'd by: _____
Rec'd by: _____
Rec'd by: _____

Total Currency _____

Checks _____

Total Cash & Checks _____

* Less Beg. Cash Box _____

Net Proceeds _____

_____
Signature

_____
Signature

_____
Signature

* This amount remains in cash box competed.

E-5 CONDUCTING A FINANCIAL REVIEW

An annual financial review of the organization's records should be completed at the end of the year, and prior to turning records over to new officers. The financial review may be completed by an internal audit committee, if the organization has gross receipts of less than $250,000 per year. Below are step-by-step guidelines to help your financial review committee complete the review. Remember, this review should be conducted by 2 or more volunteers without signature authority on the bank account(s) and who were not regularly involved with the day-to-day financial operations of your organization. This review provides a new set of eyes on the books.

Step #1: Gather financial documents including:

- Copies of all written financial policies
- Copies of treasurer's reports for the year (or other period) to be reviewed
- List of all bank and investment accounts, including names of persons authorized to sign on each account
- Copies of all bank and other financial statements for the period to be reviewed
- Copies of all bank and investment account reconciliations for the period to be reviewed
- Cash tally sheets or Cash receipts journal
- Invoices, receipts, and other documents
- Documentation of any restrictions on the use of any particular funds or donor gifts
- IRS letter documents, including most recent Form 990, IRS letter recognizing tax-exempt status, and IRS letter assigning an EIN (employer identification number) to the organization.

Step #2: Review financial documents and processes.

- Check the organization's EIN (employer identification number) as assigned by the IRS against the EIN used on the organization's bank and other financial accounts. Make sure the school's EIN is not being used.
- Check names of persons authorized to (a) approve transactions and (b) sign checks, against:

  a. persons authorized to conduct these activities in the organization's minutes; and,
  b. bank records indicating who is authorized as a signatory.

- Check to ensure that the person(s) who sign checks are not the same, or only, person(s) reviewing monthly bank statements.
- Check all bank reconciliations to determine that the beginning balance of one month is the same as the ending balance of the previous month. Also note whether the balance listed on financial statements is the same as the balance listed on the treasurer's reports presented to the organization.
- Pick one month and perform a bank reconciliation using the original records. If you find a discrepancy between your reconciliation and the reconciliation provided by the person who performed the original reconciliation, research the discrepancy to find the error or explanation for the discrepancy.
- Count all cash in petty cash accounts to ensure that the count agrees with the books.
- Check to see if the organization carries fidelity bond coverage on people handling the organization's funds; if insurance is not held, propose that the organization consider obtaining bonding coverage.

Step #3: Review income and receipts.

Determine if the deposits listed on the financial reports provided to the organization match deposits listed on bank statements. Check to see if cash tally sheets match the amount of cash reported as received from an event on financial reports, and also match the deposit indicated on bank statements.

Step #4: Review disbursements.

- Test to be sure that payments made were properly authorized—by a line item in the approved budget, an approved amendment to the budget, or an appropriate vote authorizing the expenditure.
- Test purchase orders to be sure that they were properly approved and match the actual disbursement or invoice.
- Review records to ensure that there is an invoice, receipt, or other appropriate written documentation for each disbursement, and that the amounts match.

Step #5: Review Tax/information returns.

Review financial records to ensure that appropriate federal (IRS Form 990) and state income tax/information returns have been timely filed.

Step #6: Review financial control systems.

- Check to evaluate whether financial duties have been appropriately separated. Although it can be difficult for small organizations to separate financial duties, certain separations are essential for appropriate financial controls. These separations protect both the organization, and the individuals handling the finances. Specifically:
  - Individuals with signature authority should NEVER approve the transactions/disbursements for which they sign. All expenditures should be approved in an annual budget, as originally approved or amended, or by a vote of the board or membership as appropriate. All disbursements should be documented by an invoice, receipt or other appropriate written documentation.

- The individual(s) with signature authority may reconcile bank statements. However, at least one additional officer or director should review monthly bank statements, or bank statements may be included with the treasurer's report to the board/membership.
- Finances should be reviewed annually by an audit committee that consists of two or more individuals who do not routinely handle the organization's finances, such as by being a signatory on the accounts.
- Cash should always be counted by at least 2 persons at/near the time received, and then recounted by the treasurer or other individual prior to deposit.

Step #7: Review reporting systems to ensure adequate information is provided for the organization and its officers/directors to make reasonable decisions.

- Are reports from the treasurer timely and complete?
- Are financial policies, including separation of financial controls, being followed?
- Are all records being gathered (invoices, receipts, cash records, checks and disbursement records, bank records, treasurer's reports) so that they can be reviewed as needed, and only discarded in accordance with the organization's record retention guidelines?

Step #8: Write a report.

The financial review/audit report should document at a minimum:

- Steps taken in the financial review
- Current fund(s) balance and balance sheet
- Comments, if any, on any concerns or discrepancies found and the audit committee's recommendations to correct these concerns or discrepancies.

E-6 IRS AUDIT WORKSHEET

Following are the key do's and don'ts with respect to each of the 5 nonprofit organization areas of compliance that the IRS often audits.

1. Private benefit—the rules
Officers/directors/key employees receiving inappropriate financial benefit—unreasonable salaries/benefits

Do

- ✔ Document board approval of salaries
- ✔ Document comparability data used
- ✔ Document details of any transactions between the organization and officers/directors/key employees and/or their for-profit businesses

Don't

- ✔ Approve your own (or a family members') salary
- ✔ Approve excessive benefits
- ✔ Approve transactions that provide excess value to officers/directors/employees

2. Commercial activities—the rules
Nonprofit organizations may not compete with for-profit entities

Do

- ✔ Know & document how your organization's activities differ from a commercial/for-profit entity
- ✔ Price your services at or below fair market value; document
- ✔ Know if your services are "for the convenience" of your members; document
- ✔ Know & document how any joint ventures with for-profit companies benefit the nonprofit; make sure that the board of directors approves the transaction; ensure that the transaction does not provide excess benefit to the for-profit

Don't

✔ Engage in the same or similar activities as for-profits

✔ Charge the same fees for the same activities of for-profits

✔ Undertake a contract with a board member at a fee higher than you may obtain the same services from another source

3. Change in activities—the rules

IRS rules provide that you must notify the IRS of any significant change(s) in your organization's activities.

• by written notice

• on next filed 990-series return

Do

✔ Have the board approve any change in your activities

✔ Notify the IRS of the change

✔ Document the foregoing in the minutes and organization records

Don't

✔ Make changes that require a new exemption application

✔ Make changes without board approval/documentation/IRS notice

4. Lobbying and political activities—the rules

• 501(c)(3)s may engage in an "insubstantial amount" of lobbying, but may not engage in any political activities.

• Lobbying requires a request for action (draft bill, vote yes/no) on a specific piece of legislation.

• Political activity is assisting someone to run for office.

Do

✔ Make the 501(h) election if your organization does any substantial lobbying

✔ Track all lobbying expenditures

✔ Set up a separate 501(c)(4) or political action committee if you plan to engage in lobbying and/or political campaign activity

5. Board of directors—the rules
Nonprofit organizations must have an independent board of directors.

Do

✔ Document officer/director elections in the minutes
✔ Document board actions in the minutes
✔ Keep minutes concise—record actions only

Don't

✔ Include only family/related members on board
✔ Compensate board members as board members

Recommended Documentation Tips:

Keeping the following records is good business practice, and will help ensure you are ready if the IRS ever makes a house call.

Board minutes

- Record actions and no-vote counts
- Record evidence of arms-length transactions (joint ventures)
- Record comparability data examined (salaries)
- 990 review
- Conflict of interest policy
- Whistleblower policy

Contracts with board/officers/key employees

- Record arms-length steps
- Reviewed/signed by disinterested persons
- Comparability data

Financial records

Provide only what is requested

Consider paper versus electronic

Adopt policies for what you keep/destroy; document in writing

- *IRS 990-returns*   7 years
- *Year-end financial report*   Permanent
- *Periodic financial reports*   3 years
- *Bank statements & related* 7 years

It helps to **Know IRS Rules and Procedures**:

- Know the IRS rules
- Request a delay
  - Request time whenever needed
  - IRS must complete audit within three years of the tax return in question
- Don't agree to host the audit at your office (field audit)
  - Ask that the audit be conducted at the IRS office
  - Field audits, on average, result in higher adjustments
- Don't agree to repetitive audits
  - IRS may not examine the same issue(s) if an IRS audit of either of the two preceding years resulted in a no-change

It is essential to **Review IRS Publications**:

- IRS publications
  - Compliance Guide for 501(c)(3) Public Charities
  - A Day in the Life of an Exempt Organization Audit
  - The Examination Process, Audits by Mail (Publication 3498-A)
  - The Examination Process (Publication 3498)
  - Your Rights as a Taxpayer (Publication 1)
  - How to Appeal an IRS Decision on Tax-Exempt Status (Publication 892)
  - IRS Web Pages

- http://www.irs.gov/Businesses/Small-Businesses-&-Self-Employed/IRS-Audits
- http://www.irs.gov/Individuals/Forms-and-Publications-About-Your-Appeal-Rights

E-7 CLOUD-BASED ACCOUNTING AND RECORDING KEEPING SOFTWARE

Using cloud-based software is a tremendous help to animal rescues and other organizations where volunteer turnover is high. No more changing recordkeeping methods or software each year. Pass on the password and the financial records are moved instantly to next year's treasurer, along with the all the organization's financial history. And using financial software makes creating reports, and distributing them, much easier.

Here are a few of the providers of cloud-based recordkeeping and accounting software.

Wave is the fastest growing online accounting software provider and offers FREE accounting software to small businesses. Made specifically for entrepreneurs, freelancers, consultants and small businesses with 9 employees or less.

intuit **quickbooks**.

QuickBooks is the gold standard in accounting solutions with millions of subscribers worldwide, giving you access to excellent features and customization. Quickbooks has a variety of accounting packages intended to meet the needs of different types and sizes of organizations.

APPENDIX F

FUNDRAISING TOOLS

CONTENTS

F-1 BEST PRACTICES FOR RUNNING A FUNDRAISER

1. **Ensure proper financial controls are in place before the fundraiser begins:**

Finances / Financial Controls

- Ensure all funds raised are used for the tax-exempt purpose of the organization.
- Approve a budget of anticipated revenue and expenses for the year (to include each fundraiser).
- Authorize someone to enter into contracts or agreements for the purchase of materials or services for the fundraiser on behalf of the organization (usually the Executive Director or the Board Treasurer or Chair)
- Update signature cards for the animal welfare organization bank accounts with names of those who have check-signing authority.
- Appoint two unrelated people to count cash.
- Designate two people, one without check signing authority, to review all bank statements.
- Do not make loans from the organization to any officers or members.

Treasurer

- Appoint a Treasurer who is responsible for all funds of the organization in accordance with the organization's financial policies, including but not limited to, the following:
  - Receives all funds and gives receipts for monies due and payable to the organization from all sources.
  - Deposits such funds in a bank or other organization as selected by the Executive Board, as soon as practicable upon receipt of the funds.
  - Signs checks, makes disbursements as authorized by the budget, as approved, or amended, by the membership.
  - Presents a financial report at each membership meeting detailing all financial transactions related to the fundraising event.

2. Promote your 501(c)(3) status to potential donors/buyers:
Prove your 501(c)(3) status by providing your IRS determination letter to potential donors.

F-2 SAMPLE DONATION REQUEST LETTER

Date

Potential Donor Name
Company
Street Address
City, State, Zip

Dear _____,

The (name of organization) is proud to support our pets. We invite you to support your local community by making a donation. We depend on the generosity of the surrounding community to provide the best opportunities for our pets in their time of greatest need.

Only with your help can we continue to provide the level of support our pets need and deserve. All donations are tax-deductible to the extent allowed by law. (Name of organization) is exempt from federal taxes under section 501(c)(3) of the Internal Revenue Code.

Thank you for considering a donation to this very worthy cause. For questions or further information, please contact _____

.

Sincerely,

Name of contact person
Name of organization

> Please send gift certificates, monetary donations,
> and correspondence to:
>
> Name and address of contact person
> (Name of Organization) EIN#: XX-XXXXXXX

F-3 SAMPLE CASH/IN-KIND DONATION FORM

Cash/In-Kind Donation Form

Yes! We want to help the (name of organization). The (name of organization) is tax-exempt under section 501(c)(3). All donations are tax-deductible.

Date: _____

Cash Donation: $_____

In-Kind Donation: Please describe your donation (including deductible value):

_____

_____

[An in-kind donation is deductible to the extent of your cost, and not fair market value, if it is being sold by our organization at an auction or other event, or used as a prize. Only items used by our organization to further our mission (other than for fundraising purposes) are deductible at full fair market value.]

Please PRINT clearly and list your name(s) as you would like to be recognized on our (website, program, handout, etc.)**:**

Company/Organization Name: _____

Contact Name(s): _____

Phone: _____

Email: _____

Address: _____

Contact information is needed to send a tax receipt for donations. If you do not receive a response from us within 30 days, please e-mail (contact person within your organization) so we can verify that your donation has been received.

Please mail this form to:

(Name and address of contact person)
Thank you for your support!

Name of organization
Address
City, State, Zip
EIN #

F-4 SAMPLE DONOR RECEIPT

Name of organization

Date

Donor Name
Company
Street Address
City, State, Zip

Dear _____,

Thank you for supporting (name of organization). Your generosity is greatly appreciated and will go a long way to continue our operations.

[Select and insert only the one paragraph that applies]

OPTION 1 (fully deductible contribution)
We appreciate your donation of $_____. The (name of organization) is recognized by the Internal Revenue Service as a 501(c)(3) organization. As a result, your donation is fully tax-deductible to the extent provided by law and based on your tax situation. No goods or services were received in exchange for your donation.

OPTION 2 (partially deductible contribution)
We appreciate your donation of $_____. We are happy to provide you with (describe benefit or gift given) in appreciation for your contribution. The value of this gift is (value of gift). The (name of organization) is recognized by the Internal Revenue Service as a 501(c)(3) organization. As a result, the amount of your donation, less the value of the gift ($100), is tax-deductible to the extent provided by law and based on your tax situation.

OPTION 3 (in-kind contribution)

We appreciate your donation of [e.g., dog food] valued at $_____

The (name of organization) is recognized by the Internal Revenue Service as a 501(c)(3) organization. IRS rules provide that the fair market value of your in-kind donations is tax-deductible.

Thank you again for your donation.

Sincerely,

Name of contact person
Contact information

CPSIA information can be obtained
at www.ICGtesting.com
Printed in the USA
BVHW071729021219
565404BV00022B/3584/P